Warman's

Depression Glass

4th edition

Ellen T. Schroy

Identification and Price Guide

©2006 by Krause Publications
Published by

krause publications
An Imprint of F+W Publications

700 East State Street • Iola, WI 54990-0001
715-445-2214 • 888-457-2873

Our toll-free number to place an order or obtain
a free catalog is (800) 258-0929.

Cover photo: Old Colony pink pieces, clockwise from top left: tumbler, 9 oz, 4-1/2" h, **$22**; cup, **$24**, and saucer, **$15**; and dinner plate, 10-1/2" d, **$36**. Courtesy of James Hintz.

Library of Congress Catalog Number: 2006922203

ISBN 10-digit: 0-89689-360-X
ISBN 13-digit: 978-089689-360-3

Designed by Donna Mummery
Edited by Kristine Manty

Printed in China

CONTENTS

*Moonstone, crystal relish, cloverleaf shape, **$14**; and heart-shaped bonbon with handle, **$15.** More Moonstone is on P. 172. Photo is courtesy of James Hintz.*

INTRODUCTION

Welcome to *Warman's® Depression Glass*, 4th edition, the latest edition in the Warman's price guides series. This edition is designed to assist collectors, appraisers, auctioneers, and those trying to identify that special piece of heirloom Depression-era glassware. A selection of 170 of the most popular patterns of American glass dinnerware manufactured between the 1920s and 1970s is featured. The fourth edition includes the standard Adam to Windsor patterns, plus other patterns most eagerly sought after by the collectors of the new millennium.

Each pattern is represented by one or more color photographs and a line drawing to help with the identification process, along with a listing of known manufactured items and current prices to help establish the value. The pattern name listed is the one given by the manufacturer, except in the case of numbered patterns, which have now developed more easily recognizable names. A Shape Library has been included to give you an idea of the myriad of shapes plates were manufactured in during this exciting period of American glassware production.

A quick identification guide has also been developed which sorts Depression-era glassware by motif, such as circles, fruits, florals, etc. By using this quick identification guide, you may be able to discern the pattern you are trying to identify.

What is Depression glass?

There are two categories of glassware that really have the wrong names: Depression glass and carnival class. Why and how did this happen? The names we use today were coined by folks in the late 1940s and early 1950s when collecting antiques was coming into vogue. It was when the automobile allowed people to travel freely about and enjoy Sunday rides into the country that collecting antiques became popular. Almost every little town had a dusty shop or two filled with old things and the sign out front simply read "Antiques." If it was old, belonged to someone's great aunt, or had lived out its usefulness, it was described as an antique. Most Americans lived in places where, when one generation died off, their belongings were usually dispersed among the younger generation, or sold at house auctions. These kinds of venues allowed the young people to pay a few pennies for useful household goods that they hopefully could use for a few more years. As the country grew, and the machine age became part of every day life, some began to realize that the early culture and tools of our ancestors were becoming lost and so efforts were made to save these things, either in a museum setting, or as private investors gathered them up.

As our culture started to embrace using old items as decorative accessories, dealers and shops began to spring up. By the early 1950s, entrepreneurs such as E. G. Warman realized that this vastly unregulated hobby was growing and perhaps publishing a price guide would help this new breed of collector realize that those old things they had in their cupboards, stashed in the barn, etc. had some value. However, to be able to organize things, you've got to name them.

By this time, people had begun to call old antique pressed glass "pattern glass" because of the hundreds of patterns associated with that, and also because a new name for the pretty colored glassware had to be developed. Because many people associated this pretty colored glassware as being made later than early American pattern glass, they began to call it "Depression glass," as that was the economic period that had most affected their lives. Today's Depression glass collectors embrace colored glassware that was made from the early 1920s up to the 1970s as Depression glass—stretching that period much longer than the name implies. Carnival glass was made from 1905 up to the early 1930s as the affordable answer to expensive art glass for the average consumer, but because much of it was sold as remainders to carnival vendors, the name "carnival glass" stuck.

Much of what we know today about Depression glass is thanks to a dedicated researcher, Hazel Marie Weatherman. Mrs. Weatherman was noticing that no one really knew the origins of the pretty colored glass she nicknamed "candy glass." She also knew that many of the manufacturers of this pretty glassware were going out of business and some had already disappeared. By the early 1970s, Weatherman decided someone had to document these glassmakers and their wares and through her efforts, she ended up writing *Colored Glassware of the Depression Era*, which has become a Holy Grail for Depression glass collectors. She actually had enough material for two books, but it is her first book that remains a standard reference today.

Weatherman was a fierce researcher and she personally went to the areas where the factories were located. She spent time with the owners and the designers, documenting their remembrances and copying factory catalogs. Weatherman was known to literally go door-to-door trying to find workers who had created her pretty candy glass.

As she recorded their stories, she learned much about the rich history of the glassmaking industry that was centered in western Pennsylvania, West Virginia, and Ohio. Weatherman and her assistant spent long hours in libraries scouring through newspapers, trade journals and company materials. As with many types of oral histories, sometimes contradictions surfaced, but Weatherman wouldn't give up until she got to the root of the history and tried to use original company documents as often as possible.

By the time she was finished, she had uncovered and written about more than 40 different glassmakers, where they were located, what they made, what colors they used, and everything else she could find out. Weatherman's research uncovered that the peak period of production for this pretty "candy glass" was between the 1920s and the late 1930s, and the label "Depression glass" became part of the collecting vocabulary. From the time this definition was coined, it became popular with collectors, rather than saying they were collecting Jeannette Glass or Hocking Glass. By collecting "Depression glass," they opened the door to hundreds of patterns, shapes, and colors.

What Weatherman discovered was that as the pattern glass industry was winding down, American glassware manufacturers were starting to look ahead to creating new glassware they hoped would end up on everyone's table. The manufacturers thought that through industrialization of the glassware craft, they could provide more products less expensively.

By the beginning of the 1900s, innovations were starting to come onto the scene that would allow mass-produced glass in more brilliant colors than ever before. American consumers trusted glassware to be sturdy, sanitary, and a big part of their every day lives. When manufacturers began to experiment with color, intricate impressed patterns, and more forms than ever before, the American consumer was delighted. By the early 1920s, the heavy financial investment made by the glass manufacturers looked like it might work; well, that was until the stock market crashed and the world seemed to come to a screeching halt. When the resulting economic depression caused these manufacturers to cut back in their design department and forced them to make their ingredients go further, their colors became washed out and pale. The glass that was pressed became as thin as possible so that it could be made quickly, but also less raw materials were going into each piece. Many manufacturers found themselves so strapped financially they were forced to declare bankruptcy. When that happened, it wasn't unusual to find another company buying molds, equipment, and luring trained employees to their factories.

Another thing that was changing in the glassware marketplace was how the word was getting out about what patterns, colors, and forms were being introduced by each company. For years before the Depression and even afterward, it was common practice for many glass companies to send their brightest sales people to a trade show held annually in Pittsburgh, PA. The trade journals of the time ran articles about who was there, what was new in their lines, who the top salesmen were and who was buying. Here they eagerly waited with their order blanks for the buyers from merchandisers such as Wanamakers to come and see what was new. The new mass-marketers, like F. W. Woolworth, also came and began to order glassware.

While the companies were fiercely competitive, one must assume that ideas for patterns and colors were often copied and intimated. One example of this is the Cube pattern, made by Jeannette Glass Company from 1929 to 1933. Jeannette made this pattern in several colors, but it was Fostoria's American pattern that caught on with many more collectors. Fostoria created this pattern in 1915 and continued it until 1986. Its production was mostly in a brilliant crystal, but Fostoria certainly created more forms and shapes than ever found in Cube pattern. Fostoria took its production up a notch, too, when it began to advertise in the new ladies magazines of the day. For the first time, ladies could use their leisure time to browse through magazines that taught them how to cook, how to dress, how to keep house, and on those same pages were advertisements luring them to buy Fostoria's American pattern as well as the company's other beautiful patterns. The Fenton Glass Company also soon mastered the new world of print ads and these two giant American glassmakers were able to last long after the economic depression had wrought such havoc with the industry.

When you combine savvy marketing with new colors and designs and more forms than ever before, it was easy to understand how the American consumers were eager to embrace this pretty new glassware and buy bridge sets, liquor sets, and all kinds of tableware. These new patterns were made to use from breakfast until bedtime and the manufacturers were as eager to sell as consumers were to buy, until the bottom fell out of the stock market and the average consumer's buying power diminished quickly. However, again clever marketing stepped in and events such as "dish night" at the local movies became a way for glass lovers to add new pieces to their sets. Soap manufacturers packed tumblers and all sorts of glassware pieces as giveaways in their boxes. The bubble that was the Depression glass market collapsed and while many manufacturers tried to revive it, the marketplace never embraced it so enthusiastically again, until it became fashionable to "collect Depression glass" and the trend we know today as a secondary market started.

The era of collecting this beautiful glass blossomed quickly as collectors wanting to create a whole table service bought up bits and pieces. Many collectors specialized in one pattern or maker, or even one color; others chose to collect by form, such as creamers and sugars. As the secondary market expanded, price guides devoted to just that segment of the market began to appear. Weatherman's books were used as identification guides, but the new price guides developed by authors such as Carl F. Luckey, Kent Washburn and Gene Florence began to establish a firm pricing tier.

Depression glass prices began to be traded by "book value" more and more until it was almost impossible to buy any Depression glass at all without paying established prices. Collectors and dealers were easily spotted at auctions and flea market as they scoured their favorite price guides to determine how much they could afford to pay and how much profit they could hope to achieve. A wonderful newspaper devoted to the Depression glass market was founded by Nora Koch called *The Daze*. Koch filled its pages with articles about patterns and companies, the activities of many collector clubs and show highlights, as well as print ads for Depression glass dealers all over the country. Sadly, when the Internet came roaring onto the scene, *The Daze* days were numbered.

Today with the advent of online buying and more educated buyers, the Depression glass marketplace is beginning to level out and bargains can be found. Before the advent of the Internet, it was quite common to find pockets all across America where certain patterns were more prevalent and regional pricing was in effect. Today, that is pretty much dissolved. Readers using this new edition of *Warman's*® *Depression Glass* should remember it is a price guide and they should be guided to paying a fair price, and selling for an honest profit.

Timelines

A Company Timeline that highlights the beginnings, major events, and endings of American glassware manufacturers is included in this edition to show the scope of the companies which helped produce glassware in this era. Also included in this edition is a Color Timeline designed to help identify colors and when they were manufactured. Combining all these clues, along with the pattern identification sketches, will help determine when a pattern was made, by what manufacturer, when, and in what colors.

Prices

The prices in *Warman's*® *Depression Glass* have been established by careful research and compiling data from various sources, which include advertisements of glassware listed for sale in such publications as *Antique Trader Weekly*. Visits to auctions, antiques shops, malls, and flea markets yielded still another source of pricing data. Many specialized Depression-era glassware shows and general antiques shows were visited. The newest, and probably most up-to-date, pricing venue is the Internet. Several sites were visited daily to observe what patterns were being offered, as well as which colors seemed most popular and which forms were being sold.

Regional differences were noted and it seemed apparent that advertised prices were fairly constant. Of course, some patterns are more popular in certain areas, but there is no clear definition of what patterns are being collected by any particular geographic area—collectors remain individual in their tastes and preferences for certain patterns and colors.

Some colors in some patterns are just not being offered for sale in large enough quantities to get a true reading for the price structure. In those cases, a note as to availability has been included to guide the collector in establishing a value. The antiques and collectibles business is based on comparables, and great amounts of data must be analyzed to accurately attribute pricing condition. Unlike many other aspects of the antiques and collectibles marketplace, Depression-era glass is rarely sold at large specialized auctions; rather, collections are dispersed through dealers and to other collectors.

This is an area of the antiques and collectibles marketplace where developing a good relationship with reputable Depression-era dealers is good. Many times dealers will retain "want lists" to help collectors fill in their patterns. And remember that although pricing for Depression-era glass has been driven by the major price guides for years, today the market is a buyer's market: expect to be able to pay less than "book value" if buying at auction, flea markets, etc. Bargains are out there, but it may take a little more searching to find interesting pieces at good prices.

Research

Depression-era glassware is one of the best-researched collecting areas available to the American marketplace. This is due in large part to the careful research of several people besides Weatherman, including Gene Florence, Carl F. Luckey, and Kent Washburn. Their volumes are held in high regard by researchers and collectors today. Many Depression-era glass collectors find their libraries grow as fast as their collections as they search to find what was manufactured in a particular pattern. By carefully researching company records and archives, these authors have allowed us to view what forms were popular, what colors delighted housewives of the era, and what sizes and shapes the patterns include.

Warman's® Depression Glass has responded to these authors by incorporating the best information they offer

into a new source for collectors.

Reproductions

Reproductions of Depression-era glassware have greatly impacted the market. Whole patterns have fallen in value because collectors are wary of continuing to invest in patterns beset by reproductions. Some patterns, like Miss America, are now experiencing reproductions of reproductions. The well-known clues to identifying the Miss America butter dish are now being compounded by having to recognize the second-generation reproduction and its identification clues.

Known reproductions, as of late 2005, are identified in the introduction of each pattern as well as being marked in the listing with †. Fantasy pieces, items not originally produced or produced in another color, are also listed as reproductions.

Collectors are encouraged to subscribe to the *Antique and Collectors Reproduction News*, P.O. Box 71174, Des Moines, IA 50325. This excellent publication, also online at www.reponews.com, covers all areas of the antiques and collectibles marketplace, and provides information about Depression-era glassware.

What's Included

Depression-era glassware, as defined by this edition, designates "patterns" produced between 1920 and the late 1970s. Such an expansive time span allows patterns to be included from many manufacturers. The patterns selected reflect dinnerware patterns as opposed to elegant patterns or stemware only patterns. To be included in this edition, a pattern had to meet several criteria:

· Be readily available on the marketplace
· Include a basic place setting, such as a cup and saucer, and plates
· Be manufactured during the time frame established
· Be manufactured in America
· Be eagerly sought by collectors

Several patterns were included that are considered "handmade," such as Fostoria's American and Tiffin's Flower Garden with Butterflies. These patterns actually cross over into the elegant glassware associated with

Depression glass. Because these patterns are currently popular with collectors, they were chosen to be included along with the machine-made patterns.

As our tastes in fashion change from year to year, so do the styles of glassware. These style changes have spanned many years and helped to create the lovely patterns we consider Depression-era glassware. Today's collectors seek out the traditional patterns as well as those like Indiana Glass' Constellation pattern, Imperial's Monticello, and Westmoreland's Paneled Grape.

Very expensive items have been included in some patterns to give collectors a comparable value. Depression-era collectors are referred to other volumes that list rare and expensive Depression glass to firmly establish prices on those rare items. As in some other areas of the antiques and collectibles marketplace, rare does not always equate to a high dollar amount. And, some more readily found items command lofty prices because of high demand or other factors, not because they are necessarily rare. As collectors' tastes range from the simple patterns to the more elaborate ones, so does the ability of their budget to invest in inexpensive patterns to ones that cost hundreds of dollars per form.

To maintain the fine tradition of extensive descriptions typically found in Warman's® price guides, as much information as possible has been included as far as sizes, shapes, colors, etc. Whenever possible, the original manufacturer's language has been maintained, and a glossary is included to help you identify some of those puzzling names. As the patterns evolved, sometimes other usage names were assigned to pieces. Collectors and dealers today face the constant challenge of identifying not only the pattern, but also understanding the original usage. It takes careful attention to detail to be able to discern the differences between berry, dessert, fruit, sauce, and cereal bowls. Color names are also given as the manufacturers originally named them.

The Depression-era glassware researchers have many accurate sources, including company records, catalogs, magazine advertisements, oral and written histories from sales staff, factory workers, etc. The dates included in the introductions are approximate, as are some of the factory locations. When companies had more than one factory, usually only the main office or factory is listed. With fine reference books available

to collectors, *Warman's® Depression Glass* concentrates on the pricing aspects of this segment of the antiques and collectibles market, rather than repeat the known company histories.

Today's Collectors

It has become quite evident that collectors of Depression-era glassware tend to use their treasures. Whether it's for everyday use, or for just special occasions, most reported on enjoying their collections and using them. Some collectors noted that they mix and match patterns, although most seem devoted to one color in a particular pattern. Sometimes colors will be mixed and matched as a collection is created for use purposes. Often collectors later sell off those pieces that no longer match or go with their patterns. Many Depression-era glass collectors become dealers to support their habit and to lessen their groaning cupboards!

Depression glass has been identified as being one of the hottest areas of interest on the Internet. The ever-growing number of sites available to the serious collector and first-time buyer verifies this statement. Information about company histories, interesting articles, listings of shows, and shops is becoming more easily accessible as this World Wide Web gathers collectors together.

Purchasing Depression-era glassware via the Internet is a fun way to expand a collection, locate objects not normally found in a region, etc. However, care must be exercised when bidding or purchasing glassware online. Buyers should ask the seller the same questions online as they would when making a live purchase, i.e. what is the history of the piece, more details about the description, are there any areas of damage, and what is the return policy. Because there are hundreds of Depression-era patterns, sometimes items are misidentified, so a savvy collector must learn to recognize the intricacies of the pattern they are seeking.

Many Depression-era collectors consistently look to each other for support and knowledge. This is one area where the Internet has answered a need in that some collectors correspond or "chat" daily at online message boards and forums about their collections, sharing experiences and dreams. During Depression glass antiques shows, it is not uncommon to see a dealer or collector offering their opinion about the source of a particular piece, what colors are available, etc. Perhaps this helps explain why so many young collectors are drawn to this colorful glassware: Information is readily available, standard price guides are used to establish prices, and knowledge is freely shared. Add to that excellent reference books, and you have an ever-increasing pool of collectors. Many exciting treasures await those who actively search for the rainbow of sparkling colors known today as Depression-era glass.

Thanks

Working on the 4th edition of this book has been a wonderful experience. Hopefully, it will continue to be a work in progress as readers share their discoveries, stories of special pieces, etc. with me. No book of this nature can ever be 100 percent complete; there will always be some unknown or unusual pieces, or unreported colors. Company records and catalogs are still to be discovered and shared with collectors.

Artist Jerry O'Brien's patience and attention to detail have resulted in the superb line drawings that accompany each pattern. Whenever possible, he worked from an actual example, measuring details and analyzing the pattern from an artist's point of view. Sometimes an actual plate, saucer, or other piece was photocopied and then the lines meticulously traced and enhanced to show the details. Other patterns, those with a design in a more geometric arrangement, were created using more technical drawing skills. Where the pattern repeats evenly around the piece, only a portion is shown, allowing more room for pertinent information. In other patterns, such as Parrot (Sylvan), the whole pattern is shown so that collectors can get a proper prospective as to the location of the parrots, foliage, etc. It's our hope that these detailed drawings will help give you a clearer view of the details associated with these beautiful patterns.

After Jerry completed the task of drawing the pattern, he then provided us with a drawing of a typical plate to be included in our Shape Library. As the book progressed, we were delighted to see the variations of the Depression-era glassware.

Support and guidance for *Warman's® Depression Glass* has been terrific and freely given by many. Through daily chats online, e-mails, conversations, and letters, I have received encouragement and guidance. Add to that an understanding family willing to pitch in. To all those, I say thanks!

A special thanks also goes to James Hintz and Tina Trautman, both of whom provided some new photos of pieces in their Depression glass collections for this edition.

And, most important, thanks to you, the collectors, dealers, and those who read books such as *Warman's® Depression Glass*. For it is all of you who keep the Depression glass market glittering.

COMPANY TIMELINE

19th C Ohio Flint Glass founded, later becomes part of National Glass Company conglomerate.

Indiana Glass Company established in 1907.

Bottle plant at Jeannette, Pennsylvania, which becomes Jeannette Glass Company.

1853 McKee and Brothers founded in Pittsburgh, Pennsylvania.

1887 Fostoria Glass Company founded in Fostoria, Ohio, but moves to Moundsville, West Virginia, when fuel supply is depleted.

1888 McKee moves to Jeannette, Pennsylvania.

1890 Westmoreland Specialty Company established in Grapeville, Pennsylvania. Early manufacture includes bottles and food containers. During World War I, glass candy containers are made. The plant continues on to make colored and opaque glassware in both Depression patterns and later a giftware line.

1891 U.S. Glass Company organizes by combining 18 different glass houses located in Pennsylvania, Ohio, and West Virginia. The main offices are in Pittsburgh, as well as some manufacturing.

1899 Macbeth merges with Evans, creating Macbeth-Evans. Main factory located in Charleroi, Pennsylvania, with others located in Marion, Bethevan, and Elwood, Indiana, as well as Toledo, Ohio.

1900 Federal Glass Company opens Columbus, Ohio, plant. First wares are crystal with needle etching, various decorations, and crackle finish. After switching to automation, it soon begins production of tumblers and many Depression-era patterns, as well as restaurant wares, all at an economical price.

1901 Imperial Glass Company organizes. Produces first glass at Bellaire, Ohio, plant in 1904.

Morgantown Glass Works begins production in Morgantown, West Virginia.

New Martinsville Glass Manufacturing Company is established at New Martinsville, West Virginia.

1902 Hazel Atlas Glass Company established in Washington, Pennsylvania, a result of the merger of the Hazel Glass Company and its neighboring factory, Atlas Glass and Metal Company. Corporate offices are later established at Wheeling, West Virginia.

1903 Morgantown Glass Works reorganizes as Economy Tumbler Company and operates using that name.

Liberty Cut Glass Works established in Egg Harbor, New Jersey. Primarily a cutting house for years, pressed glass is also made.

McKee Brothers reorganizes into McKee Glass Company and continues until 1951.

1905 Anchor Hocking Glass Company established in Lancaster, Ohio. Well known by the mid-1920s for its tumbler and tableware production.

1906 Fenton Art Glass Company builds new factory, Williamstown, West Virginia. While its giftware lines are well known, some Depression-era glassware is produced.

1907 Indiana Glass Company established at Dunkirk, Indiana. Early production is hand pressed. Assembly line patterns evolve during the 1920s, although some still require handwork. Later produce automobile glassware items, become a subsidiary of Lancaster Colony.

1908 Lancaster Glass Company, Lancaster, Ohio, built by first president of Fostoria.

1911 L.E. Smith begins in the glass trade. A lot of the production of this company remains utilitarian in nature as well as making lenses for automobiles.

1916 Paden City Glass Manufacturing Company established at Paden City, West Virginia. Production includes some Depression-era patterns, but is better known for its elegant lines, vases, lamps and restaurant wares.

1923 Economy Tumbler Company changes name to Economy Glass Company.

1924 Fostoria introduces color and starts national magazine advertising campaign.

Jeannette touted by trade as "one of the most complete automatic factories in the country." Lancaster becomes subsidary of Hocking Glass Company. Continues to make kitchenware, cut and decorated tableware under the Lancaster name until 1937. Also makes colored blanks for Standard Glass Company, another Hocking subsidiary, where the glass is etched and cut. Known as Plant #2 to Anchor Hocking.

1927 Jeannette management ceases all hand operations.

1928 Jeannette makes green and pink glass automatically in a continuous tank, a first!

Trade journals proclaim Clarksburg, West Virginia, Hazel-Atlas factory the "World's Largest Tumbler Factory," which accurately describes the fully automated factory.

1929 Economy Glass Company changes name back to Morgantown Glass Works, Inc.

1932 Liberty Cut Glass Works destroyed by fire, never to rebuild.

1937 Corning Glass Works purchases Macbeth-Evans.

Hocking Glass Company merges with Anchor Cap and Closure Corporation, Long Island City, New York, creating the huge Anchor-Hocking Glass Company, which has continued to have a major impact on the glassware industry.

Morgantown Glass Works, Inc., closes.

1938 U.S. Glass moves main offices to Tiffin, Ohio, and production decreases.

1939 Morgantown Glassware Guild organizes and reopens factory.

1944 New Martinsville sold and reorganizes as Viking Glass Company.

1949 Westmoreland Glass Company begins to use impressed intertwined "W" and "G" mark.

1951 The only operating company of the former U.S. Glass is Tiffin. The rest have all closed.

McKee sold to Thatcher Manufacturing Co.

1952 Fire destroys Belmont plant, Bellaire, Ohio, and with the fire goes company records.

1955 Duncan and Miller molds acquired by Tiffin, which begins to produce colors and crystal wares with these molds.

1956 Continental Can purchases Hazel-Atlas and continues to sell tableware under name "Hazelware."

1958 Federal Glass becomes a division of Federal Paper Board Company, and continues glassware production.

1961 Jeannette buys old McKee factory in Jeannette and moves there to continue production.

1964 Brockway Glass Company buys out Continental Can's interest in Hazel-Atlas and begins operation.

1965 Fostoria Glass Company purchases Morgantown Glassware Guild.

1966 Continental Can takes over operation of Tiffin until 1969, with glass production continuing.

1971 Glass production terminated at Fostoria's Morgantown facility, ending the Morgantown Glassware Guild.

1973 Imperial Glass Company sold to Lenox, Inc.

1980 Tiffin Glass discontinues operation.

1982 Westmoreland Glass Company closes factory in May. Reorganizes in July.

1983 Lancaster Glass purchases Fostoria.

Westmoreland begins to use full name as imprinted mark.

1984 Westmoreland Glass Company again closes Grapeville plant.

1999 L.G. Wright discontinues operation. Molds, factory equipment liquidated at public auction in May.

2000 Indiana Glass goes out of business in November.

2004 L. E. Smith ceases production in June, but manages to re-organize and production later resumes.

COLOR TIMELINE

AMBER
1923: McKee
1923: New Martinsville
1924: Paden City
1924: Westmoreland's Transparent Amber
1924-1941: Fostoria
1925: Indiana
Mid-1920s: Hocking, Imperial and L.E. Smith
1926: Jeannette
Late 1920s: Liberty
1931-1942: Federal's Golden Glow
1960: Westmoreland's Golden Sunset

AMETHYST
1923: McKee
1924: New Martinsville
Mid-1920s: L.E. Smith
1926: Morgantown's Old Amethyst
1933: Paden City
1939: Morgantown's Light Amethyst

APPLE GREEN
1925: Jeannette

BLACK
1920s-1930s: L.E. Smith
1922: Morgantown's India Black
1923 and 1930s: Paden City
1923: New Martinsville
1924: Fostoria
1930: McKee
1931: Hazel-Atlas, Imperial, Lancaster

BLUE
1920s: Lancaster
1923: McKee's Jap Blue and Transparent Blue
1923: New Martinsville
1924: Paden City
1924-1928: Fostoria
1925: McKee's Sky Blue and Westmoreland's
Mid-1920s: Hocking
1926: Imperial, Morgantown's Azure and transparent blue
1927: Imperial's Blue-Green, Morgantown's Ritz
1928: New Martinsville's Alice Blue (medium shade)
1928-1943: Fostoria's Azure Blue (lighter shade)
Late 1920s: Liberty's pale shade
1930: Hocking's Mayfair Blue (medium shade), McKee's Ritz Blue and Chalaine Blue
1931: Imperial's Ritz Blue, Lancaster's pale blue, Westmoreland's Belgian Blue
1933: Fostoria's Regal Blue
1933-1934: Federal's Madonna Blue (medium shade)
1933-1942: New Martinsville's Ritz Blue
Mid-1930s: Macbeth-Evans' Ritz Blue
1936: Hazel-Atlas' Ritz Blue, McKee's opaque Poudre Blue, Paden City's Ceylon Blue
1939: Morgantown's Copen Blue and Gloria Blue
1940: Anchor-Hocking's Fire King
1950s: Indiana's Blue-Green

BURGUNDY
1933: Fostoria
1936: Hazel-Atlas (deep shade)

CANARY YELLOW
1923: McKee
Mid-1920s: Hocking, L.E. Smith
1924: New Martinsville
1924-1927: Fostoria
1925: Lancaster

COBALT BLUE
1930: Liberty
1936: Paden City
1939: Morgantown

CREMAX
1939: Macbeth-Evans

CRYSTAL
1923: Paden City
1930s: Imperial
1935: New Martinsville and Westmoreland—most companies produced crystal throughout their years of production

DELPHITE, DELFITE
1936: Jeannette

FIRED-ON COLORS
1920s: Federal and Lancaster
1923: Westmoreland
1926: New Martinsville
Mid-1930s: Macbeth-Evans

FRENCH IVORY (OPAQUE)
1933: McKee

GREEN
1920s: Lancaster
1921: Morgantown's Venetian Green
1922: Morgantown's Meadow Green
1923: McKee
1924: Paden City
1924-1941: Fostoria
Mid-1920s: Hocking, Imperial and L.E. Smith
1925: Indiana, McKee's Grass Green and New Martinsville
1926: New Martinsville's Emerald Green
1926-1936: Federal's Springtime Green
1928: Macbeth-Evans' Emerald
Late 1920s: Liberty
1929: Hazel-Atlas, Imperial
1931: Morgantown's Stiegel Green
1931-1933: New Martinsville's Stiegel Green
1933: Fostoria's Empire Green, Hazel-Atlas' Killarney Green, New Martinsville's Evergreen (dark shade)
1936: Paden City's Forest Green
1939: Morgantown's Shamrock Green
1950s: Anchor-Hocking's Forest Green

IRIDESCENT
1920s: Federal
1920s to present: Jeannette
1934-1935: Federal's Iridescent Amber

IVORY
1929: Imperial
1933: Indiana (opaque)
1940: Anchor-Hocking

IVRENE
1930s: Macbeth-Evans

JADE
1930: McKee
1931: New Martinsville

JADE YELLOW
1923: McKee

JADITE
1932: Jeannette

MONAX
1920s: Macbeth-Evans

MULBERRY
1924: Paden City

OPALESCENT
1923: Morgantown's Alabaster
1931: Westmoreland's Moonstone (blue)
1942: Anchor-Hocking's Moonstone

ORCHID
1927: McKee
1927-1929: Fostoria
1929: Imperial

PINK
Mid-1920s: Imperial's Rose Marie, Rose
1925: Paden City's Cheriglo
1926: McKee's Rose Pink, Morgantown's Anna

RED-AMBER
1930: Liberty

ROSE
1926: Indiana and Westmoreland
1926-1942: Hocking's Rose (later called Flamingo or Cerise), New Martinsville's Peach Melba (later known as Rose)
1927: Jeannette's Wild Rose, L.E. Smith
1928: Macbeth-Evans
1928-1941: Fostoria's Rose or Dawn
Late 1920s: Liberty
1930: Hazel-Atlas, Lancaster's deep pink
1931-1942: Federal's Rose Glow
1933: Hazel-Atlas' Sunset Pink
1939: Morgantown's Pink Champagne
1947-1949: Jeannette

ROYAL BLUE
1932: Paden City

RUBY
1925: Morgantown
1927: McKee
1931: Imperial
1932: Paden City
1933-1942: New Martinsville
Mid-1930s: Macbeth-Evans
1935: Fostoria's Ruby
1939: Anchor-Hocking's Royal Ruby

SEA FOAM
1931: Imperial, Harding Blue, Moss Green or Burnt Almond with opal edge

SEVILLE YELLOW
1931: McKee

SHELL PINK
1958: Jeannette

SKOKIE GREEN
1931: McKee

TAN
1931: McKee's Old Rose

TOPAZ
1921: Morgantown's 14K Topaz
1925: Jeannette
1928: Hocking
1929: Fostoria
1930: Lancaster, Westmoreland (sometimes combined with crystal or black)
1930 to mid-1930s: Indiana
1931: Imperial, Liberty, Macbeth-Evans, McKee, Paden City's Golden Glow
1933: Hazel-Atlas
1938-1940s: Fostoria's Golden Tint
1939: Morgantown's Topaz Mist

ULTRAMARINE
1937-1938: Jeannette

VASELINE
Mid-1920s: Imperial

WHITE
1930s: Hazel-Atlas' Platonite (opaque)
1932: Hocking (Vitrock)
1937-1942: McKee (opal) and after World War II

WINE
1923: New Martinsville

WISTERIA
1931-1938: Fostoria

COLOR IDENTIFICATION GUIDE

Blue, back row from left: Laced Edge, Radiance and Bubble; front row from left: Mayfair and Ships.

Green #1, from left: Floral and Diamond Band, Colonial, U.S. Swirl, Thistle, Pyramid, Daisy, and Fire King Restaurant Ware.

Green #2, from left: Laurel, Rosemary, Westmoreland Vaseline basket, Parrot and Thumbprint.

Pink #1, back row from left: Nora Bird, Fire-King Swirl, Petalware and Diana; front row from left: Fortune and Hobnail.

Pink #2, back row from left: Lincoln Inn, Open Lace and Ovide; front row from left: Moondrops (cup and saucer), Sharon, Diana (coaster), and Peacock & Wild Rose.

Yellow #1, from left: Madrid, Patrick, Jubilee, Parrot, Orchid, Madrid and Roxanna.

Yellow #2, from left: Crow's Foot, Princess (apricot grill plate), Daisy, and Rock Crystal (front).

SHAPE GUIDE

American Sweetheart

Avocado

Beaded Edge

Bowknot

Bubble

Candlewick

Cherry Blossom

Chinex Classic

Christmas Candy

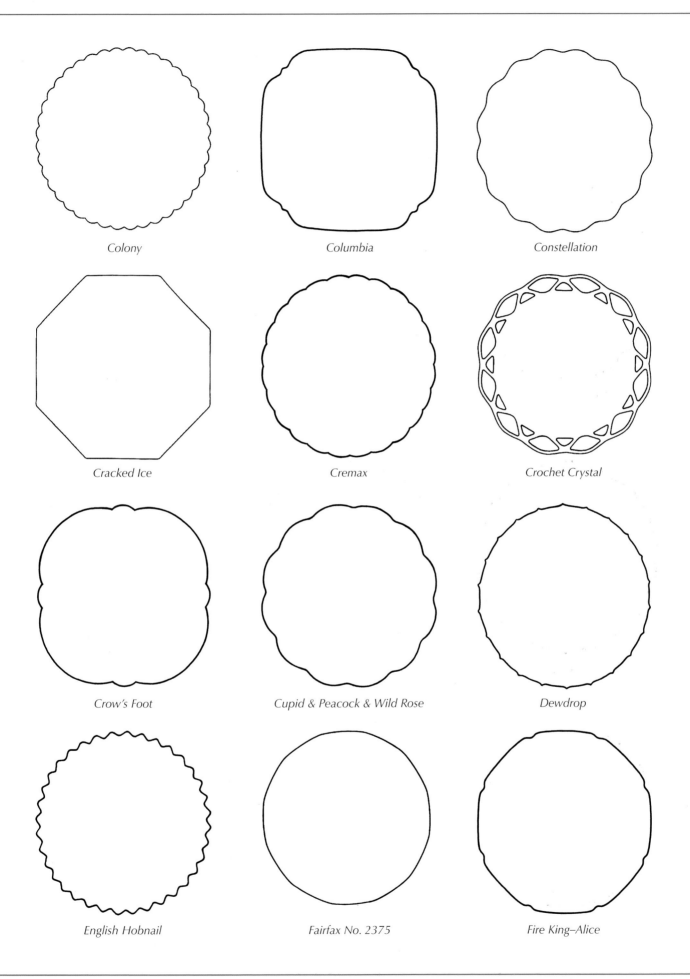

Colony

Columbia

Constellation

Cracked Ice

Cremax

Crochet Crystal

Crow's Foot

Cupid & Peacock & Wild Rose

Dewdrop

English Hobnail

Fairfax No. 2375

Fire King–Alice

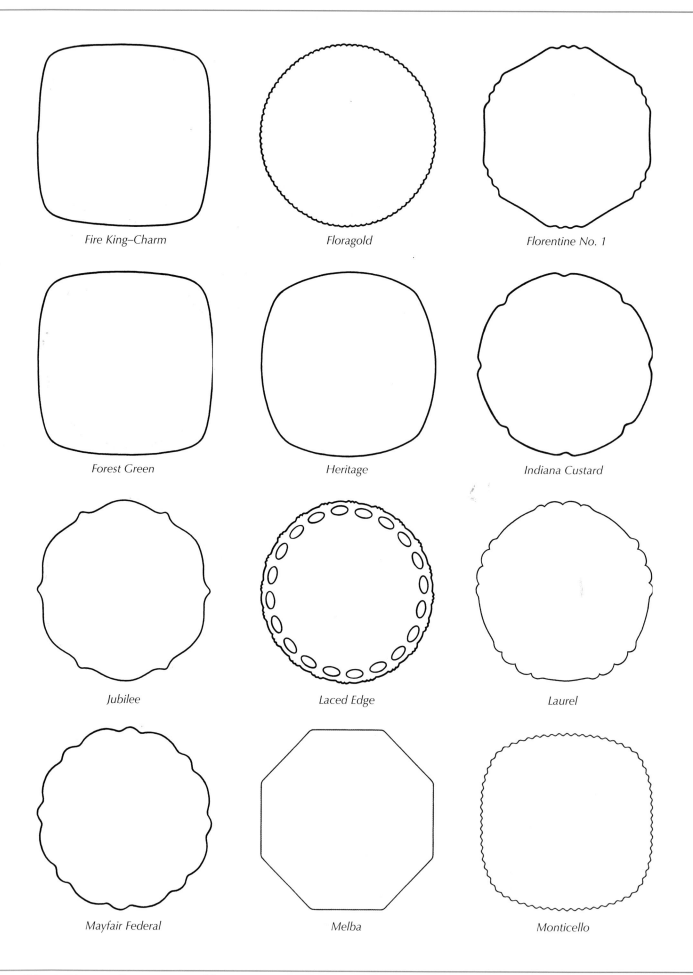

Fire King–Charm

Floragold

Florentine No. 1

Forest Green

Heritage

Indiana Custard

Jubilee

Laced Edge

Laurel

Mayfair Federal

Melba

Monticello

Moonstone

Mt. Pleasant

Nora Bird

Old Café

Orchid

Oyster & Pearl

Paneled Grape

Parrot

Patrick

Pineapple & Floral

Pioneer

Pretzel

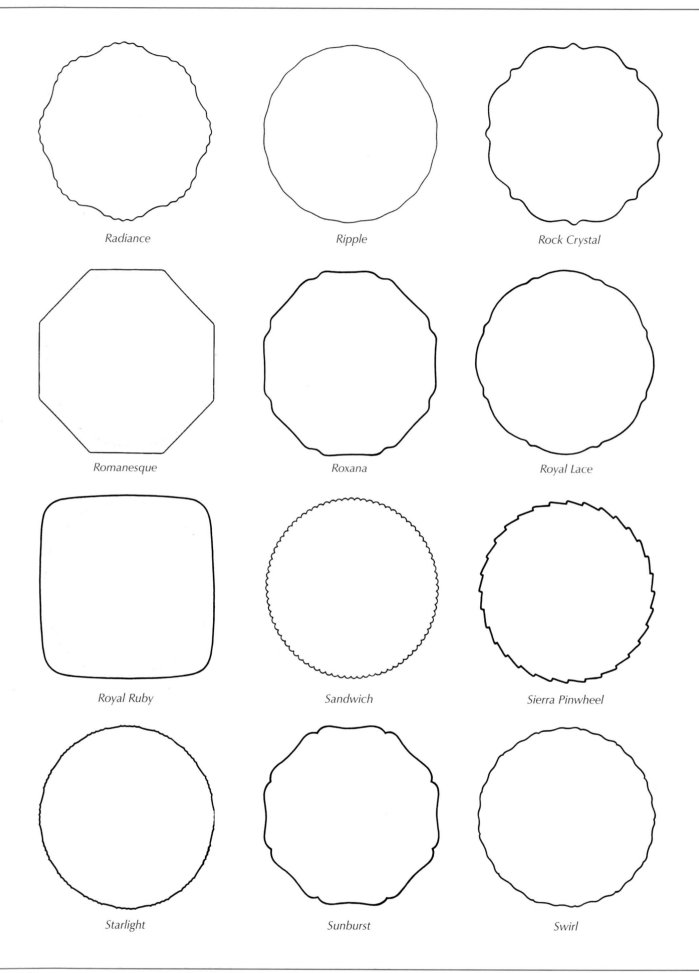

Radiance

Ripple

Rock Crystal

Romanesque

Roxana

Royal Lace

Royal Ruby

Sandwich

Sierra Pinwheel

Starlight

Sunburst

Swirl

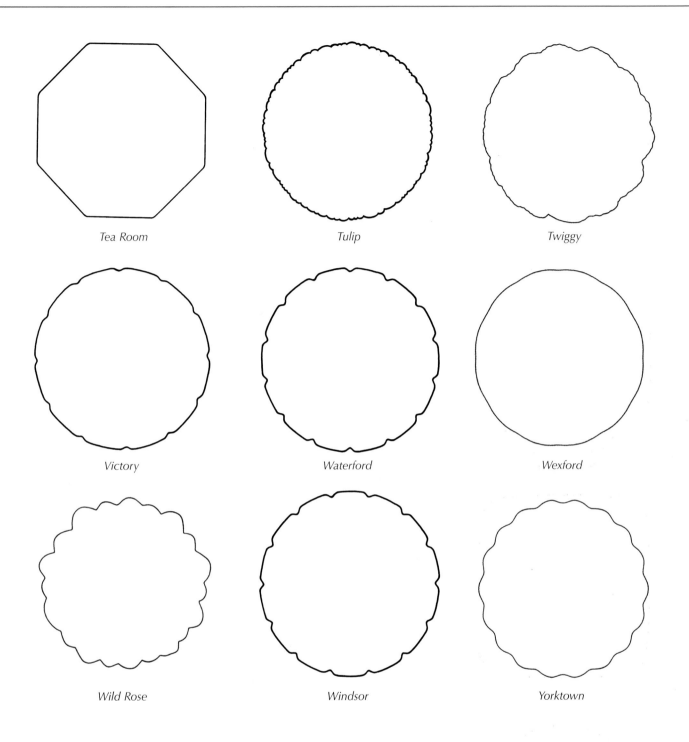

Tea Room   Tulip   Twiggy

Victory   Waterford   Wexford

Wild Rose   Windsor   Yorktown

THUMBNAIL GUIDE

Depression-era glassware can be confusing. Many times one manufacturer came up with a neat new design and as soon as it was successful, other companies started to make patterns that were similar. To help you figure out what pattern you might be trying to research, here's a quick identification guide. The patterns are broken down into several different classifications by design elements. Try comparing your piece to these and then consult the detailed pattern listing and larger drawing for more information.

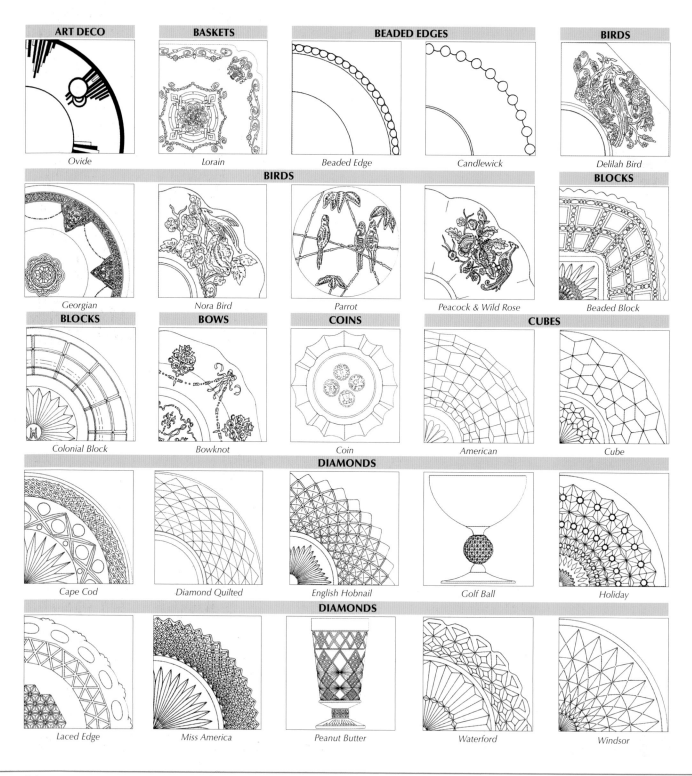

ART DECO	BASKETS	BEADED EDGES		BIRDS
Ovide	Lorain	Beaded Edge	Candlewick	Delilah Bird

BIRDS / **BLOCKS**

| Georgian | Nora Bird | Parrot | Peacock & Wild Rose | Beaded Block |

BLOCKS / **BOWS** / **COINS** / **CUBES**

| Colonial Block | Bowknot | Coin | American | Cube |

DIAMONDS

| Cape Cod | Diamond Quilted | English Hobnail | Golf Ball | Holiday |

DIAMONDS

| Laced Edge | Miss America | Peanut Butter | Waterford | Windsor |

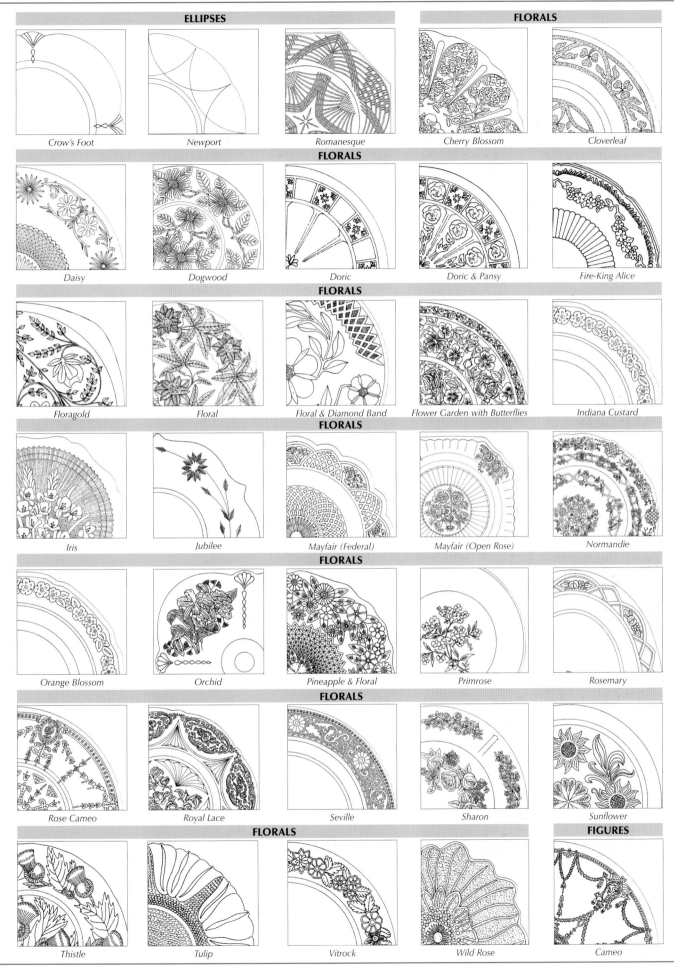

ELLIPSES

Crow's Foot

Newport

Romanesque

FLORALS

Cherry Blossom

Cloverleaf

FLORALS

Daisy

Dogwood

Doric

Doric & Pansy

Fire-King Alice

FLORALS

Floragold

Floral

Floral & Diamond Band

Flower Garden with Butterflies

Indiana Custard

FLORALS

Iris

Jubilee

Mayfair (Federal)

Mayfair (Open Rose)

Normandie

FLORALS

Orange Blossom

Orchid

Pineapple & Floral

Primrose

Rosemary

FLORALS

Rose Cameo

Royal Lace

Seville

Sharon

Sunflower

FLORALS

Thistle

Tulip

Vitrock

Wild Rose

FIGURES

Cameo

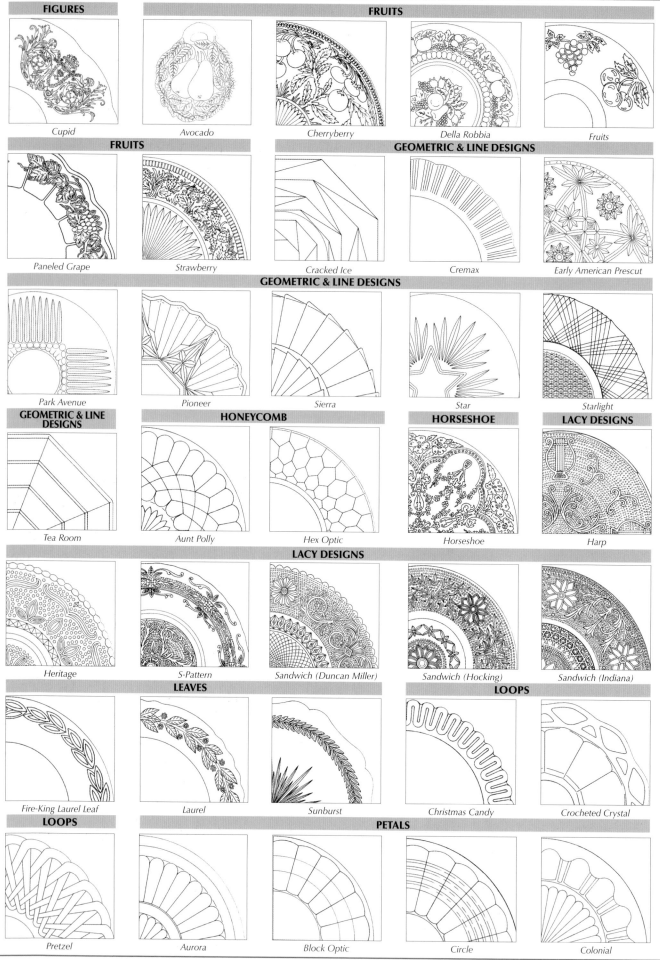

FIGURES

Cupid

Avocado

FRUITS

Cherryberry

Della Robbia

Fruits

FRUITS

Paneled Grape

Strawberry

GEOMETRIC & LINE DESIGNS

Cracked Ice

Cremax

Early American Prescut

GEOMETRIC & LINE DESIGNS

Park Avenue

Pioneer

Sierra

Star

Starlight

GEOMETRIC & LINE DESIGNS

Tea Room

HONEYCOMB

Aunt Polly

Hex Optic

HORSESHOE

Horseshoe

LACY DESIGNS

Harp

LACY DESIGNS

Heritage

S-Pattern

Sandwich (Duncan Miller)

Sandwich (Hocking)

Sandwich (Indiana)

LEAVES

Fire-King Laurel Leaf

Laurel

Sunburst

LOOPS

Christmas Candy

Crocheted Crystal

LOOPS

Pretzel

PETALS

Aurora

Block Optic

Circle

Colonial

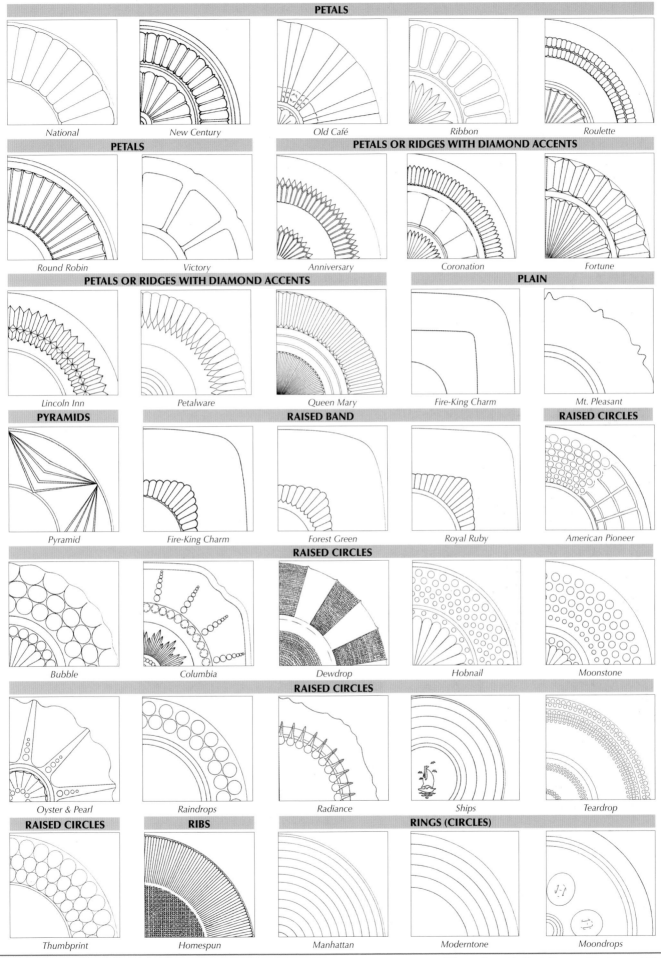

PETALS

National · New Century · Old Café · Ribbon · Roulette

PETALS — **PETALS OR RIDGES WITH DIAMOND ACCENTS**

Round Robin · Victory · Anniversary · Coronation · Fortune

PETALS OR RIDGES WITH DIAMOND ACCENTS — **PLAIN**

Lincoln Inn · Petalware · Queen Mary · Fire-King Charm · Mt. Pleasant

PYRAMIDS — **RAISED BAND** — **RAISED CIRCLES**

Pyramid · Fire-King Charm · Forest Green · Royal Ruby · American Pioneer

RAISED CIRCLES

Bubble · Columbia · Dewdrop · Hobnail · Moonstone

RAISED CIRCLES

Oyster & Pearl · Raindrops · Radiance · Ships · Teardrop

RAISED CIRCLES — **RIBS** — **RINGS (CIRCLES)**

Thumbprint · Homespun · Manhattan · Moderntone · Moondrops

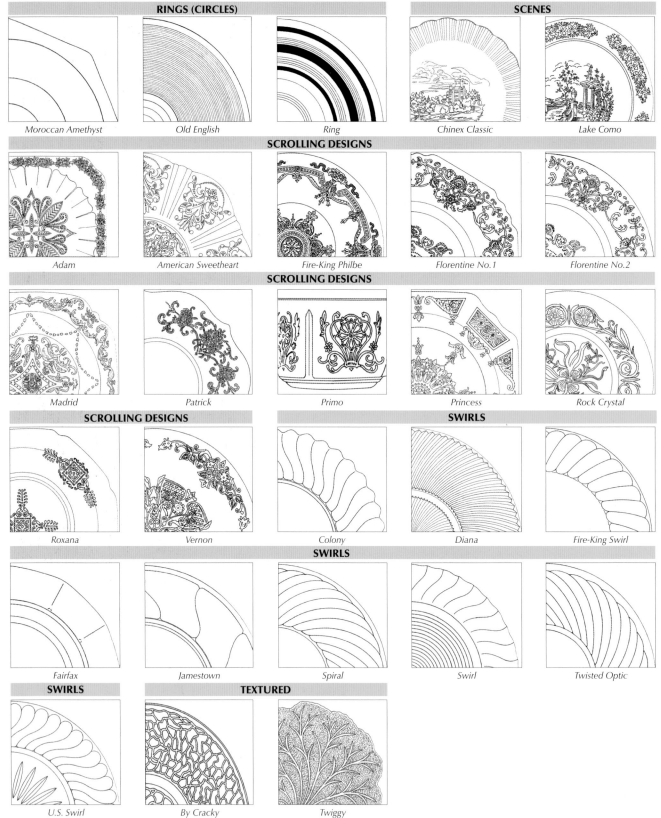

RINGS (CIRCLES)

Moroccan Amethyst

Old English

Ring

SCENES

Chinex Classic

Lake Como

SCROLLING DESIGNS

Adam

American Sweetheart

Fire-King Philbe

Florentine No.1

Florentine No.2

SCROLLING DESIGNS

Madrid

Patrick

Primo

Princess

Rock Crystal

SCROLLING DESIGNS

Roxana

Vernon

SWIRLS

Colony

Diana

Fire-King Swirl

SWIRLS

Fairfax

Jamestown

Spiral

Swirl

Twisted Optic

SWIRLS

U.S. Swirl

TEXTURED

By Cracky

Twiggy

ADAM

Manufactured by Jeannette Glass Company, Jeannette, Pa., from 1932 to 1934.

Pieces are made in crystal, Delphite blue, green, pink, some topaz and yellow. Delphite 4-inch high candlesticks are valued at $250 a pair. A yellow cup and saucer are valued at $200, and a 7-3/4-inch diameter yellow plate is valued at $115. Production in topaz and yellow was limited. Crystal prices are approximately 50 percent of the prices listed for green.

Reproductions: † Butter dish in pink and green.

Item	Green	Pink
Ashtray, 4-1/2" d	28.00	30.00
Berry bowl, small	22.50	18.50
Bowl, 9" d, cov	90.00	75.00
Bowl, 9" d, open	45.00	30.00
Bowl, 10" l, oval	40.00	40.00
Butter dish, cov †	395.00	135.00
Cake plate, 10" d, ftd	38.00	40.00
Candlesticks, pr, 4" h	125.00	100.00
Candy jar, cov, 2-1/2" h	120.00	135.00
Casserole, cov	95.00	80.00
Cereal bowl, 5-3/4" d	50.00	40.00
Coaster, 3-1/4" d	32.00	35.00
Creamer	30.00	35.00
Cup	30.00	28.00
Dessert bowl, 4-3/4" d	25.00	25.00
Iced tea tumbler, 5-1/2" h	72.00	75.00
Lamp	500.00	500.00
Pitcher, 32 oz, round base	—	125.00
Pitcher, 32 oz, 8" h	48.00	45.00
Plate, 6" d, sherbet	15.00	18.00
Plate, 7-3/4" d, salad, sq	18.50	19.50
Plate, 9" d, dinner, sq	37.50	42.00
Plate, 9" d, grill	37.50	35.00
Platter, 11-3/4" l, rect	38.00	38.00
Relish dish, 8" l, divided	27.00	20.00
Salt and pepper shakers, pr, 4" h	130.00	95.00
Saucer, 6" sq	12.00	10.00
Sherbet, 3"	40.00	38.00
Sugar, cov	48.00	65.00
Tumbler, 4-1/2" h	35.00	40.00
Vase, 7-1/2" h	60.00	550.00
Vegetable bowl, cov, 7-3/4" d	95.00	75.00
Vegetable bowl, open, 7-3/4" d	30.00	40.00

*Adam, green ashtray, **$45**; pink pitcher, **$28**.*

*Adam, green plate, **$18.50**.*

AMERICAN
Line #2056

Manufactured by Fostoria Glass Company, Moundsville, Va., from 1915 to 1986.

Pieces are made in crystal, some amber, blue, green, yellow, pink, pink tinting to purple in the late 1920s, white, red in 1980s, and currently in red and crystal for Lancaster Colony by Dalzell Viking. Prices for colors fluctuate greatly.

Item	Crystal
Almond bowl, 3-3/4" l, oval	18.00
Appetizer insert, 3-1/4"	30.00
Appetizer tray, 10-1/2" l, six inserts	250.00
Ashtray, 2-7/8" w, sq	10.00
Ashtray, 3-7/8" l, oval	25.00
Ashtray, 5" w, sq	35.00
Ashtray, 5-1/2" l, oval	20.00
Banana split, 9" x 3-1/2"	900.00
Basket, open handle	125.00
Basket, 10", c1988	40.00
Basket, 7" x 9", reeded handle	95.00
Beer mug, 4-1/2" h, 12 oz	70.00
Bell	650.00
Biscuit jar, cov	800.00
Bitter bottles, 5-3/4" h, 4-1/2 oz, two-pc set	310.00
Boat, 8-1/2" d	15.00
Boat, 9" d, two parts	12.00
Boat, 12" l	17.50

Item	Crystal
Bonbon, 6" d, three ftd	15.00
Bonbon, 7" h, three ftd	15.00
Bonbon, 8" d, three ftd	17.50
Bowl, 4-1/2" d, one handle, round or square	12.00
Bowl, 4-1/2" d, oval	15.00
Bowl, 5" d, handle, tricorner	15.00
Bowl, 7" d, 4-1/2" h, cupped	50.00
Bowl, 8" d, ftd	55.00
Bowl, 8-1/2" d, two handles	65.00
Bowl, 9" l, oval #4836	25.00
Bowl, 9-1/2" d, 6" w, three parts	60.00
Bowl, 10" d, deep	48.00
Bowl, 10" d, 14" d liner	50.00
Bowl, 11-1/2" d rolled edge	75.00
Box, cov, 4-1/2" x 4-1/2"	200.00
Brush tray	50.00
Bud vase, 6" h, flared	45.00
Bud vase, 6" h, ftd	40.00
Bud vase, 8-1/2" h, cupped	40.00
Bud vase, 8-1/2" h, flared	45.00
Butter dish, cov, 1/4 lb	45.00
Butter dish, cov, 7-1/4" d, round plate	135.00
Cake plate, 10" d, two handles	24.00
Cake plate, 12" d, three ftd	20.00
Cake stand, 10" round, pedestal foot	165.00
Cake stand, 10" sq, pedestal foot	295.00
Cake stand, 11" d, round, pedestal foot	195.00
Cake tray, 10-1/2" d, crook-shaped handle	45.00
Candelabrum, 6-1/2", two-light, bell base, bobeche, pr	125.00
Candle lamp, 8-1/2" h, chimney, candle part, 3-1/2"	170.00
Candlestick, 2", chamber, fingerhold	60.00
Candlesticks, pr, 3", round, ftd	24.00
Candlesticks, pr, 4-3/8", two-light, round foot	95.00
Candlesticks, pr, 6", octagon foot	65.00
Candlesticks, pr, 6-1/2", two-light, bell base	265.00
Candlesticks, pr, 6-1/4", round foot	360.00
Candlesticks, pr, 7", sq, column	225.00

American, crystal bowl, 10" d $48.

Item	Crystal
Candlesticks, pr, 7-1/4", Eiffel Tower	375.00
Candy box, cov, three parts, triangular	95.00
Candy box, cov, 7" x 5"	500.00
Catsup bottle	145.00
Celery tray, 10" l, oblong	35.00
Centerpiece bowl, 9-1/2" d	45.00
Centerpiece bowl, 11" d	45.00
Centerpiece bowl, 11" d, tricorner	45.00
Centerpiece bowl, 15" d, hat-shape	165.00
Cheese and cracker, 5-3/4" comport, 11-1/2" d plate	125.00
Chocolate tray, 7" x 5" x 1-7/8" deep	695.00
Cigarette box, cov, 4-3/4"	60.00
Claret, 4-5/8" h, 3-1/2 oz, plain bowl, #5056	65.00
Claret, 4-7/8" h, 7 oz, #2056	75.00
Coaster, 3-3/4" d	20.00
Cocktail, 2-7/8" h, cone, ftd, 3 oz, #2506	20.00
Cocktail, 4" h, 3-1/2 oz, plain bowl, #5056	18.00
Cologne bottle, orig stopper, 5-3/4" h, 6 oz	95.00
Cologne bottle, orig stopper, 7-1/4" h, 9 oz	90.00
Comport, 5" d, covered	25.00
Comport, 8-1/2" d, 4" h	45.00
Comport, 9-1/2" d, #3237	75.00
Condiment bottle	115.00
Condiment set, two oils, two shakers, mustard, tray	325.00
Condiment tray, clover leaf	375.00
Cookie jar, cov, 8-3/4" h	600.00
Cordial, 3-1/8" h, 1 oz, plain bowl, #5056	25.00
Cordial bottle, 7-1/4" h, 9 oz	95.00
Cordial set, four decanters, chrome holder	2,285.00
Cosmetic box	850.00
Cream soup bowl, 5" d, two handles	95.00
Cream soup liner	20.00
Creamer and sugar tray, 6-3/4" l, handle	15.00
Creamer, 3 oz, 2-3/8" h, tea size	10.00
Creamer, 4-3/4 oz, individual size	11.50
Creamer, 9-1/2 oz	14.00
Cruet, orig stopper, 5 oz	32.00
Cruet, orig stopper, 7 oz	35.00
Crushed fruit, cov, spoon, 9-1/2" h	2,125.00
Crushed fruit, cov, spoon, 10" h	1,425.00
Cup, flat	8.50
Cup, ftd, 7 oz	7.50
Decanter, stopper, 24 oz, 9-1/4" h	150.00
Dresser set, pr cov powder boxes, tray	500.00
Dresser tray, 11"	450.00
Finger bowl, 4-1/2" d, underplate	110.00
Float bowl, 10" d	45.00
Float bowl, 10" l, oval	35.00
Float bowl, 11-1/2" d	55.00
Flower pot, orig flower frog center, 5-1/2" h, 9-1/2" w ..	2,700.00
Fruit bowl, 10-1/2" d, three ftd	40.00
Fruit bowl, 11-1/2" d, 2-3/4" h, rolled edge	45.00
Fruit bowl, 13" d, shallow	65.00
Fruit bowl, 4-3/4" d, flared	18.00
Fruit bowl, 16" d, pedestal foot	250.00
Fruit cocktail, 4-3/4" h, 4-1/2 oz, hex foot, #2506	40.00

American, crystal bowl, flared, $75.

Item	Crystal
Glove box, cov, 9-1/2" x 3-1/2"	325.00
Goblet, 9 oz, 4-3/8" h, low foot, #2056	12.00
Goblet, 10 oz, 6-1/8" h, plain bowl, #5056	12.50
Goblet, 10 oz, 6-7/8" h, hex foot, #2056	16.00
Hair receiver, 3" x 3"	1,000.00
Hairpin box, cov, 3-1/2" x 1-3/4"	1,700.00
Handkerchief box, cov, 5-5/8" x 4-5/8"*	700.00
Hat, 2-1/8"	30.00
Hat, 3" h	35.00
Hat, 4" h	45.00
Hat, western style	200.00
Hurricane lamp, 12" h, complete	425.00
Ice bucket, tongs	90.00
Ice cream saucer, two styles	55.00
Ice cream tray, 13-1/2" l, oval	300.00
Ice dish for 4-oz crab or 5-oz tomato liner	65.00
Ice dish insert	18.00
Ice tub, with liner, 5-3/8"	95.00
Ice tub, with liner, 6-1/2"	100.00
Iced tea tumbler, handle	215.00
Iced tea tumbler, 12 oz, 5-3/4" h, 12 oz, low foot, #2056	26.00
Jam pot, cov	125.00
Jelly bowl, 4-1/4" d, 4-1/4" h	20.00
Jelly bowl, cov, 4-1/2" d, 6-3/4" h	40.00
Jelly comport, 4-1/2" d	25.00
Jelly comport, 5" d, flared	70.00
Jelly comport, cov, 6-3/4" d	35.00
Jewel box, cov, 3-1/2" x 6"	1,600.00
Jewel box, cov, 4-1/4" x 3-1/4", two drawers	1,800.00
Jewel box, cov, 5-1/4" x 2-1/4"	325.00
Juice tumbler, 5 oz, straight sides, flat	15.00
Juice tumbler, 4-1/8" h, 5 oz, ftd, plain bowl	15.00
Juice tumbler, 4-3/4" h, 5 oz, ftd, #2056	15.00
Ketchup bottle, orig stopper	160.00
Lemon bowl, cov, 5-1/2" d	45.00
Lemonade tumbler, 11 oz, 5-3/4" h, ftd	500.00
Lily pond bowl, 12" d	95.00
Marmalade, cov, chrome spoon	125.00

Item	Crystal
Mayonnaise, div	25.00
Mayonnaise, ladle, pedestal foot	45.00
Mayonnaise, liner, ladle	35.00
Molasses can, 11 oz, 6-3/4" h, one handle	450.00
Muffin tray, 10" l, two upturned sides	45.00
Mustard, cov	45.00
Napkin ring	45.00
Nappy, 4-1/2"	15.00
Nappy, 4-3/4" x 8"	150.00
Nappy, 5" d, cov	30.00
Nappy, 6" d	15.00
Nappy, 8" d	20.00
Old fashioned tumbler, 3-3/8" h, 6 oz, flat	10.00
Olive, 6" l, oblong	22.00
Oyster cocktail, 3-1/2" h, 4-1/2 oz, #2056	18.00
Oyster cocktail, 3-1/2" h, 4 oz, plain bowl	16.50
Pastry server, orig spoon, orig box	45.00
Pastry stand, ftd, 8-1/2" or 9-3/4" d	500.00
Perfume bottle, orig stopper ****	100.00
Pickle jar, pointed cov, 6" h	650.00
Pickle, 8" l, oblong	25.00
Picture frame	18.00
Pin tray, oval, 5-1/2" x 4-1/2"	120.00
Pitcher, one pt, 5-3/8" h, flat	35.00
Pitcher, one qt, flat	75.00
Pitcher, 1/2 gal, 8", ftd	90.00
Pitcher, 1/2 gal, ice lip, 8-1/4", flat bottom	165.00
Pitcher, 1/2 gal, without ice lip	265.00
Pitcher, two-pt, 7-1/4" h, ftd	70.00
Pitcher, three-pt, 8", ftd	75.00
Pitcher, three-pt, ice lip, 6-1/2", ftd, fat	65.00
Plate, 6" d, bread and butter	12.00
Plate, 7" d, salad	15.00
Plate, 7-1/2" x 4-3/8", crescent salad	45.00
Plate, 8" d, sauce liner, oval	28.00
Plate, 8-1/2" d, lunch	18.00
Plate, 9-1/2" d, dinner	28.00
Platter, 10-1/2" l, oval	40.00
Platter, 12" l, oval	55.00
Platter, 13-1/2" l	850.00
Pomade box, 2" sq	365.00
Preserve bowl, cov, 5-1/2" d, two handles	85.00
Puff box, cov, round	950.00
Puff box, cov, square	2,700.00
Punch bowl, 14" d, high foot, base, two gallon	250.00
Punch bowl, 14" d, low foot, base	275.00
Punch bowl, 18" d, low, 3-3/4 gallon	325.00
Punch cup, flared rim	12.50
Punch cup, straight edge	10.00
Relish boat, 12" l, two parts	16.50
Relish tray, 6-1/2" x 9", four parts	42.00
Relish/celery, 11" l, three parts	48.00
Ring holder	750.00
Rose bowl, 3-1/2" d	50.00
Rose bowl, 5" d	40.00
Salt and pepper shakers, pr, tray, 2" h	24.00

Item	Crystal
Salt shaker, 3" h	20.00
Salt shaker, 3-1/2" h	7.50
Salt shaker, 3-1/4" h	9.50
Salt, individual	15.00
Sandwich plate, 9" d, small center	20.00
Sandwich plate, 10-1/2" d, small center	22.00
Sandwich plate, 11-1/2" d, small center	22.00
Sandwich tray, 12" d, center handle	35.00
Sauce boat	50.00
Saucer	3.25
Service tray, 9-1/2", two handles	32.00
Sherbet, 4-1/2 oz, 3-1/2" h, handle	95.00
Sherbet, 4-1/2 oz, 4-3/8" h, flared, #2056	9.00
Sherbet, 4-1/2 oz, 4-1/2" h, #2056-1/2	9.00
Sherbet, 5 oz, 3-1/2" h, low, #2056-1/2	12.00
Sherbet, 5-1/2 oz, 4-1/8" h, plain bowl, #5056	8.50
Shrimp bowl, 12-1/4" d	395.00
Spooner, 3-3/4" h	60.00
Strawholder, 10" h, cov	395.00
Sugar shaker	50.00
Sugar, cov, two handles	22.00
Sugar, cov, 6-1/4" h	65.00
Sugar cube holder	450.00
Sugar, handle, 3-1/4" h	55.00
Sugar, tea, 2-1/4" h	15.00
Sundae, 3-1/8" h, 6 oz, low foot, #2056	8.50
Sweet pea vase, 4-1/2" h	75.00
Syrup, drip-proof top	95.00
Syrup, 6 oz, non-pour screw top, 5-1/2" h	200.00
Syrup, 6-1/2 oz, Sani-cut server, #2056-1/2	175.00
Syrup, 10 oz, glass cov, 6" liner plate	145.00
Tea tumbler, 5" h, 12 oz, #2056-1/2	17.50
Tea tumbler, 5-1/2" h, plain bowl, #5056	15.00
Tea tumbler, 5-1/4" h, 12 oz, flat, flared	17.50
Tidbit tray, metal crook-shaped handle	30.00
Toddler set, baby tumbler, bowl	85.00
Tom and Jerry mug, 3-1/4" h, 5-1/2 oz	42.00
Tom and Jerry, 12" d, small punch bowl, pedestal foot**	240.00
Toothpick holder	25.00
Torte plate, 13-1/2" d, oval	65.00
Torte plate, 14" d	90.00
Torte plate, 18" d	150.00
Torte plate, 24" d	275.00
Tray, cloverleaf	250.00
Tray, 5" x 2-1/2", rect	80.00
Tray, 6", oval, handle	45.00
Tray, 10" w, sq	115.00
Tray, 10" w, sq, four parts	85.00
Tray, 10-1/2" x 5", oval, handle	48.00
Tray, 10-1/2" x 7-1/2", rect	75.00
Tray, 10-3/4" sq, four parts	175.00
Tray, 12" d, round	185.00
Tray, 14-1/8", five parts***	160.00
Trifle bowl, 8" d, 4" h	300.00
Trophy cup, 8" d, ftd, two handles	145.00
Tumbler, 3-7/8" h, straight sides, #2056-1/2	17.50

*American, crystal relish, **$16.50**; luncheon plate, 8-1/2" d, **$18**; and footed tumbler, **$12**.*

Item	Crystal
Tumbler, 4-1/8" h, 8 oz, flat, flared	16.00
Tumbler, 4-7/8" h, 9 oz, ftd	12.00
Urn, 6" h, sq, pedestal foot	32.00
Urn, 7-1/2" sq, pedestal foot	60.00
Vase, 6" h, straight side	38.00
Vase, 6-1/2" h, flared rim	18.00
Vase, 7" h, flared	75.00
Vase, 8" h, flared	85.00
Vase, 8" h, porch, 5" d	315.00
Vase, 8" h, straight side	45.00
Vase, 9" h, sq pedestal foot	60.00
Vase, 9-1/2" h, flared	300.00
Vase, 10" h, cupped in top	250.00
Vase, 10" h, flared	95.00
Vase, 10" h, porch, 8" d	3,600.00

Item	Crystal
Vase, 10" h, straight side	95.00
Vase, 10" h, swung	295.00
Vase, 12" h, straight side	125.00
Vase, 12" h, swung	295.00
Vase, 20" h, swung	395.00
Vase, 22-1/2" h, swung	1,000.00
Vegetable bowl, 9" l, oval	32.00
Vegetable bowl, 10" l, oval, two parts	35.00
Wash bowl and pitcher	2,650.00
Water bottle, 9-1/4" h, 44 oz	750.00
Wedding bowl, cov, 6-1/2" w, 5-1/4" h, sq, pedestal	160.00
Whiskey, 2 oz	12.00
Whiskey tumbler, 2-1/4" h, 6 oz, #2056	16.00
Wine, 4-3/8" h, 2-1/2 oz, hex foot, #2056	22.00

* Handkerchief box, cov, 5-5/8" x 4-5/8" in blue is valued at $800.

** Tom and Jerry, 12" d, small punch bowl, pedestal foot in blue sold in 1999 for $12,000.

*** Tray, 14-1/8" d, five parts, in blue, is valued at $425.

**** Perfume bottle, orig stopper, 5-1/2" h, in amber, $425.

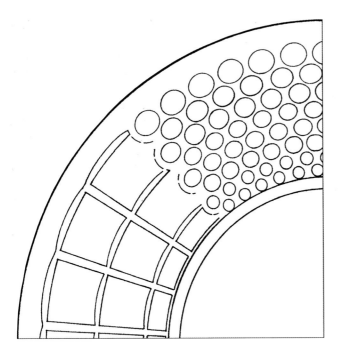

AMERICAN PIONEER

Manufactured by Liberty Works, Egg Harbor, N.J., from 1931 to 1934.

Pieces are made in amber, crystal, green, and pink.

Item	Amber	Crystal	Green	Pink
Bowl, 5" d, handle	45.00	24.00	27.50	24.00
Bowl, 8-3/4" d, cov	—	115.00	125.00	115.00
Bowl, 9" d, handle	—	24.00	30.00	24.00
Bowl, 9-1/4" d, cov	—	120.00	150.00	120.00
Bowl, 10" d	—	50.00	70.00	60.00
Candlesticks, pr, 6-1/2" h	—	75.00	95.00	75.00
Candy jar, cov, 1 pound	—	100.00	115.00	110.00
Candy jar, cov, 1-1/2 pound	—	70.00	125.00	95.00
Cheese and cracker set, indented plate and compote	—	50.00	65.00	55.00
Coaster, 3-1/2" d	—	30.00	35.00	32.00
Cocktail, 3 oz, 3-13/16" h	45.00	—	—	—
Cocktail, 3-1/2 oz, 3-15/16" h	45.00	—	—	—
Console Bowl, 10-3/4" d	—	50.00	75.00	60.00
Creamer, 2-3/4" h	—	20.00	22.00	25.00
Creamer, 3-1/2" h	60.00	30.00	32.00	30.00
Cup	24.00	10.00	12.00	12.00
Dresser set, two cologne bottles, powder jar, 7-1/2" tray	—	300.00	345.00	365.00
Goblet, 8 oz, 6" h, water	—	40.00	45.00	40.00
Ice bucket, 6" h	—	90.00	95.00	95.00
Juice tumbler, 5 oz	—	40.00	45.00	40.00
Lamp, 1-3/4", metal pole, 9-1/2"	—	—	85.00	—
Lamp, 5-1/2" round, ball shape	175.00	—	—	70.00
Lamp, 8-1/2" h	—	90.00	115.00	110.00
Mayonnaise, 4-1/4"	—	75.00	115.00	95.00
Pilsner, 5-3/4" h, 11 oz	—	100.00	110.00	100.00
Pitcher, cov, 5" h	295.00	150.00	225.00	165.00
Pitcher, cov, 7" h	325.00	175.00	250.00	195.00
Plate, 6" d	—	12.50	17.50	12.50
Plate, 6" d, handle	25.00	12.50	17.50	12.50

Item	Amber	Crystal	Green	Pink
Plate, 8" d	28.00	10.00	13.00	14.00
Plate, 11-1/2" d, handle	40.00	20.00	24.00	20.00
Rose bowl, 4-1/4" d, ftd	—	40.00	50.00	45.00
Saucer, 6" sq	10.00	4.50	5.00	5.50
Sherbet, 3-1/2" h	—	20.00	25.00	20.00
Sherbet, 4-3/4" h	65.00	32.50	40.00	30.00
Sugar, 2-3/4" h	—	20.00	27.50	25.00
Sugar, 3-1/2" h	50.00	20.00	27.50	25.00
Tumbler, 8 oz, 4" h	—	32.00	55.00	35.00
Tumbler, 12 oz, 5" h	—	60.00	65.00	60.00
Vase, 7" h, four styles	—	115.00	145.00	125.00
Vase, 9" h, round	—	—	245.00	—
Whiskey, 2 oz, 2-1/4" h	—	50.00	100.00	50.00

*American Pioneer, green plate, **$13**; cup, **$15**; and saucer, **$5**.*

AMERICAN SWEETHEART

Manufactured by Macbeth-Evans Glass Company, Charleroi, Pa., from 1930 to1936.

Pieces are made in blue, Monax, pink, and red. There is limited production in Cremax and color-trimmed Monax.

Item	Blue	Cremax	Monax	Monax with Color Trim	Pink	Red
Berry bowl, 3-1/4" d, flat	—	—	—	—	90.00	—
Berry bowl, 9" d	—	140.00	85.00	200.00	75.00	—
Cereal bowl, 6" d	—	19.50	20.00	50.00	28.00	—
Chop plate, 11" d	—	—	26.00	—	—	—
Console bowl, 18" d	1,450.00	—	550.00	—	—	1,200.00
Cream soup, 4-1/2" d	—	—	135.00	—	100.00	—
Creamer, ftd	195.00	—	15.00	110.00	20.00	175.00
Cup	160.00	—	15.00	100.00	20.00	95.00
Lamp shade	—	450.00	995.00	—	—	—
Pitcher, 60 oz, 7-1/2" h	—	—	—	—	995.00	—
Pitcher, 80 oz, 8" h	—	—	—	—	795.00	—
Plate, 6" d, bread and butter	—	—	7.50	24.00	10.00	—

American Sweetheart, Monax open sugar, $15; and creamer, $11.50.

*American Sweetheart, Monax dinner plate, 10-1/4" d, **$30**.*

Item	Blue	Cremax	Monax	Monax with Color Trim	Pink	Red
Plate, 8" d, salad	135.00	—	12.00	30.00	15.00	145.00
Plate, 9" d, luncheon	—	—	19.50	48.00	—	—
Plate, 9-3/4" d, dinner	—	—	25.00	90.00	45.00	—
Plate, 10-1/4" d, dinner	—	—	30.00	—	45.00	—
Platter, 13" l, oval	—	—	85.00	225.00	75.00	—
Salt and pepper shakers, pr, ftd	—	—	395.00	—	500.00	—
Salver plate, 12" d	275.00	—	30.00	—	30.00	200.00
Saucer	25.00	—	7.00	18.00	7.50	45.00
Serving plate, 15-1/2" d	450.00	—	250.00	—	—	350.00
Sherbet, 3-3/4" h, ftd	—	—	25.00	—	30.00	—
Sherbet, 4-1/4" h, ftd	—	—	25.00	110.00	25.00	—
Soup bowl, flat, 9-1/2" d	—	—	95.00	170.00	85.00	—
Sugar, open, ftd	195.00	—	15.00	110.00	15.00	175.00
Tidbit, two-tier	350.00	—	95.00	—	250.00	—
Tidbit, three-tier	750.00	—	275.00	—	—	600.00
Tumbler, 5 oz, 3-1/2" h	—	—	—	—	130.00	—
Tumbler, 9 oz, 4-1/4" h	—	—	—	—	95.00	—
Tumbler, 10 oz, 4-3/4" h	—	—	—	—	185.00	—
Vegetable bowl, 11"	—	—	90.00	—	85.00	—

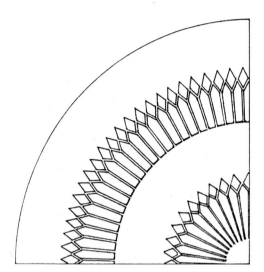

ANNIVERSARY

Manufactured by Jeannette Glass Company, Jeannette, Pa., from 1947 to 1949, late 1960s to mid-1970s.

Pieces are made in crystal, iridescent, and pink.

Item	Crystal	Iridescent	Pink
Berry bowl, 4-7/8" d	6.50	5.50	12.00
Butter dish, cov	25.00	—	50.00
Cake plate, 12-3/8" w, square	7.00	—	16.50
Cake plate, 12-1/2" d, round	18.00	—	18.50
Cake plate, metal cover	15.00	—	—
Candlesticks, pr, 4-7/8" h	20.00	25.00	—
Candy jar, cov	24.00	—	45.00
Comport, open, three legs	5.00	5.00	16.00
Comport, ruffled, three legs	6.50	—	—
Creamer, ftd	6.00	6.50	14.00
Cup	5.00	4.00	9.00
Fruit bowl, 9" d	15.00	14.50	24.50
Pickle, 9" d	5.50	7.50	12.00
Plate, 6-1/4" d, sherbet	2.00	3.50	4.00
Plate, 9" d, dinner	8.00	8.50	18.00
Plate, 10" d, dinner	15.00	—	—
Relish dish, 8" d	10.00	12.50	16.00
Sandwich server, 12-1/2" d	6.50	10.00	20.00
Saucer	1.00	1.50	6.00
Sherbet, ftd	10.00	—	12.00
Soup bowl, 7-3/8" d	8.00	7.50	18.00
Sugar, cov	12.00	10.00	20.00
Sugar, open, gold trim	4.50	—	—
Tidbit, metal handle	14.00	—	—
Vase, 6-1/2" h	20.00	—	30.00
Wall pocket	65.00	—	90.00
Wine, 2-1/2 oz	12.00	—	25.00

Anniversary, iridescent dinner plate, $8.

AUNT POLLY

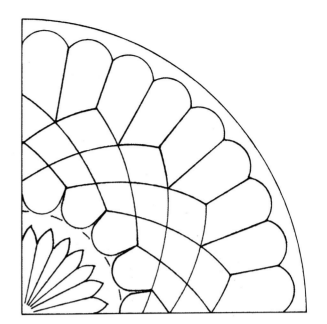

Manufactured by U.S. Glass Company, Pittsburgh, Pa., in the late 1920s.

Pieces are made in blue, green, and iridescent.

Item	Blue	Green	Iridescent
Berry bowl, 4-3/4" d, individual	20.00	15.00	15.00
Berry bowl, 7-1/8" d, master	45.00	22.00	22.00
Bowl, 4-3/4" d, 2" h	—	15.00	15.00
Bowl, 5-1/2" d, one handle	25.00	15.00	15.00
Bowl, 8-3/8" l, oval	100.00	42.00	42.00
Butter dish, cov	225.00	210.00	200.00
Candy jar, cov, two handles	50.00	30.00	30.00
Candy jar, ftd, two handles	—	27.50	27.50
Creamer	60.00	32.00	32.00
Pickle, 7-1/4" l, oval, handle	45.00	20.00	20.00
Pitcher, 48 oz, 8" h	200.00	—	—
Plate, 6" d, sherbet	16.00	6.00	6.00
Plate, 8" d, luncheon	20.00	—	—
Salt and pepper shakers, pr	245.00	—	—
Sherbet	15.00	12.00	12.00
Sugar	195.00	95.00	95.00
Tumbler, 8 oz, 3-5/8" h	35.00	—	—
Vase, 6-1/2" h, ftd	55.00	35.00	38.00

*Aunt Polly, blue sherbet, **$15**.*

AURORA

Manufactured by Hazel Atlas Glass Company, Clarksburg, West Virginia, and Zanesville, Ohio, in the late 1930s.

Pieces are made in cobalt (Ritz) blue, crystal, green, and pink.

Item	Cobalt Blue	Crystal	Green	Pink
Bowl, 4-1/2" d	85.00	—	—	75.00
Breakfast set, 24 pcs, service for four	500.00	—	—	—
Cereal bowl, 5-3/8" d	20.00	12.00	9.50	15.00
Cup	20.00	6.00	10.00	15.00
Milk pitcher	27.50	—	—	25.00
Plate, 6-1/2" d	12.50	—	—	12.50
Saucer	7.50	2.00	3.00	6.00
Tumbler, 10 oz, 4-3/4" h	32.50	—	—	35.50

*Aurora, cobalt blue cereal bowl, **$20**; bowl, 4-1/2" d, **$85**; and milk pitcher, **$27.50**.*

AVOCADO

Manufactured by Indiana Glass Company, Dunkirk, Ind., from 1923 to 1933.

Pieces are made in crystal, green, pink, and white.

Reproductions: † Creamer, 8-inch pickle, a 64-oz pitcher, plates, sherbet, sugar, and tumblers. Reproductions can be found in amethyst, blue, dark green, frosted green, frosted pink, pink, red, and yellow, representing several colors not made originally.

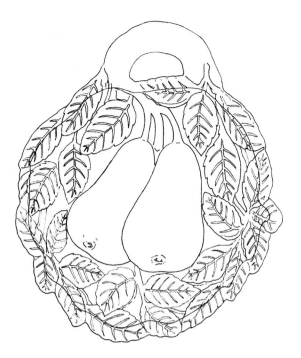

Item	Crystal	Green	Pink	White
Bowl, 5-1/4" d, two handles	12.00	42.00	45.00	—
Bowl, 8" d, two handles, oval	17.50	35.00	30.00	—
Bowl, 8-1/2" d	20.00	60.00	50.00	—
Bowl, 9-1/2" d, 3-1/4" deep	25.00	175.00	150.00	—
Cake plate, 10-1/4" d, two handles	17.50	70.00	40.00	—
Creamer, ftd †	17.50	50.00	45.00	†
Cup, ftd	—	40.00	45.00	—
Pickle bowl, 8" d, two handles, oval †	17.50	30.00	25.00	—
Pitcher, 64 oz †	385.00	950.00	900.00	425.00
Plate, 6-3/8" d, sherbet †	6.00	24.00	22.00	—
Plate, 8-1/4" d, luncheon †	7.50	27.00	20.00	—
Preserve bowl, 7" l, handle	10.00	32.00	28.00	—
Relish, 6" d, ftd	10.00	38.00	28.00	—
Salad bowl, 7-1/2" d	18.00	80.00	55.50	—
Saucer	6.00	24.00	15.00	—
Sherbet, ftd †	—	75.00	65.00	†
Sugar, ftd †	17.50	40.00	45.00	—
Tumbler †	25.00	250.00	150.00	35.00

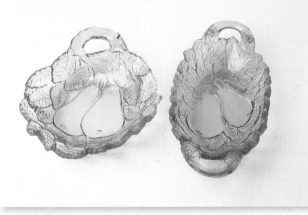

*Avocado, green preserve bowl with handle, **$32**; and bowl with two handles, **$30**.*

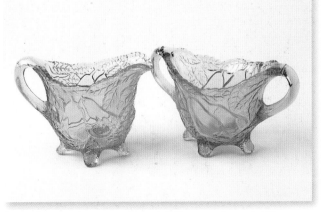

*Avocado, green creamer, footed, **$40**; sugar, footed, **$40**.*

BEADED BLOCK

Manufactured by Imperial Glass Company, Bellaire, Ohio, from 1927 to the 1930s.

Pieces are made in amber, crystal, green, ice blue, iridescent, milk white (1950s), opalescent, pink, red, and Vaseline. Some pieces are still being made in pink and are embossed with the "IG" trademark. The only form known in red is the 4-1/2-inch lily bowl, valued at $300. The secondary market for milk white is still being established.

Item	Amber	Crystal	Green	Ice Blue
Bowl, 4-1/2" d, lily	22.00	18.00	20.00	26.00
Bowl, 4-1/2" d, two handles	18.00	10.00	22.00	28.00
Bowl, 5-1/2" sq	18.00	8.00	20.00	12.00
Bowl, 5-1/2" d, one handle	18.00	8.00	20.00	12.00
Bowl, 6" deep	24.00	12.00	24.00	15.00
Bowl, 6-1/4" d	24.00	8.50	20.00	12.00
Bowl, 6-1/2" d, two handles	24.00	8.50	20.00	12.00
Bowl, 6-3/4" d	27.50	12.00	28.00	14.00
Bowl, 7-1/4" d, flared	30.00	12.00	28.00	14.00
Bowl, 7-1/2" d, fluted	30.00	22.00	30.00	24.00
Bowl, 7-1/2", plain	30.00	20.00	30.00	22.00
Candy dish, cov, pear shaped	—	—	395.00	—
Celery, 8-1/4" d	35.00	18.00	35.00	18.00
Creamer, ftd	25.00	25.00	25.00	24.00
Jelly, 4-1/2" h, stemmed	20.00	10.00	20.00	12.00
Jelly, 4-1/2" h, stemmed, flared lid	24.00	20.00	24.00	30.00
Pitcher, one pt, 5-1/4" h	95.00	115.00	125.00	115.00
Plate, 7-3/4" sq	20.00	7.50	20.00	10.00
Plate, 8-3/4"	30.00	24.00	30.00	30.00
Sugar, ftd	25.00	24.00	30.00	30.00
Syrup	—	—	—	—
Vase, 6" h, ftd	25.00	20.00	35.00	35.00

*Beaded Block, Vaseline square plate, **$10**; iridescent round plate, **$20**.*

*Beaded Block, ice blue vase, **$35**; crystal jelly, stemmed, **$10**.*

Item	Iridescent	Opal	Pink	Vaseline
Bowl, 4-1/2" d, lily	18.00	30.00	18.00	24.00
Bowl, 4-1/2" d, two handles	20.00	30.00	12.00	28.00
Bowl, 5-1/2" sq	10.00	15.00	10.00	12.00
Bowl, 5-1/2" d, one handle	10.00	15.00	20.00	12.00
Bowl, 6" deep	12.00	24.00	18.00	15.00
Bowl, 6-1/4" d	12.00	18.00	10.00	12.00
Bowl, 6-1/2" d, two handles	12.00	18.00	28.00	12.00
Bowl, 6-3/4" d	15.00	20.00	14.00	14.00
Bowl, 7-1/4" d, flared	15.00	20.00	14.00	14.00
Bowl, 7-1/2" d, fluted	20.00	24.00	24.00	24.00
Bowl, 7-1/2", plain	24.00	24.00	20.00	22.00
Candy dish, cov, pear shaped	—	—	—	650.00
Celery, 8-1/4" d	18.00	30.00	16.50	18.00
Creamer, ftd	24.00	50.00	30.00	24.00
Jelly, 4-1/2" h, stemmed	12.00	15.00	12.00	12.00
Jelly, 4-1/2" h, stemmed, flared lid	15.00	24.00	15.00	12.00
Pitcher, one pt, 5-1/4" h	115.00	125.00	195.00	115.00
Plate, 7-3/4" sq	10.00	15.00	8.00	10.00
Plate, 8-3/4"	20.00	24.00	20.00	20.00
Sugar, ftd	20.00	60.00	30.00	20.00
Syrup	—	—	—	165.00
Vase, 6" h, ftd	25.00	20.00	36.00	30.00

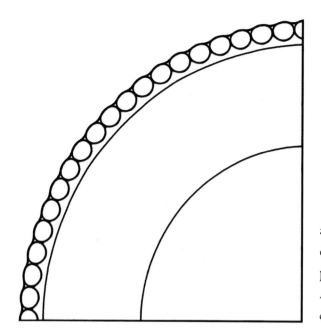

BEADED EDGE

Pattern #22 Milk Glass

Made by Westmoreland Glass Co., late 1930s-1950s.

Pieces are made in white milk glass. Painted decorations add interesting variety to this pattern. Collectors can find eight different fruit patterns and eight different floral patterns; others include birds and Christmas designs. Another variation incorporates a red edge or band into the design.

Beaded Edge, white luncheon plate, $8.50.

Item	Decorated	Plain	Red Edge
Creamer, cov, ftd	35.00	20.00	25.00
Creamer, open, ftd	18.00	10.00	14.00
Cup	12.00	5.00	6.50
Nappy, 5" d	16.00	4.50	10.00
Nappy, 6" d, crimped	22.00	7.50	12.00
Plate, 6" d, bread and butter	19.00	5.00	7.00
Plate, 7" d, salad	15.00	8.00	9.00
Plate, 7-1/2" d, coupe	15.00	10.00	12.00
Plate, 8-1/2" d, luncheon	25.00	8.50	10.00
Plate, 10-1/2" d, dinner	45.00	12.00	20.00
Platter, 12" l, tab handles	90.00	75.00	45.00
Relish, three-part	90.00	25.00	50.00
Salt and pepper shakers, pr	75.00	30.00	35.00
Saucer	5.00	2.00	2.50
Sherbet, ftd	18.00	8.50	12.00
Sugar, cov, ftd	35.00	20.00	25.00
Sugar, open, ftd	18.00	10.00	14.00
Torte plate, 15" d	70.00	25.00	40.00
Tumbler, ftd, 8 oz	15.00	10.00	15.00

BLOCK OPTIC

Block

Manufactured by Hocking Glass Company, Lancaster, Ohio, from 1929 to 1933.

Pieces are made in amber, crystal, green, pink, and yellow. Production in amber was limited. A console bowl that is 11-3/4-inch in diameter is valued at $50, while a pair of matching 1-3/4-inch high candlesticks is valued at $110.

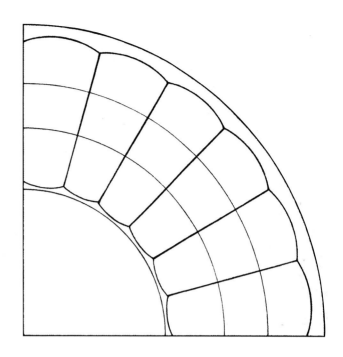

Item	Crystal	Green	Pink	Yellow
Berry bowl, 8-1/2" d	24.00	40.00	45.00	—
Bowl, 4-1/4" d, 1-3/8" h	6.00	15.00	10.00	—
Bowl, 4-1/2" d, 1-1/2" h	—	28.00	—	—
Bowl, 8-5/8" d, low, ruffled	—	150.00	—	—
Butter dish, cov	—	50.00	—	—
Cake plate, 10" d, ftd	18.00	—	—	—
Candlesticks, pr, 1-3/4" h	—	120.00	100.00	—
Candy jar, cov, 2-1/4" h	30.00	60.00	55.00	75.00
Candy jar, cov, 6-1/4" h	42.00	80.00	60.00	—
Cereal bowl, 5-1/2" d	—	25.00	30.00	—
Champagne, 4-3/4" h	12.50	30.00	18.50	24.00
Cocktail, 4" h	—	35.00	45.00	—
Comport, 4" wide	—	36.00	70.00	—
Console bowl, 11-3/4" d, rolled edge	55.00	75.00	125.00	—
Creamer*	12.00	20.00	18.00	20.00
Cup*	7.50	9.00	12.00	12.00
Goblet, 9 oz, 5-3/4" h	12.00	40.00	45.00	—
Goblet, 9 oz, 7-1/2" h, thin	24.00	—	30.00	45.00
Ice bucket	—	40.00	48.00	—
Ice tub, open	—	65.00	120.00	—
Mug	—	75.00	—	—
Pitcher, 54 oz, 7-5/8" h, bulbous	—	95.00	85.00	—
Pitcher, 54 oz, 8-1/2" h	25.00	45.00	40.00	—
Pitcher, 80 oz, 8" h	—	90.00	85.00	—
Plate, 6" d, sherbet	2.50	7.00	5.00	6.50
Plate, 8" d, luncheon	3.50	6.00	8.50	9.50
Plate, 9" d, dinner	11.00	35.00	38.00	45.00
Plate, 9" d, dinner, snowflake center	—	16.50	—	—
Plate, 9" d, grill	15.00	27.50	30.00	60.00
Salad bowl, 7-1/4" d	—	155.00	—	—
Salt and pepper shakers, pr, ftd	—	42.00	90.00	95.00
Salt and pepper shakers, pr, squatty	—	100.00	—	—
Sandwich plate, 10-1/4" d	—	27.50	30.00	—

Item	Crystal	Green	Pink	Yellow
Sandwich server, center handle	—	65.00	50.00	—
Saucer, 5-3/4" d	—	12.00	10.00	—
Saucer, 6-1/8" d	2.00	10.00	10.00	4.00
Sherbet, cone	—	12.00	6.00	—
Sherbet, 5-1/2 oz, 3-1/4" h	—	12.00	9.50	7.50
Sherbet, 6 oz, 4-3/4" h	8.00	28.00	17.50	20.00
Sugar, cone	—	19.50	15.00	15.00
Sugar, flat	—	20.00	10.00	—
Sugar, round, ftd	10.00	12.00	18.00	16.00
Tumbler, 3 oz, 2-5/8" h	—	27.50	30.00	—
Tumbler, 3 oz, 3-1/4" h, ftd	—	27.50	25.00	—
Tumbler, 5 oz, 3-1/2" h, flat	—	24.00	20.00	—
Tumbler, 5-3/8" h, ftd	—	—	24.00	18.00
Tumbler, 9" h, ftd	—	—	17.50	22.00
Tumbler, 9-1/2 oz, 3-13/16" h, flat	—	17.50	15.00	—
Tumbler, 10 oz, 6" h, ftd	12.00	—	—	—
Tumbler, 10 or 11 oz, 5" h, flat	—	30.00	35.00	—
Tumbler, 12 oz, 4-7/8" h, flat	—	35.50	30.00	—
Tumbler, 15 oz, 5-1/4" h, flat	—	32.50	30.00	—
Tumble-up, 3" h tumbler and bottle	—	130.00	75.00	—
Vase, 5-3/4" h, blown	—	350.00	—	—
Whiskey, 1 oz, 1-5/8" h	20.00	40.00	45.00	—
Whiskey, 2 oz, 2-1/4" h	15.00	35.00	30.00	—
Wine, 3-1/2" h	—	400.00	400.00	—
Wine, 4-1/2" h	25.00	35.00	32.00	—

*There are five styles of creamers and four styles of cups, and each have a relative value.

*Block Optic, green sherbet, **$28**; sugar, **$12**, and creamer, **$17.50**; and Hazel Atlas look-alike covered candy dish.*

*Block Optic, green large berry bowl, 8-1/2" d, **$35**; cereal bowl, 5-1/4" d, **$12**; and individual berry bowl, 4-1/4" d, **$15**.*

BOWKNOT

Unknown maker, late 1920s.
Pieces are made in green.

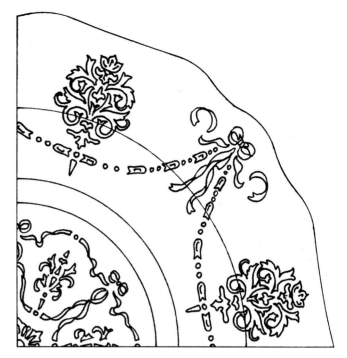

Item	Green
Berry bowl, 4-1/2" d	25.00
Cereal bowl, 5-1/2" d	30.00
Cup	20.00
Plate, 7" d, salad	18.00
Sherbet, low, ftd	25.00
Tumbler, 10 oz, 5" h, flat	20.00
Tumbler, 10 oz, 5" h, ftd	25.00

*Bowknot, green tumbler, **$12**; footed berry bowl, **$25**.*

BUBBLE

Bullseye, Provincial

Manufactured originally by Hocking Glass Company, and followed by Anchor Hocking Glass Corporation, Lancaster, Ohio, from 1937 to 1965.

Pieces are made in crystal (1937); forest green (1937); pink, Royal Ruby (1963); and sapphire blue (1937). Production in pink was limited. The current value for a pink cup and saucer is $175.

Item	Crystal	Forest Green	Royal Ruby	Sapphire Blue
Berry bowl, 4" d	4.00	—	6.50	20.00
Berry bowl, 8-3/4" d	12.00	15.00	15.00	20.00
Bowl, 9" d, flanged	8.00	—	—	335.00
Candlesticks, pr	18.00	40.00	—	—
Cereal bowl, 5-1/4" d	10.00	20.00	—	17.50
Cocktail, 3-1/2 oz	4.50	15.00	18.00	—
Cocktail, 4-1/2 oz	4.50	16.00	16.00	—
Creamer	7.50	15.00	18.00	45.00
Cup	4.50	9.75	12.50	15.00
Fruit bowl, 4-1/2" d	5.00	11.00	9.00	12.00
Goblet, 9 oz, stem, 5-1/2" h	7.50	15.00	15.00	—
Goblet, 9-1/2 oz, stem	8.00	15.00	18.00	—
Goblet, 10-3/4 oz, 5-3/8" h	—	14.50	—	—
Iced tea goblet, 14 oz	8.00	17.50	—	—
Iced tea tumbler, 12 oz, 4-1/2" h	12.50	—	19.50	—
Juice goblet, 4 oz	3.00	14.00	—	—
Juice goblet, 5-1/2 oz	5.00	12.50	15.00	—
Juice tumbler, 6 oz, ftd	4.00	12.00	10.00	—
Lamp, three styles	42.00	—	—	—
Lemonade tumbler, 16 oz, 5-7/8" h	16.00	—	16.00	—
Old fashioned tumbler, 8 oz, 3-1/4" h	6.50	16.00	16.50	—
Pitcher, 64 oz, ice lip	60.00	—	65.00	—
Plate, 6-3/4" d, bread and butter	4.00	4.50	—	3.75
Plate, 9-3/8" d, dinner	7.50	28.00	27.50	10.00
Plate, 9-3/8" d, grill	—	20.00	—	22.00
Platter, 12" l, oval	10.00	—	—	18.00
Sandwich plate, 9-1/2" d	7.50	25.00	22.00	8.00
Saucer	1.50	5.00	5.00	1.50
Sherbet, 6 oz	5.00	9.00	12.00	—
Soup bowl, flat, 7-3/4" d	10.00	—	—	16.00
Sugar	6.00	14.50	—	35.00
Tidbit, two tiers	—	—	35.00	—
Tumbler, 9 oz, water	6.00	—	16.00	—

*Bubble, forest green sugar, **$14.50**.*

*Bubble, blue grill plate, **$22**; platter, **$18**; soup bowl, **$16**; berry bowl, 4" d, **$18**.*

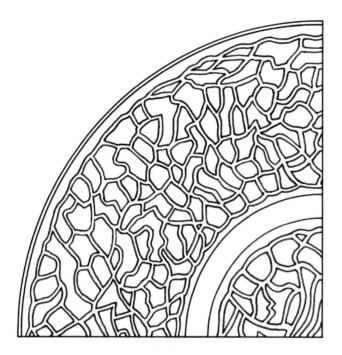

BY CRACKY

Manufactured by L.E. Smith Glass Company, Mount Pleasant, Pa., in the late 1920s.

Pieces have been made in amber, canary, crystal, and green.

Item	Amber	Canary	Crystal	Green
Cake plate, ftd	35.00	40.00	30.00	30.00
Candleholder, octagonal base	7.50	10.00	5.00	5.00
Candleholder, round base	5.00	7.50	5.00	5.00
Candy box, cov	17.50	20.00	15.00	17.50
Candy jar, cov	20.00	25.00	17.50	17.50
Center bowl, 12", octagonal	15.00	17.50	12.00	15.00
Cup	5.00	5.00	5.00	5.00
Goblet	18.00	18.00	10.00	15.00
Flower block, 3"	15.00	17.50	7.50	10.00
Plate, 8", octagonal	15.00	17.50	7.50	10.00
Saucer	3.00	5.00	2.00	2.00
Sherbet	7.50	10.00	5.00	5.00
Sherbet plate	12.00	15.00	5.00	7.50
Vase, fan shape	20.00	25.00	15.00	15.00
Violet bowl	20.00	25.00	15.00	15.00

*By Cracky, green goblet, **$15***.

*By Cracky, crystal sherbet plate, **$5***.

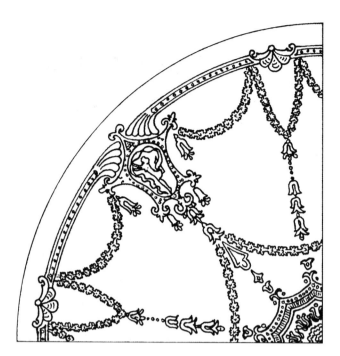

CAMEO

Ballerina, Dancing Girl

Manufactured by Hocking Glass Company, Lancaster, Ohio, from 1930 to 1934.

Pieces are made in crystal, green, pink, and yellow. Only the crystal has a platinum rim.

Reproductions: † Salt shakers made in blue, green and pink. Children's dishes have been made in green and pink, but were never part of the original pattern. Recently, a squatty candy dish in cobalt blue has also been made, but this was not an original color.

Item	Crystal	Green	Pink	Yellow
Berry bowl, 4-1/4" d	18.00	—	—	—
Berry bowl, 8-1/4" d	—	48.00	175.00	—
Butter dish, cov	—	250.00	—	1,500.00
Cake plate, 10" d, three legs	—	50.00	—	—
Cake plate, 10-1/2" d, flat	—	120.00	165.00	—
Candlesticks, pr, 4" h	—	150.00	—	—
Candy jar, cov, 4" h	—	110.00	495.00	125.00
Candy jar, cov, 6-1/2" h	—	195.00	—	—
Cereal bowl, 5-1/2" d	9.50	45.00	160.00	35.00
Champagne	—	45.00	—	—
Cocktail shaker	600.00	—	—	—
Comport, 5" w	—	65.00	200.00	—
Console bowl, three legs, 11" d	—	90.00	45.00	125.00
Cookie jar, cov	—	85.00	—	—
Cream soup bowl, 4-3/4" d	—	215.00	—	—
Creamer, 3-1/4" h	—	30.00	110.00	25.00
Creamer, 4-1/4" h	—	30.00	115.00	—
Cup	10.00	20.00	85.00	10.00
Decanter, 10" h	235.00	225.00	—	—
Domino tray, 7" l	165.00	275.00	265.00	—
Goblet, 6" h, water	—	95.00	195.00	—
Ice bowl, 3" h, 5-1/2" d	265.00	300.00	750.00	—
Jam jar, cov, 2" h	185.00	275.00	—	—
Juice pitcher, 6" h, 36 oz	—	110.00	—	—
Juice tumbler, 3 oz, ftd	—	65.00	90.00	—
Juice tumbler, 5 oz, 3-3/4" h	—	60.00	—	—
Mayonnaise, ftd	—	60.00	—	—
Pitcher, 8-1/2" h, 56 oz	550.00	70.00	1,450.00	—
Plate, 6" d, sherbet	6.00	12.50	90.00	4.00
Plate, 7" d, salad	12.00	13.50	—	—
Plate, 8" d, luncheon	8.00	18.00	36.00	12.50

Cameo, green vegetable bowl, $50.

Cameo, crystal tumbler with platinum trim, $16.

Item	Crystal	Green	Pink	Yellow
Plate, 8-1/2", luncheon, sq	—	70.00	—	250.00
Plate, 9-1/2" d, dinner	—	30.00	85.00	15.00
Plate, 10-1/2" d, dinner, rimmed	—	115.00	175.00	—
Plate, 10-1/2" d, grill	—	20.00	55.00	14.50
Platter, 12" l	—	35.00	—	42.00
Relish, 7-1/2" l, ftd, three parts	175.00	40.00	—	—
Salad bowl, 7-1/4" d	—	70.00	—	—
Salt and pepper shakers, pr, ftd †	—	95.00	90.00	—
Sandwich plate, 10" d	—	30.00	45.00	—
Saucer	4.00	4.00	90.00	4.50
Sherbet, 3-1/8" h, blown	—	18.00	75.00	—
Sherbet, 3-1/8" h, molded	—	18.00	75.00	40.00
Sherbet, 4-7/8" h	—	40.00	100.00	45.00
Soup bowl, rimmed, 9" d	—	100.00	135.00	85.00
Sugar, 3-1/4" h	—	25.00	—	22.00
Sugar, 4-1/4" h	—	32.50	125.00	—
Syrup pitcher, 20 oz, 5-3/4" h	—	250.00	—	2,000.00
Tumbler, 9 oz, 4" h	16.00	32.00	80.00	—
Tumbler, 9 oz, 5" h, ftd	—	30.00	115.00	22.00
Tumbler, 10 oz, 4-3/4" h, flat	—	35.00	95.00	—
Tumbler, 11" oz, 5" h, flat	—	30.00	90.00	60.00
Tumbler, 11 oz, 5-3/4" h, ftd	—	75.00	135.00	—
Tumbler, 15 oz, 5-1/4" h	—	80.00	145.00	—
Tumbler, 15 oz, 6-3/8" h, ftd	—	495.00	—	—
Vase, 5-3/4" h	—	375.00	—	—
Vase, 8" h	—	75.00	—	—
Vegetable, oval, 10" l	—	55.00	—	48.00
Vinegar bottle	—	55.00	—	—
Wine, 3-1/2" h	—	1,200.00	950.00	—
Wine, 4" h	—	95.00	250.00	—

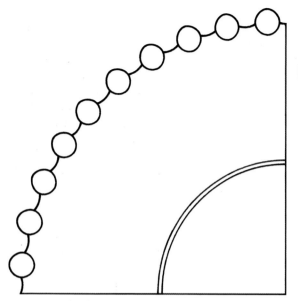

CANDLEWICK

Manufactured by Imperial Glass Company from 1936 to 1984.

Pieces are made in black, blue, cobalt blue, crystal, green, pink, red, and yellow, with crystal being the most prevalent. Some etched designs are known.

Reproductions: † Reproduction Candlewick has been made in caramel slag and jadeite. Cobalt blue and red items were made by Dalzell Viking.

Item	Crystal
After dinner cup and saucer, 400/77, 5-1/2" d beaded saucer	25.00
Ashtray, 400/118	18.00
Ashtray, 400/150, 6" d, round, large beads	8.00
Ashtray, 400/176, 3-1/4" sq, large beads	12.50
Ashtray, 400/450, nested set, 4", 5", and 6" sq	125.00
Ashtray, 400/60, match holder center	100.00
Ashtray, 400/650, nested set, orig Imperial sticker	135.00
Atomizer, 400/96 shaker, atomizer top, made by DeVilbiss	125.00
Baked apple dish, 400/53X, 6-1/2"	30.00
Banana stand, 400/103E, 11" d, two turned-up sides, four-bead stem	1,500.00
Basket, 400/273, 5" h	300.00
Basket, 400/273, 5", beaded top, beads on top of handle	225.00
Basket, 400/37/0, 11", applied handle	200.00
Basket, 400/40/0, 6-1/2", turned-up sides, applied handle	50.00
Bell, 400/108, 4", 4-bead handle	85.00
Bonbon, 400/51T, 6", heart shape, curved-over center handle, beaded edge	35.00
Bonbon, 400/149F, 7-1/2"	200.00
Bouillon cup, two handles	50.00
Bowl, 400/5F, 7" d	50.00
Bowl, 400/7F, 7-5/8" d	65.00
Bowl, 400/427B, 4-3/4" d, 6" d, 7" d and 8-1/2" d, nested	75.00
Bowl, 400/49H, 5" d, heart shaped	175.00
Bowl, 400/52, 6" d, divided	80.00
Bowl, 400/73H, 9" d, heart shape	55.00
Bowl, 400/74SC, 9" d, four ball toes, crimped	60.00
Bowl, 400/75B, 10-1/2" d	40.00
Bowl, 400/84, 6-1/2" d, divided	20.00
Bowl, 400/182, 6" d, three toes	75.00
Bud vase, 400/107, 5-1/4" h, beaded foot, large beads, crimped top	50.00
Bud vase, 400/227, 8-1/2" h, beaded ball bottom, narrowed top slants, applied handle	140.00

Item	Crystal
Bud vase, 400/25, 3-3/4" h, beaded foot, ball shape, crimped top	35.00
Bud vase, 400/28C, 8-1/2", trumpet shaped top, crimped, beaded ball bottom	75.00
Buffet set, 400/9266, 14" d 400/92D plate, 5-1/2" d 400/66E cheese compote, plain stem, two pcs	70.00
Butter, cov, 400/161, quarter pound, graduated beads on cov	25.00
Butter, cov, 400/276, 6-3/4" x 4", California, beaded top, c1960	100.00
Butter, cov, 400/276, 6-3/4" x 4", California, plain top, c1951	125.00
Butter pat	12.00
Cake stand, 400/103D, 11" h, three-bead stem	140.00
Cake stand, 400/160, 14" d, 72 candle holes	725.00
Cake stand, 400/67D, 10" d, wedge marks on plate, one-bead stem, dome foot, c1939	85.00
Cake stand, 400/67D, 10" d, wedge marks on plate, one-bead stem, flat foot, c1943	70.00
Candleholder, 400/175, 6-1/2" h, three-bead stem	95.00
Candleholder, 400/175, 9" h, three-bead stem, adapter, prisms	250.00
Candleholder, 400/207, 4-1/2" h	120.00
Candleholder, 400/40CV, 5" h, round bowl, beaded or fluted vase insert	75.00
Candleholder, 400/79R, 3-1/2" h, rolled saucer, small beads	15.00
Candleholder, 400/81, 3-1/2" h, dome ftd, small beads, round handle	75.00
Candleholders, pr, 400/147, three lite	210.00
Candleholders, pr, 400/86, mushroom	92.00
Candy dish, cov, 400/110, three parts	165.00
Candy dish, cov, 400/110, 7" d, three-part, two-bead finial	195.00
Candy dish, cov, 400/140, 8" d, one-bead stem, domed beaded foot, c1942	500.00

Item	Crystal
Candy dish, cov, 400/140, 8" d, one-bead stem, flat plain foot, c1944	275.00
Candy dish, cov, 400/245, 6-1/2" d, round bowl, sq cov, two-bead finial	300.00
Candy dish, cov, 400/259, 6-3/4" w, beaded rim, two-bead finial on cov	135.00
Candy dish, cov, 400/59, 5-1/2" d, two-bead finial	40.00
Candy dish, cov, 400/59, small	80.00
Celery tray, 400/105, 13" l, oval, two curved beaded handles	40.00
Celery tray, 400/46, 11" l, oval, scalloped edge	80.00
Champagne, 3400, flared belled top, 5 oz, four graduated beads in stem	24.00
Cheese and cracker set, 400/88, 5-1/2" ftd 400/88 cheese compote, 10-1/2" d 400/72D handled plate	125.00
Cheese, toast or butter dish, 400/123, 7-3/4" d plate with cupped edge, domed cov with bubble knob	350.00
Chip and dip, 400/228	795.00
Cigarette set, 400/29/64/44 or 400/29/6, dome ftd 3" 400/44 cigarette holder, small beads, four nested 400/64 2-3/4" d ashtrays, 400/29 kidney-shaped tray	95.00
Clock, 4", large beads, New Haven works	400.00
Coaster	8.00
Cocktail, 3400, 4 oz	20.00
Cocktail, 4000/190, bell-shaped bowl, beads around foot, 4 oz, three-bead stem	32.00
Cocktail pitcher, 400/19, 40 ounce, 8-1/2"	250.00
Cocktail set, 400/97, 6" d 400/39 plate with 2-1/2" off-center indent, #111 one-bead cocktail glass	35.00
Coffee cup and saucer, 400/37, slender 40/37 cup, 400/35 saucer	15.00
Compote, 400/103F, 10" d, crimped, three-bead stem, hp pink roses, blue ribbons	350.00
Compote, 400/220, 5", arch beaded trim-stem	150.00
Compote, 400/48F, 8" d, beaded edge, four-bead stem	75.00
Compote, 400/48F, 8" d, beaded edge, five-bead stem	200.00
Compote, 400/67B, 9" d, flat, large bead stem, c1943	100.00
Condiment set, 400/1589, jam set, two cov 400/89 marmalade jars, three-bead ladles, oval 400/159 tray	95.00
Condiment set, 400/1769, 6-ounce 400/119 cruet, pr 400/96 salt and pepper shakers, 8" 400/171 tray	100.00
Console set, 400/100, 12" 400/92F flat bowl, cupped edge, pr 400/100 two-lite candleholders, center circle of large beads	—
Console set, 400/8063B, bowl and pr candleholders	95.00
Console set, 400/8692L, 13" 400/92L mushroom bowl on 400/127B 7-1/2" d base, pr 400/86 mushroom candleholders	125.00
Cordial bottle, 400/82, 15 oz, beaded foot, three-bead stopper, handle, c1938	225.00
Cordial bottle, 400/82, 15 oz, beaded foot, c1941	200.00
Cordial, 3400, flared belled top, four graduated beads stem	90.00
Cream soup bowl	60.00
Creamer and sugar, 400/122, individual, pr	22.00

Item	Crystal
Creamer and sugar, 400/18, domed foot, large beads, creamer with plain handle attached at bottom, no handle on sugar, 1954-55	125.00
Creamer and sugar, 400/29/30, flat base, beaded question mark handles, 400/30, 7" l 400/29 tray	35.00
Creamer and sugar, 400/31, beaded foot, plain handles, c1937	85.00
Creamer and sugar, 400/31, plain foot, question mark handles, c1941	50.00
Cruet, 400/119, orig stopper	160.00
Cup and saucer, 400/35/252, no beads on question mark handle	25.00
Decanter, 400/163, beaded foot, round stopper	475.00
Dessert tumbler, 400/18, domed beaded foot, rounded top, 6 oz	40.00
Dessert tumbler, 400/19, beaded base, straight sides, 5 oz	14.00
Deviled egg server, 400/154, 11-1/2" d	150.00
Deviled egg tray, 400/154, 11-1/2" d, 12 indents for eggs, heart-shaped center handle	190.00
Dresser set, I. Rice Co., 400/151 round mirrored tray, powder jar, beaded base, three-bead cover, two round perfume bottles, beaded base, four-bead stoppers, 1942, four-pc set	250.00
Eggcup, large beaded base	70.00
Epergne set, 400/196, 9" ftd 400/196FC flower candle holder, one-bead stem, 7-3/4" h two-bead peg vase, beaded top, peg to fit into candle cut	295.00
Float bowl, 400/92B, 11" d, cupped edge, fuchsia cutting	75.00
Float bowl, 400/92B, 11" d, cupped edge, plain	55.00
Float bowl, 400/101, 13" d	225.00
Fruit bowl, 400/103C, 10" d, ftd	375.00

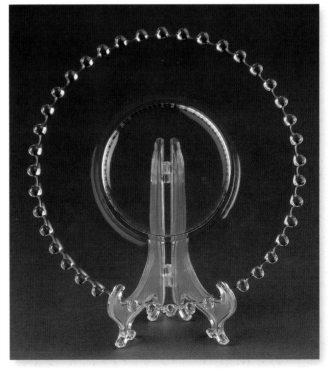

*Candlewick, crystal luncheon plate, 9" d, **$18**.*

Item	Crystal
Goblet, water, 3400 line, flared bell bowl, four graduated beads in stem, 9 oz	15.00
Goblet, water, 400/190 Line, bell-shaped bowl, hollow trumpet-shaped stem with beads around foot, 10 oz	35.00
Gravy boat, liner	200.00
Hurricane lamp, 400/152R, candleholder, chimney, and 100/152 adapter, three pcs	350.00
Iced tea tumbler, 12 oz, ftd, 3400 line	15.00
Iced tea tumbler, 12 oz, ftd, 400/18, domed beaded foot, rounded top	65.00
Iced tea tumbler, 12 oz, ftd, 400/19, beaded base, straight sides	18.00
Ice tub, 400/63, 8" d	110.00
Jelly server, 400/157, 4-3/4" d, ftd, one-bead stem, two-bead cov	65.00
Jelly server, 400/157, 4-3/4" d, ftd, one-bead stem, no cover	35.00
Jelly server, 400/52, 6" d, divided dish, beaded edge, handles	20.00
Juice tumbler, 400/18, domed beaded foot, straight sides, 5 oz	35.00
Ladle, 400/139, 6-3/8" l	42.00
Lemon tray, 400/221, 5-1/2" l, arched handle	45.00
Marmalade jar, 400/130, round 400/89 base, beaded cover with notch, two-bead finial, 400/130 three-bead ladle	135.00
Marmalade jar, 400/8918, 400/18 old fashion tumbler, beaded notched cover with two-bead finial, 400/130 three-bead ladle	175.00
Mayonnaise set, 400/52/3, 400/23D 7-1/2" d handled plate with indent, 400/52B 5-1/2" d handled bowl, 400/135 ladle	40.00
Mayonnaise set, 400/84, 6-1/4" divided bowl with silver overlay, 8-1/4" underplate	85.00
Mint dish, 400/51F, 5" d, round, applied handle	28.00
Mirror, domed beaded base, brass holder and frame, two-sided mirror flips on hinges, made for I. Rice Co., 1940s	250.00
Muddler	25.00
Mustard jar, 400/156, beaded foot, notched beaded cov with two-bead finial, 3-1/2" glass spoon, fleur-de-lis handle	45.00
Nappy, 400/3F, 6"	12.00
Old fashion tumbler, 400/19, beaded base, straight sides, 7 oz	20.00
Parfait, 3400, flared bell top, one-bead stem, 6 oz	60.00
Pastry tray, 400/68D, 11-1/2" d beaded plate, center heart-shaped handle	35.00
Pickle/celery, 400/57, 8-1/2" l, oval	30.00
Pitcher, 400/18, 16 oz, plain handle, beaded base	315.00
Pitcher, 400/18, 80 oz, plain handle, beaded base	300.00
Pitcher, 400/24, 80 oz, beaded question mark handle, plain base	195.00
Plate, 400/1D, 6" d, bread and butter	10.00
Plate, 400/3D, 7" d, salad	12.00
Plate, 400/5D, 8-1/2" d, salad/dessert	14.00
Plate, 400/7D, 9" d, luncheon	18.00
Plate, 400/10D, 10-1/4" d, dinner	37.50

Item	Crystal
Plate, 400/42D, 7" w handle to handle	45.00
Plate, 400/72C, 10" d, w handles, crimped	28.00
Plate, 400/145D, 12" d, two open handles	30.00
Platter, 12-1/2" x 13"	120.00
Punch bowl set, 400/20, 13" d six-quart 400/20 bowl, 17" d 400/20V plate, 12 400/37 punch cups, 400/91 ladle, 15-pc set	375.00
Punch bowl set, 400/210, 14-1/2" d 10-quart 400/210 bowl, 9" belled 400/210 base, 12 400/211 punch cups with round beaded handles, 400/91 ladle, 15-pc set	800.00
Punch bowl, ladle	1,500.00
Punch bowl, set, 400/128, 13" d 400/20 bowl, 10" 400/128 belled base, 12 400/37 punch cups, 400/91 ladle	300.00
Relish and dressing set, 400/1112, 10-1/2" five-part 400/112 relish, 400/89 jar fits center well; long ladle, c1941	95.00
Relish and dressing set, 400/1112, 10-1/2" five-part 400/112 relish, 400/289 jar fits center well, three-bead ladle, c1945	70.00
Relish, 400/56, 10-1/2" d	50.00
Relish, 400/213, 10" l, three parts	95.00
Relish, 400/213, three-part, 10" l, handle	75.00
Relish, 400/215, three-part on one side, one section on other, 5-1/2" l, two tab handles	90.00
Relish, 400/234, two-part, 7" sq	140.00
Relish, 400/262, three-part, 10-1/2" l, two tab handles	100.00
Relish, 400/54, two-part, 6-1/2" l, two tab handles	15.00
Relish, five parts	130.00
Relish, cov, 400/214, 10" l, oblong, cover with beaded top handle	250.00
Salad plate, crescent, 8-1/2" l	70.00
Salad set, 400/106B/75, 12" d bell 400/106B bowl, graduated beads on both side, fork and spoon	110.00
Salad set, 400/17, 14" 400/92D plate, 10-1/2" 400/17F bowl, Old-style ribbed fork and spoon	85.00
Salad set, 400/735, 9" d handled heart-shaped 400/73H bowl, 700/75 fork and spoon set	150.00
Salt and pepper shakers, pr, 400/116, one-bead stem, no beads on foot, plastic or metal tops	75.00
Salt and pepper shakers, pr, 400/190, trumpet foot, chrome tops	65.00
Salt and pepper shakers, pr, 400/96, nine beads, flat bottom, plastic tops, c1941	30.00
Salt and pepper shakers, pr, 400/96, bulbous, eight beads, chrome tops	20.00
Salt dip, 400/61, 2"	12.00
Sauce boat set, 400/169, oval gravy boat with handle, 9" oval plate with indent	175.00
Seafood icer, 400/190, one-pc coupette	90.00
Sherbet, 3400 line, flared bell top, low, 5 oz	24.00
Sherbet, 3400 line, flared bell top, tall, 5 oz	24.00
Tea cup and saucer, 400/35, round 400/35 cup, 400/35 saucer	15.00
Tidbit server, 400/2701, two tiers, 7-1/2" d and 10-1/2" d plates joined by metal rod, round handle at top	60.00
Tidbit set, 400/750, three-pc nested hearts, 4-1/2", 5-1/2", 6-1/2", beaded edges	40.00

Item	Crystal
Torte plate, 400/20D, 17" d, flat	40.00
Torte plate, 400/20V, 17" d, cupped	60.00
Tray, 400/51	45.00
Tray, 400/159, 9" oval, concentric circles in bottom, rect Farberware chrome holder with cut-out lacy pattern on each corner	65.00
Tumbler, 400/18, domed beaded foot, rounded top, 9 oz	45.00
Tumbler, 400/19, beaded base, straight sides, ftd, 10 oz, 4-3/4" h	18.00

Item	Crystal
Tumbler, 3400, 10 oz, ftd	24.00
Vase, 400/87C, 8" h, crimped beaded top	35.00
Vase, 400/87F, 8" h, fan shaped	65.00
Vase, 400/87R, 7" h, rolled over beaded top	40.00
Wine, 3400 line, flared belled bowl, four graduated stems in base, 9 oz	35.00
Wine, 400/190 line, belled bowl, hollow trumpet stem with beads, 5 oz	45.00

Prices for colored pieces:

Ashtray, 400/150, 6" d, round, large beads: blue, $50; pink, $15.

Ashtray, 400/450, nested set, 4", 5", and 6", patriotic dec: blue, yellow, pink, $75; red, white, and blue, $175.

Atomizer, 400/167 shaker, atomizer top: in amethyst or aqua, $175.

Bonbon, 400/51T, 6", heart shape, curved-over center handle, beaded edge: blue, $90; ruby: $250.

Bowl, 400/74SC, 9" d, four ball toes, crimped: blue, $100; black with painted flowers, $475; ruby: $395.

Center bowl, 11" d, light blue, $250.

Cordial bottle, 400/82, 15 oz, beaded foot, three-bead stopper, handle, c1938, ruby stopper: $275.

Creamer and sugar, 400/31, beaded foot, plain handles, c1937, Viennen blue, $225.

Cup and saucer, 400/35/252, no beads on question mark handle: blue, $40.

Goblet, water, 3400 line, flared bell bowl, four graduated beads in stem, 9 oz, solid colors: Verde Green, Ultra Blue, Sunshine Yellow, Nut Brown, c1977-80, $40.

Iced tea tumbler, 12 oz, ftd, 3400 line, solid colors: Verde Green, Ultra Blue, Sunshine Yellow, Nut Brown, c1977-80, $40.

Plate, 400/52E, two handles, 7" d, ebony, $325.

Sherbet, 6 oz, Viennen Blue, $100.

Tidbit server, 400/2701, two tiers, 7-1/2" d and 10-1/2" d plates joined by metal rod, round handle at top: emerald green, $750.

Wine, 3400 line, flared belled bowl, four graduated stems in base, 9 oz; solid colors: Verde Green, Ultra Blue, Sunshine Yellow, Nut Brown, c1977-80, $40 each; red: $125.

*Candlewick, green relish, three parts, **$195.** Photo courtesy of Tina Trautman.*

CAPE COD

Manufactured by Imperial Glass Company, Bellaire, Ohio, from 1932 to 1984.

Pieces are made in amber, azalea (pink), black, blue, crystal, evergreen (dark green), milk glass, Ritz blue, ruby and Verde (green). The colored wares were manufactured in the late 1960s and 1970s. Values for most colors are about 50 percent higher than crystal, with Ritz Blue and ruby often commanding even higher values.

Item	Crystal
Ashtray, 160/130, 5-1/2" d	18.50
Ashtray, 160/134/1, 4" d	15.00
Baked apple, 160/53X, 6" d	10.00
Basket, 160/221/0, 9"	200.00
Basket, 160/40, 11"	150.00
Birthday cake plate, 160/72, 13" d	395.00
Bitters bottle, 160/223, 4 oz	60.00
Bouillon cup, 160/250	30.00
Bowl, 160/10F, 7-3/4" d	24.00
Bowl, 160/137B, 10" d, ftd	70.00
Bowl, 160/199, 6-1/2" d, tab handle	25.00
Bowl, 160/62B, 7-1/2" d, two handles	27.50
Bowl, 160/75B, 12" d	40.00
Bread plate, 160/222, 12-1/2" d	65.00
Butter dish, cov, 1/4 pound	48.00
Butter dish, cov, 160/144, handle	32.00
Cake plate, 160/220, 10" d	165.00
Cake stand, 160/67D, 10-1/2" d	90.00
Cake stand, 160/103D, 11" d	95.00
Candlesticks, pr, 160/48BC, 6" h	150.00
Candlesticks, pr, 160/81, 4" h	50.00
Candlesticks, pr, 160/100, 2-lite	145.00
Candlesticks, pr, 160/170, 3" h	35.00
Candlesticks, pr, 160/175, 4-1/2" h, saucer base	50.00
Candy jar, cov, 160/194, wicker band	85.00
Candy, cov, 160/110	65.00
Celery tray, 160/105, 8" l	32.00
Celery tray, 160/189, 10-1/2" l	45.00
Champagne, 1602	10.00
Cigarette box, 160/134	45.00
Cigarette holder, 1602	14.00
Cigarette lighter, 1602	32.50
Claret, 1602, 5 oz	15.00
Coaster, 160/1R, 4-1/2" d	14.00

Item	Crystal
Coaster, 160/76, spoon rest, 4" d	12.50
Coaster, 160/78, 4" d, round	14.00
Coaster, 160/85, 3" w, sq	14.00
Cocktail, 1602, 3-1/2 oz	12.00
Coffee cup, 160/37	15.00
Coffee saucer, 160/37	3.50
Cologne bottle, stopper	65.00
Comport, 160/45, 6"	27.50
Comport, 160/48B, 7"	35.00
Comport, 160F, 5-1/4"	30.00
Comport, 160X, 5-3/4"	32.00
Comport, 1602, 11-1/4" d, 6-1/2" h	175.00
Comport, cov, 160/140, 6", ftd	72.00
Condiment bottle, 160/224	68.00
Console bowl, 160/75L, 13" d	45.00
Console bowl, 1601/0L, 15" d	65.00
Cookie jar, 160/195, wicker band	120.00
Cordial, 1602, 1-1/2 oz	12.00
Cordial bottle, 160/256, 18 oz	120.00
Creamer, 160/30	12.00
Creamer, 160/31, ftd	17.50
Creamer, 160/190	32.00
Cruet, stopper, 160/70, 5 oz	35.00
Cruet, stopper, 160/119, 4 oz	30.00
Cruet, stopper, 160/241, 6 oz	40.00
Decanter, 160/163, 30 oz	70.00
Decanter, 160/212, 24 oz	75.00
Decanter, 160/244	120.00
Decanter, 160/260, bourbon	90.00
Decanter, 160/260, rye	90.00
Dessert bowl, 160/197, 4-1/2" d, tab handle	24.00
Dessert bowl, 160/49H, 5" d, heart shape	20.00
Eggcup, 160/225	35.00
Epergne, 160/196	225.00

Item	Crystal
Finger bowl, 4" or 4-1/2"	12.50
Flower bowl, 5" d	24.00
Fork, 160/701	12.00
Fruit bowl, 160/23B, 5-1/2" d	15.00
Fruit bowl, 160/3F, 6" d	10.00
Fruit bowl, 160/67/F, 9" d, ftd	60.00
Goblet, 160, 8 oz	12.00
Goblet, 1600, 10 oz	25.00
Goblet, 1602, 9 oz or 11 oz	10.00
Gravy boat, 160/202	70.00
Horseradish jar, 160/226	80.00
Ice bucket, 160/63	185.00
Iced tea tumbler, 1600, 12 oz	15.00
Iced tea tumbler, 1602, 12 oz, ftd	30.00
Jelly, 160/33, 3"	15.00
Juice tumbler, 1602, 6 oz, ftd	15.00
Ketchup bottle, 160/237	225.00
Marmalade ladle, 160/130	12.00
Marmalade, 160/89/3, three-pc set	35.00
Martini pitcher, 160/178, blown, 40 oz	200.00
Mayonnaise ladle, 160/165	12.00
Mayonnaise, 160/52H, three-pc set	30.00
Milk pitcher, 160/240, 1 pint	45.00
Mint bowl, 160/183, 3" d	20.00
Mint bowl, 160/51F, 6" d, handle	35.00
Mug, 160/188, 12 oz	48.00
Mustard, cov, spoon, 160/156	24.00
Nappy, 160/5F, 7" d	24.00
Nut dish, 160/183, 3" d, handle	27.50
Nut dish, 160/184, 4" d, handle	27.50
Old Fashioned tumbler, 1600, 6 oz	25.00
Oyster cocktail, 1602	12.00
Parfait, 1602, 6 oz	16.50
Pastry tray, 160/68D, 11" l	70.00
Peanut jar, 160/210, 12 oz	70.00
Pepper mill, 160/236	32.50
Pitcher, 160/19, 40 oz, ice lip	80.00
Pitcher, 160/176, 5 pint	150.00
Pitcher, 160/239, 2 qt, ice lip	100.00
Plate, 4-1/2" d, butter	8.50
Plate, 6-1/2" d, bread and butter	8.50
Plate, 8" d, salad	10.00
Plate, 9" d, luncheon	20.00
Plate, 10" d, dinner	40.00
Platter, 160/124D, 13-1/2" l, oval	60.00
Puff box, cov, 1601	48.00
Punch bowl, 160/20B, 12" d	65.00
Punch cup, 160	8.00
Punch ladle	25.00
Relish, 160/55, 9-1/2" l, oval, three parts	35.00
Relish, 160/56, 9-1/2" d, four parts	35.00
Relish, 160/102, 11" d, five parts	50.00
Relish, 160/223, 8" d, two parts, handle	40.00
Salad bowl, 1608D, 11" d	42.00
Salad crescent, 160/12, 8"	50.00
Salt and pepper shakers, pr, 160/96	20.00

Item	Crystal
Salt and pepper shakers, pr, 160/109	24.00
Salt and pepper shakers, pr, 160/116, ftd	24.00
Salt and pepper shakers, pr, 160/243, stemmed	42.00
Salt and pepper shakers, pr, 160/251, individual size	18.00
Salt, open, 160/61	18.00
Salt spoon, 1600	10.00
Sherbet, 1600, 6 oz	30.00
Sherbet, 1602, 6 oz, tall	20.00
Soup bowl, 160/198, 5-1/2" d, tab handle	20.00
Spoon, 160/701	15.00
Sugar, 160/30	8.50
Sugar, 160/31, ftd	18.00
Sugar, 160/190	35.00
Sundae, 1602, 6 oz, low	8.50
Tea cup, 160/35	8.50
Tea saucer, 160/35	3.00
Toast, cov, 160/123	165.00
Tom and Jerry bowl, 160/200	375.00
Torte plate, 1608F, 13" d	40.00
Torte plate, 1608V, 13" d, cupped	40.00
Tray, 160/51T, 6" d, handle	20.00
Tumbler, 160, 10 oz	12.00
Tumbler, 1602, 10 oz, ftd	18.50
Urn, 160/186, 10-1/2" h, handle	175.00
Vase, 160/143, flip, 8-1/2" h	55.00
Vase, 160/192, 10" h	80.00
Vase, 160/21, 11-1/2" h, ftd	65.00
Vase, 160/22, 6-1/4" h, ftd	35.00
Vase, 160/22, 7-1/2" h, ftd	42.00
Vase, 160/87F, 8" h, fan	200.00
Vase, 1603, 11" h, flip	175.00
Whiskey, 160, 2-1/2 oz	15.00
Wine carafe, 160/185	200.00
Wine, 1602, 3 oz	17.50

*Cape Cod, crystal bread and butter plate, 6-1/2" d, **$8.50**.*

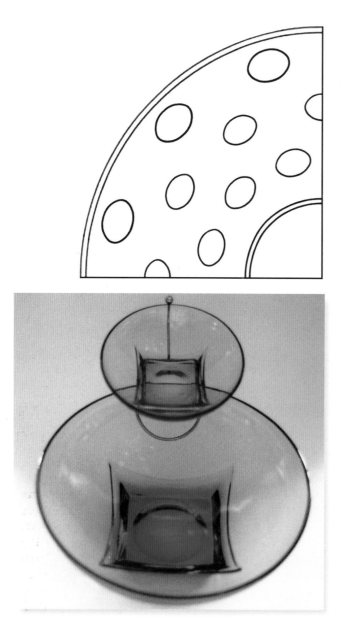

CAPRI

Manufactured by Hazel Ware, division of Continental Can, 1960s. Collectors are starting to divide these wares into several distinct patterns, based on the shape. All are the same pretty azure blue color and have the same market value. Original "Capri" paper labels are found on most of the styles.

Pieces are made in azure blue.

Item	Azure Blue
Ashtray, 3-1/2" sq, emb flower center	15.00
Ashtray, 3-1/4" w, triangular or round	6.00
Ashtray, 5" d, round	7.50
Ashtray, 6-7/8" w, triangular	10.00
Bowl, 4-3/4" d, octagonal or swirled	6.50
Bowl, 4-7/8" d, round, Dots	7.50
Bowl, 5-3/4" w, sq	10.00
Bowl, 5-5/8", Colony Swirl	6.50
Bowl, 6" d, Dots, Colony Swirl	6.00
Bowl, 6" d, Tulip	12.00
Bowl, 7-3/4" l, oval	14.00
Bowl, 8-3/4" d, swirled	18.00
Bowl, 9-1/2" d	18.00
Candy jar, cov, ftd	35.00
Celery, 8" l, oval	17.00
Chip and dip set, metal rack	30.00
Creamer	12.00
Cup, octagonal	6.50
Cup, round	5.00
Iced tea tumbler, 5" h, 12 oz	10.00
Juice tumbler, 3-5/8" h, Dots	6.00
Old fashioned tumbler, 3-5/8" h, Dots	8.50
Plate, 5-3/4" d, bread and butter	5.00
Plate, 7" d, salad	6.50
Plate, 8" w, sq	7.50
Plate, 9-3/4", dinner	10.00
Salad bowl, 5-3/8" d	7.50
Saucer, round, sq, or octagonal	1.50
Sherbet	7.50
Snack plate, fan shape	12.00
Snack plate, round	9.50
Sugar, cov	20.00
Tidbit, two bowl tiers, Colony Swirl	45.00
Tidbit, three-plate tiers	20.00
Tumbler, 2-3/4" h, Colony Swirl	7.50
Tumbler, 3" h, Dots	5.50
Tumbler, 3-1/16", Colony, Colony Swirl	8.50
Tumbler, 4-1/4" h, 9 oz	7.50
Tumbler, 5-1/4", Dots	9.00
Vase, 8" h, Dots	20.00
Vase, 8-1/2" h, ruffled rim	35.00

*Capri, Azure Blue chip and dip set, **$30**. Photo courtesy of Tina Trautman.*

*Capri, azure blue saucer with dots, **$1.50**.*

CHERRY BLOSSOM

Manufactured by Jeannette Glass Company, Jeannette, Pa., from 1930 to 1939.

Pieces are made in Crystal, Delphite, green, jadeite, pink, and red (production was very limited in crystal, jadeite and red).

Reproductions: † Reproductions include a small berry bowl, an 8-1/2-inch diameter bowl, a covered butter dish, a cake plate, a cereal bowl, cup, pitcher, 6-inch and 9-inch plates, divided 13-inch platter, salt shaker, sandwich tray, saucer, and footed tumblers that are 3-3/4-inch and 4-1/2-inch high. Reproductions have been made in cobalt blue, Delphite, green, pink, and red. A children's butter dish has also been made, which was never included in the original production.

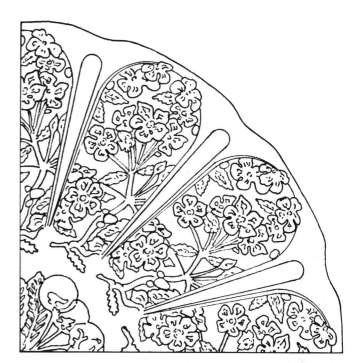

Item	Delphite	Green	Pink
Berry bowl, 4-3/4" d †	24.00	27.50	25.00
Berry bowl, 8-1/2" d †	45.00	55.00	50.00
Bowl, 9" d, two handles	27.50	95.00	48.00
Butter dish, cov †	—	115.00	75.00
Cake plate, 10-1/4" d, three legs †	—	38.00	35.00
Cereal bowl, 5-3/4" d †	—	35.00	60.00
Coaster	—	15.00	15.00
Creamer	30.00	20.00	25.00
Cup †	28.00	28.00	30.00
Fruit bowl, 10-1/2" d	32.00	120.00	135.00
Iced tea tumbler, PAT, flat	—	—	135.00
Juice tumbler, 1 oz, 3-1/2"	25.00	35.00	25.00
Mug, 7 oz	—	195.00	265.00
Pitcher, 36 oz, 6-3/4" h, 36 oz †	95.00	60.00	78.00
Pitcher, 36 oz, 8", PAT, ftd	—	65.00	75.00
Pitcher, 42 oz, 8", PAT, flat	—	65.00	95.00
Plate, 6" d, sherbet †	12.50	10.00	12.00
Plate, 7" d, salad	—	30.00	28.00
Plate, 9" d, dinner †	20.00	24.00	30.00
Plate, 9" d, grill	—	35.00	32.50
Plate, 10" d, grill	—	32.50	—
Platter, 11" l, oval	40.00	55.00	50.00
Platter, 13" d	—	150.00	150.00
Platter, 13" divided †	—	72.00	75.00
Salt and pepper shakers, pr, scalloped base †	—	995.00	1,250.00
Sandwich tray, 10-1/2" d †	20.00	30.00	45.00
Saucer †	6.00	8.00	6.50

Item	Delphite	Green	Pink
Sherbet	24.00	30.00	22.00
Soup, flat, 7-3/4" d	—	90.00	80.00
Sugar, cov	20.00	27.50	35.00
Tray, 10-1/2" w handles	—	—	35.00
Tumbler, 3-3/4" h, AOP, ftd †	—	22.00	24.00
Tumbler, 5" h	20.00	70.00	72.00
Tumbler, 8 oz, 4-1/2" h, scalloped ftd base, AOP	—	40.00	42.00
Tumbler, 9 oz, 4-1/4" h	—	24.00	20.00
Tumbler, 9 oz, 4-1/2" h †	30.00	30.00	30.00
Vegetable bowl, 9" l, oval	45.00	42.00	40.00

Children's

Item	Delphite	Pink
Creamer	50.00	50.00
Cup †	42.00	65.00
Plate, 6" d	15.00	15.00
Saucer	7.50	7.50
Sugar	50.00	50.00

Cherry Blossom, delphite berry bowls, 4-3/4" d, each $17.50.

CHERRYBERRY

Manufactured by U.S. Glass Company, Pittsburgh, Pa., early 1930s.

Pieces are made in crystal, green, iridescent, and pink.

Cherryberry, crystal berry bowl, **$17.50**.

Item	Crystal	Green	Iridescent	Pink
Berry bowl, 4" d	7.00	8.75	7.00	8.75
Berry bowl, 7-1/2" d, deep	1950	35.00	22.00	24.00
Bowl, 6-1/4" d, 2" deep	50.00	55.00	40.00	55.00
Butter dish, cov	150.00	175.00	150.00	175.00
Comport, 5-3/4"	17.50	25.00	17.50	25.00
Creamer, large, 4-5/8"	40.00	45.00	40.00	45.00
Creamer, small	15.00	20.00	15.00	20.00
Olive dish, 5" l, one handle	10.00	15.00	10.00	15.00
Pickle dish, 8-1/4" l, oval	10.00	15.00	10.00	15.00
Pitcher, 7-3/4" h	165.00	175.00	165.00	175.00
Plate, 6" d, sherbet	6.50	11.00	6.50	11.00
Plate, 7-1/2" d, salad	8.50	15.00	9.00	15.00
Salad bowl, 6-1/2" d, deep	17.50	22.00	17.50	22.00
Sherbet	10.00	12.00	12.00	14.00
Sugar, large, cov	45.00	75.00	45.00	75.00
Sugar, small, open	15.00	20.00	15.00	20.00
Tumbler, 9 oz, 3-5/8" h	20.00	35.00	20.00	35.00

CHINEX CLASSIC

Manufactured by Macbeth-Evans Division of Corning Glass Works, from the late 1930s to early 1940s.

Pieces are made in Chinex (ivory) and Chinex with Classic Bouquet or Classic Castle decal.

Item	Chinex	Chinex, Classic Bouquet decal	Chinex, Classic Castle deal
Bowl, 11" d	20.00	36.00	48.00
Butter dish, cov	55.00	80.00	135.00
Cake plate, 11-1/2" d	10.00	15.00	25.00
Cereal bowl, 5- 3/4" d	6.00	8.50	15.00
Creamer	5.00	12.00	20.00
Cup	6.00	9.50	17.50
Plate, 6-1/4" d, sherbet	4.00	6.50	10.00
Plate, 9-3/4" d, dinner	5.00	9.00	10.00
Sandwich plate, 11-1/2" d	8.50	12.00	25.00
Saucer	2.00	4.00	7.00
Sherbet, low, ftd	9.50	12.00	30.00
Soup bowl, 7-3/4" d	14.00	25.00	40.00
Sugar, open	7.50	12.50	20.00
Vegetable bowl, 7" d	15.00	25.00	35.00
Vegetable bowl, 9" d	15.00	25.00	35.00

*Chinex Classic, dinner plate with castle decal, **$18**.*

CHRISTMAS CANDY

No. 624

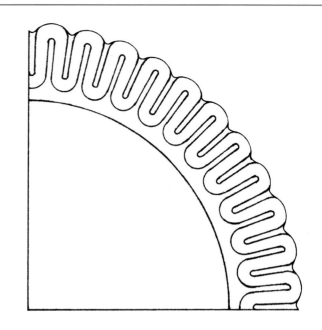

Manufactured by Indiana Glass Company, Dunkirk, Ind., 1950s.

Pieces are made in crystal and Terrace Green (teal).

Item	Crystal	Terrace Green
Bowl, 5-3/4" d	6.50	—
Creamer	17.50	45.00
Cup	8.50	38.00
Mayonnaise, ladle, liner	24.00	—
Plate, 6" d, bread and butter	6.00	16.00
Plate, 8-1/4" d, luncheon	8.00	30.00
Plate, 9-5/8"d, dinner	12.00	36.00
Sandwich plate, 11-1/4" d	24.00	65.00
Saucer	5.00	15.00
Soup bowl, 7-3/8" d	12.00	75.00
Sugar	15.00	45.00
Tidbit, two tiers	20.00	—
Vegetable bowl, 9-1/2" d	—	235.00

*Christmas Candy, crystal sugar, **$15**; creamer, **$15**.*

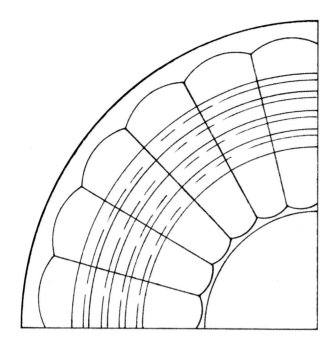

CIRCLE

Manufactured by Hocking Glass Company, Lancaster, Ohio, in the 1930s.

Pieces are made in crystal, green, and pink. Crystal is listed in the original catalogs, but few pieces have surfaced to date. A 3-1/8-inch diameter sherbet is known and valued at $4.

Item	Green	Pink
Bowl, 4-1/2" d	15.00	15.00
Bowl, 5-1/2" d, flared	17.50	17.50
Bowl, 8" d	16.00	16.00
Bowl, 9-3/8" d	18.50	18.50
Creamer, ftd	9.00	16.00
Cup	6.50	7.50
Goblet, 8 oz, 5-3/4" h	16.50	15.00
Iced tea tumbler, 10 oz	17.50	17.50
Juice tumbler, 4 oz	9.50	9.00
Pitcher, 60 oz	35.00	35.00
Pitcher, 80 oz	30.00	32.00

Item	Green	Pink
Plate, 6" d, sherbet	6.00	6.00
Plate, 8-1/4"d, luncheon	12.00	12.00
Plate, 9-1/2" d, dinner	12.00	12.00
Sandwich plate, 10" d	15.00	17.50
Saucer, 6" d	2.50	2.50
Sherbet, 3-1/8"	8.00	8.00
Sherbet, 4-3/4"	10.00	12.00
Sugar, ftd	12.00	16.00
Tumbler, 8 oz	10.00	10.00
Tumbler, 15 oz, flat	17.50	17.50
Wine, 4-1/2" h	15.00	$15.00

Circle, green cup, **$6**.

Circle, green footed creamer, **$9**; *green tumbler, flat, 15 oz,* **$17.50**. *Photo courtesy of James Hintz.*

*Circle, green berry bowl, 5", **$17.50**; green bowl, **$15**, on a sherbet plate, **$6**; associated ladle, **$10**. All photos on this page are courtesy of James Hintz.*

*Circle, from left: green tumbler, 8 oz, **$10**; green sherbet, 4-3/4" h, **$12**; green sherbet, 3-1/8" h, **$5**.*

*Circle, green pitcher, 80 oz, **$30**. A reamer is known that fits on top of the pitcher. A 60-oz pitcher is also known and rare.*

*Circle, items have frosted green stems and clear tops; from left: wine, 4-1/2" h, **$15**; sherbet, 4-3/4" h, **$10**; sherbet, 3-1/8" h, **$8**.*

*Circle, green luncheon plate, 8-1/4", **$11**; green flared cup, **$6**, on a 6" saucer, **$2.50**. Two styles of cups are known: flared sides and round sides.*

CLOVERLEAF

Manufactured by Hazel Atlas Glass Company, Clarksburg, W.V., and Zanesville, Ohio, from 1930 to 1936.

Pieces are made in black, crystal, green, pink, and yellow. Collector interest in crystal is minimal; prices would be about 50 percent of those listed for green.

Item	Black	Green	Pink	Yellow
Ashtray, match holder in center, 4" d	65.00	—	—	—
Ashtray, match holder in center, 5-3/4" d	90.00	—	—	—
Bowl, 8" d	—	95.00	—	—
Candy dish, cov	—	65.00	—	130.00
Cereal bowl, 5" d	—	50.00	—	55.00
Creamer, 3-5/8" h, ftd	25.00	12.00	—	24.00
Cup	20.00	12.00	8.00	12.00
Dessert bowl, 4" d	—	30.00	30.00	35.00
Plate, 6" d, sherbet	40.00	6.50	—	10.00
Plate, 8" d, luncheon	18.00	15.00	12.00	18.00
Plate, 10-1/4" d, grill	—	25.00	—	40.00
Salad bowl, 7" d	—	60.00	—	65.00
Salt and pepper shakers, pr	100.00	40.00	—	140.00
Saucer	10.00	10.00	7.00	5.00
Sherbet, 3" h, ftd	22.00	25.00	10.00	16.00
Sugar, 3-5/8" h, ftd	25.00	12.00	—	24.00
Tumbler, 9 oz, 4" h, flat	—	65.00	26.50	35.00
Tumbler, 10 oz, 3-3/4" h, flat	—	50.00	30.00	—
Tumbler, 10 oz, 5-3/4" h, ftd	—	50.00	—	40.00

Cloverleaf,
*green saucer, **$10**;*
*pink plate, **$12**;*
*pink cup, **$8**.*

COIN

Manufactured by Fostoria Glass Company, Moundsville, Va., from 1958 to 1982.

Pieces are made in amber, blue, crystal, emerald green, olive green, and red.

Reproductions: † Reproductions have been made in colors similar to the original colors by Lancaster Colony, using original Fostoria molds.

Item	Amber	Blue	Crystal	Emerald Green	Olive Green	Red
Ashtray, #110, cov, 3"	20.00	24.00	24.00	30.00	—	—
Ashtray, #114, 8" d	25.00	40.00	24.00	42.00	30.00	45.00
Ashtray, #115, 3" x 4" oblong	25.00	22.00	12.00	25.00	25.00	—
Ashtray, #119, 7-1/2" d, coin center	25.00	—	35.00	95.00	35.00	27.50
Ashtray, #123, 5" d	25.00	27.50	20.00	30.00	20.00	25.00
Ashtray, #124, 10" d	35.00	30.00	40.00	65.00	35.00	—
Bowl, #179, 7-1/2" d	40.00	80.00	35.00	115.00	40.00	70.00
Bowl, #189, 9" d, oval †	30.00	55.00	30.00	105.00	35.00	65.00
Bowl, #199, 8-1/2" d, ftd	75.00	125.00	75.00	125.00	65.00	85.00
Bowl, cov, #212, 8-1/2" d, ftd	225.00	425.00	95.00	225.00	—	—
Bud vase, #799, 8" h	35.00	85.00	25.00	125.00	45.00	70.00
Cake salver, #630, ftd †	135.00	315.00	135.00	300.00	125.00	—
Candlesticks, pr, #316, 4-1/2" h	60.00	80.00	50.00	60.00	50.00	95.00
Candlesticks, pr, #326, 8" h	85.00	—	48.00	—	70.00	110.00
Candy box, cov, 4-1/8", #354	45.00	65.00	40.00	135.00	32.50	70.00
Candy jar, cov, #347, 6-1/2" †	70.00	150.00	50.00	200.00	60.00	125.00
Cigarette box, cov, #374 †	50.00	85.00	75.00	120.00	—	—
Cigarette holder, ash tray cover, #372	45.00	72.00	40.00	85.00	—	—
Cigarette urn, 3-1/2", #381	35.00	45.00	35.00	48.00	35.00	40.00
Condiment set, #737, salt and pepper, cruet, tray	225.00	300.00	175.00	—	215.00	—
Creamer, #680 †	24.00	28.00	22.00	28.50	28.00	30.00
Cruet, os, #531	115.00	195.00	115.00	250.00	115.00	—
Decanter, os, #400, pint †	135.00	250.00	100.00	350.00	175.00	—
Goblet, water, #2, 6-1/2", 10-1/2" h	—	—	40.00	—	95.00	95.00
Iced tea tumbler, #58, 14 oz	—	—	40.00	—	—	—
Iced tea tumbler, #64, 12 oz	—	—	45.00	—	—	—
Jelly compote, #448 †	30.00	35.00	22.50	65.00	25.00	45.00
Juice tumbler, #81, 9 oz	—	—	40.00	—	—	—
Lamp chimney, #461, patio	50.00	60.00	40.00	—	—	—
Lamp chimney, #292, courting	48.00	65.00	—	—	—	—

Item	Amber	Blue	Crystal Green	Emerald Green	Olive	Red
Lamp, #310, courting, 9-3/4" h, oil, handle	125.00	310.00	—	—	—	—
Lamp, #311, courting, 10-3/4" h, electric	135.00	315.00	—	—	—	—
Lamp, #320, coach, 13-1/2" h, oil	165.00	355.00	100.00	—	—	—
Lamp, #321, coach, 13-1/2" h, electric	175.00	365.00	100.00	—	—	—
Lamp, #459, patio, 16-1/2", electric	185.00	500.00	145.00	—	—	—
Lamp, #466, patio, 16-1/2" h, oil	195.00	490.00	145.00	—	—	—
Nappy, #495, 4-1/2" d	—	—	24.00	—	—	—
Nappy, handle, #499, 5-3/8" †	25.00	50.00	25.00	95.00	25.00	40.00
Old Fashioned tumbler, #23, 10 oz	—	—	45.00	—	—	—
Pitcher, #453, 1 qt	95.00	125.00	95.00	330.00	95.00	145.00
Plate, 8" d, #550	—	—	45.00	—	—	—
Punch bowl set, punch bowl, base, 12 cups, #600/602, 615	650.00	—	675.00	—	—	—
Salt and pepper shakers, pr, #652	45.00	85.00	35.00	125.00	45.00	60.00
Sherbet, #7, 9 oz	—	—	25.00	—	85.00	75.00
Sugar, cov, #673 †	30.00	45.00	30.00	60.00	35.00	40.00
Tumbler, #73, 9 oz, water	—	—	45.00	—	—	—
Urn, cov, #829, 12-3/4" h †	125.00	85.00	65.00	195.00	115.00	195.00
Vase, #818, 10" h, ftd	—	—	175.00	—	—	—
Wedding bowl, cov, #162, 8-1/4" d †	70.00	125.00	55.00	125.00	65.00	95.00
Wine, #26, 5 oz	—	—	38.50	—	75.00	90.00

*Coin, red candy jar with cover, **$125**.*

COLONIAL

Knife and Fork

Manufactured by Hocking Glass Company, Lancaster, Ohio, from 1934 to 1938.

Pieces are made in crystal, green, and pink.

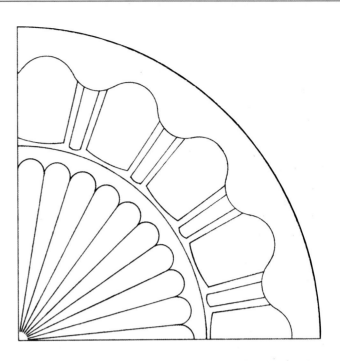

Item	Crystal	Green	Pink
Berry bowl, 3-3/4" d	—	—	60.00
Berry bowl, 4-1/2"	10.00	20.00	18.00
Berry bowl, 9" d	24.00	36.00	35.00
Butter dish, cov	45.00	60.00	700.00
Cereal bowl, 5-1/2" d	32.00	85.00	60.00
Claret, 4 oz, 5-1/4" h	21.00	31.50	—
Cocktail, 3 oz, 4" h	15.00	27.50	—
Cordial, 1 oz, 3-3/4" h	25.00	30.00	—
Cream soup bowl, 4-1/2" d	70.00	85.00	72.00
Creamer, 8 oz, 5" h	20.00	25.00	65.00
Cup	8.00	15.00	12.00
Goblet, 8-1/2 oz, 5-3/4" h	20.00	36.00	40.00
Iced tea tumbler, 12 oz	28.00	55.00	45.00
Juice tumbler, 5 oz, 3" h	17.50	27.50	24.50
Lemonade tumbler, 15 oz	47.50	75.00	65.00
Milk pitcher, 8 oz, 5" h	25.00	25.00	65.00
Mug, 12 oz, 5-1/2" h	—	825.00	500.00
Pitcher, 54 oz, 7" h, ice lip	40.00	45.00	48.00
Pitcher, 54 oz, 7" h, no lip	40.00	45.00	48.00
Pitcher, 68 oz, 7-3/4" h, ice lip	35.00	72.00	65.00
Pitcher, 68 oz, 7-3/4" h, no lip	45.00	72.00	65.00
Plate, 6" d, sherbet	4.50	10.00	7.00
Plate, 8-1/2" d, luncheon	6.00	8.00	10.00
Plate, 10" d, dinner	35.00	67.50	65.00
Plate, 10"d, grill	17.50	30.00	27.50
Plate, 12" d, oval	17.50	25.00	30.00
Platter, 12" l, oval	17.50	25.00	35.00
Salt and pepper shakers, pr	60.00	160.00	150.00
Saucer	4.50	7.50	6.50
Sherbet, 3" h	—	—	24.00
Sherbet, 3-3/8" h	10.00	18.00	12.00

Item	Crystal	Green	Pink
Soup bowl, 7" d	30.00	85.00	85.00
Spoon holder or celery vase	105.00	130.00	135.00
Sugar, cov	90.00	55.00	50.00
Sugar, 5", open	10.00	12.00	15.00
Tumbler, 3 oz, 3-1/4" h, ftd	18.00	20.00	16.00
Tumbler, 5 oz, 4" h, ftd	15.00	35.00	24.50
Tumbler, 9 oz, 4" h	15.00	20.00	25.00
Tumbler, 10 oz, 5-1/4" h, ftd	30.00	48.50	50.00
Tumbler, 11 oz, 5-1/8" h	25.00	37.50	45.00
Vegetable bowl, 10" l, oval	18.00	25.00	30.00
Whiskey, 2-1/2" h, 1-1/2 oz	9.00	20.00	18.00
Wine, 4-1/2" h, 2-1/2 oz	18.00	30.00	15.00

*Colonial, crystal wine, **$17**; cocktail, **$15**.*

*Colonial, green creamer, **$25**; sugar, **$12**.*

*Colonial, green saucer, **$7.50**.*

COLONIAL BLOCK

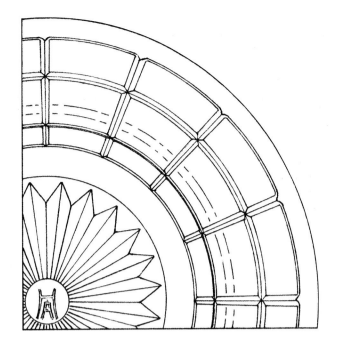

Manufactured by Hazel Atlas Glass Company, Clarksburg, W.V., and Zanesville, Ohio, early 1930s.

Pieces are made in black, cobalt blue (rare), crystal, green, pink, and white (1950s).

Item	Black	Crystal	Green	Pink	White
Bowl, 4" d	—	6.00	10.00	10.00	—
Bowl, 7" d	—	16.00	35.00	20.00	—
Butter dish, cov	—	35.00	50.00	45.00	—
Butter tub, cov	—	35.00	40.00	40.00	—
Candy jar, cov	—	30.00	45.00	40.00	—
Compote, 4" h, 4-3/4" w	—	12.00	—	—	—
Creamer	—	15.00	16.00	15.00	7.50
Goblet, 5-3/4" h	—	9.00	12.00	15.00	—
Pitcher, 20 oz, 5-3/4" h	—	40.00	50.00	50.00	—
Powder jar, cov	30.00	20.00	24.00	24.00	—
Sherbet	—	6.00	10.00	9.50	—
Sugar, cov	—	20.00	25.00	25.00	20.00
Sugar, open	—	10.00	8.00	8.00	10.00

*Colonial Block, green covered butter dish, **$50**.*

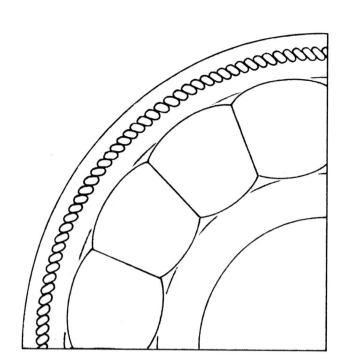

COLONIAL FLUTED

Rope

Manufactured by Federal Glass Company, Columbus, Ohio, from 1928 to 1933.

Pieces are made in crystal and green.

Item	Crystal	Green
Berry bowl, 4" d	11.00	12.00
Berry bowl, 7-1/2" d	16.00	30.00
Cereal bowl, 6" d	15.00	18.00
Creamer, ftd	12.00	14.00
Cup	5.00	7.50
Plate, 6" d, sherbet	2.50	4.50
Plate, 8" d, luncheon	5.00	10.00
Salad bowl, 6-1/2" d, 2-1/2" deep	22.00	35.00
Saucer	2.50	4.00
Sherbet	6.00	8.50
Sugar, cov	21.00	25.00
Sugar, open	8.00	10.00

*Colonial Fluted, green sugar, **$10**; creamer, **$14**.*

COLONY

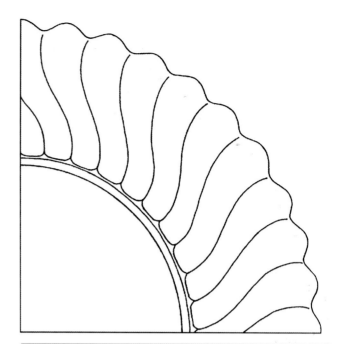

Manufactured by Fostoria Glass Company, Moundsville, Va., from the 1930s until 1983.

Pieces are made in crystal. The pattern was reissued as "Maypole" in the 1980s in the following colors: amber, blue, green, red, yellow, and white.

Item	Crystal
Almond bowl, ftd	15.00
Ashtray, 2-7/8" w, sq	8.75
Ashtray, 3" d, round	7.50
Ashtray, 3-1/2" w, sq	12.00
Ashtray, 4-1/2" d, round	15.00
Ashtray, 6" d, round	18.00
Bonbon, 5" d	12.00
Bonbon, 7"	15.00
Bowl, 4-1/2" d	32.00
Bowl, 5" d, handle	40.00
Bowl, 5-1/2" d, sq	45.00
Bowl, 8" d	35.00
Bowl, 10-1/2" d, high foot	95.00
Bowl, 10-1/2" d, low foot	75.00
Bowl, 11" l, flared	35.00
Bowl, 11" l, oval, ftd	95.00
Bud vase, 6" h	16.50
Butter dish, cov, quarter pound	60.00
Cake plate, 10" d, handle	24.00
Candlesticks, pr, 3-1/2" h	24.00
Candlesticks, pr, 6-1/2" h, two-lite	50.00
Candlesticks, pr, 7" h	25.00
Candlesticks, pr, 7-1/2" h, prisms	150.00
Candlesticks, pr, 9" h	65.00
Candlesticks, pr, 9-3/4" h, prisms	172.00
Candlesticks, pr, 14-1/2" h, prisms	400.00
Candy dish, cov, 6-1/2"	52.50
Candy dish, cov, ftd, half pound	75.00
Celery, 11-1/2"	32.00
Cheese and cracker	50.00
Cigarette box	48.00
Cocktail, 3-1/2 oz, 4"	15.00
Comport, 4" h	18.00
Comport, cov, 6-1/2" d	38.00
Console bowl, 9" d or 13" d	35.00
Cornucopia, 9" h	70.00
Cream soup bowl, 5" d	48.00
Creamer	6.50
Creamer, individual size	7.00

Colony, crystal cup, **$8**.

Colony, crystal dinner plate, **$27.50**.

Item	Crystal
Creamer and sugar tray, individual size	9.00
Cup	8.00
Finger bowl	45.00
Fruit bowl, 10" d	36.00
Fruit bowl, 14" d	45.00
Goblet, 5-1/4" h	17.50
Ice bucket	150.00
Iced tea tumbler, 12 oz	50.00
Juice tumbler, 5 oz, ftd	28.00
Lamp, electric	172.00
Lemon plate, 6-1/2" d, handle	12.50
Lily pond bowl, 10" d	57.50
Mayonnaise, three pcs	36.00
Milk pitcher, 16 oz	72.00
Oil bottle, orig stopper	40.00
Olive, 7" l, oblong	18.00
Oyster cocktail, 4 oz	14.00
Pickle	17.50
Pitcher, 48 oz, ice lip	215.00
Plate, 6" d, bread and butter	4.50
Plate, 7" d, salad	8.25
Plate, 8" d, luncheon	10.00
Plate, 9" d, dinner	27.50
Platter, 12" l	50.00

Item	Crystal
Punch bowl	695.00
Punch cup	12.00
Relish, 10-1/2" d, three-part	20.00
Rose bowl	145.00
Salad bowl, 7-3/4" d	25.00
Salad bowl, 9-3/4" d	40.00
Salt and pepper shakers, pr, 2-1/2" h	45.00
Salt and pepper shakers, pr, 3-5/8" h	15.00
Salver, 12" d, ftd	65.00
Sandwich plate, center handle	32.00
Saucer	3.00
Sherbet, 3-5/8"	9.00
Sugar	6.50
Sugar, individual	7.50
Torte plate, 13" d	32.00
Torte plate, 15" d	60.00
Torte plate, 18" d	100.00
Tumbler, 5 oz, 4-1/2" h, ftd	30.00
Tumbler, 9 oz, 3-7/8" h	25.00
Tumbler, 12 oz, 5-3/4" h, ftd	25.00
Vase, 7" h	35.00
Vase, 7-1/2" h, flared	42.00
Vase, 12" h	200.00
Wine, 4-1/4" h	32.00

*Colony, crystal pickle with two handles, **$17.50**.*

COLUMBIA

Manufactured by Federal Glass Company, Columbus, Ohio, from 1938 to 1942.

Pieces are made in crystal and pink. Several flashed (stained) colors are found, and some decaled pieces are known.

Reproductions: † The 2-7/8-inch high juice tumbler has been reproduced. Look for the "France" on the base to clearly identify the reproductions.

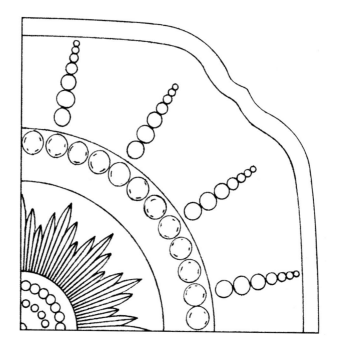

Item	Crystal	Flashed	Pink
Bowl, 8-1/2" d	20.00	—	—
Bowl, 10-1/2" d, ruffled edge	20.00	20.00	—
Butter dish, cov	22.00	25.00	—
Cereal bowl, 5" d	18.50	—	—
Chop plate, 11" d	17.00	12.00	—
Crescent shaped salad	27.00	—	—
Cup	8.50	10.00	25.00
Juice tumbler, 4 oz, 2-3/4" h †	30.00	—	—
Lamp shade, 8-1/2" d	25.00	—	—
Plate, 6" d, bread and butter	5.00	4.00	14.00
Plate, 9-1/2" d, luncheon	15.00	12.00	32.00
Salad bowl, 8-1/2" d	20.00	—	—
Saucer	4.50	4.00	10.00
Snack tray, cup	30.00	—	—
Soup bowl, 8" d, low	25.00	—	—
Tumbler, 9 oz	32.50	—	—

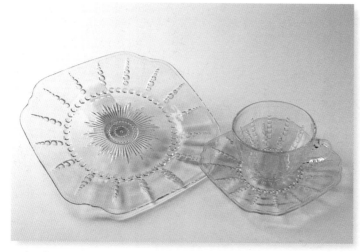

Columbia, crystal luncheon plate $15; cup, $27; saucer, $4.50.

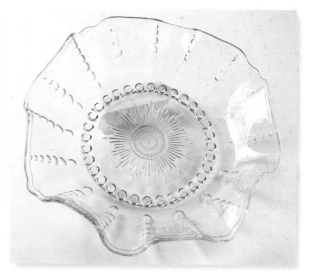

Columbia, crystal ruffled bowl, $20.

CONSTELLATION

Pattern #300

Manufactured by Indiana Glass Company, Dunkirk, Ind., c1940. Later reissued as Sunset Constellation by Tiara Home products in the 1980s.

Pieces are made in crystal and amber by Indiana. Made in amberina, emerald green, red, and yellow mist by Tiara.

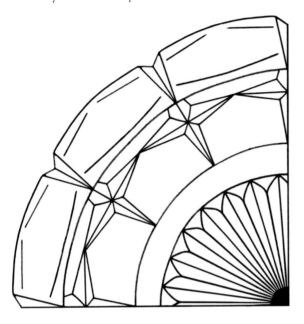

*Constellation, crystal nut bowl, **$12**.*

Item	Amber	Crystal	Tiara Colors
Basket, 11"	—	30.00	25.00
Bowl, 11" d, two handles	—	25.00	12.00
Buffet plate, 18" d	—	40.00	—
Cake stand	—	50.00	—
Candlesticks, pr	—	45.00	15.00
Candy dish, cov	—	25.00	18.00
Celery tray	—	20.00	—
Console bowl, 11-1/2" d	—	25.00	20.00
Cookie jar, cov	—	28.00	24.00
Creamer	—	10.00	—
Goblet, water	15.00	15.00	12.00
Mayonnaise bowl, ladle, underplate	—	28.00	—
Mug	—	15.00	—
Nappy, three toes	—	15.00	—
Nut bowl, 6" d, cupped	—	12.00	—
Pickle, oval	—	15.00	—
Pitcher, 7-1/2" d	65.00	45.00	60.00
Plate, dessert	—	5.00	—
Plate, lunch	—	8.00	—

Item	Amber	Crystal	Tiara Colors
Plate, salad	—	10.00	—
Platter, oval	—	20.00	—
Punch bowl	—	35.00	—
Relish, three parts	—	15.00	—
Salad bowl	—	22.00	—
Serving plate, 13-1/2" d	—	25.00	15.00
Sugar	—	10.00	—
Tumbler, 8 oz	—	15.00	—

*Constellation, amber water goblet, **$15**.*

CORONATION

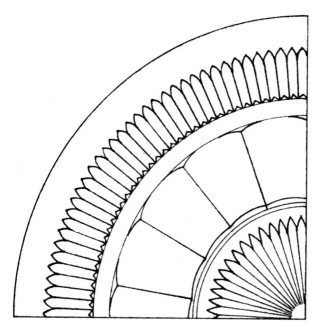

Banded Fine Rib, Saxon

Manufactured by Hocking Glass Company, Lancaster, Ohio, from 1936 to 1940.

Pieces are made in crystal, green, pink, and Royal Ruby.

Item	Crystal	Green	Pink	Royal Ruby
Berry bowl, 4-1/4" d	—	50.00	9.00	9.50
Berry bowl, 8" d, handle	—	—	18.00	20.00
Berry bowl, 8" d	—	195.00	—	—
Cup	5.00	—	6.00	7.50
Nappy bowl, 6-1/2" d	15.00	—	7.50	15.00
Pitcher, 68 oz, 7-3/4" h	—	—	500.00	—
Plate, 6" d, sherbet	2.00	—	5.00	—
Plate, 8-1/2" d, luncheon	5.00	60.00	15.00	8.50
Saucer	2.00	—	5.00	—
Sherbet	—	85.00	7.00	—
Tumbler, 10 oz, 5" h, ftd	—	195.00	35.00	—

Coronation, royal ruby handled berry bowl, $20.

CRACKED ICE

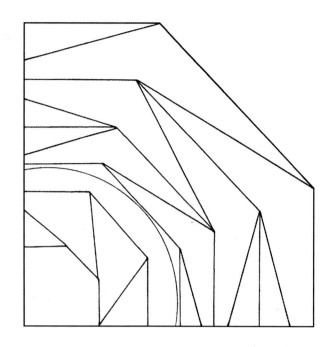

Manufactured by Indiana Glass, Dunkirk, Ind., in the 1930s.

Pieces are made in pink and green. This pattern is often mistaken for Tea Room, so look for the additional diagonal line, giving it a more Art Deco style.

Item	Green	Pink
Creamer	30.00	35.00
Plate, 6-1/2" d	15.00	18.00
Sherbet	12.00	15.00
Sugar, cov	30.00	35.00
Tumbler	30.00	32.50

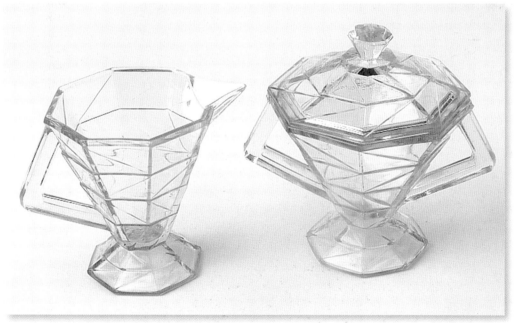

Cracked Ice, pink creamer, $35; covered sugar, $35.

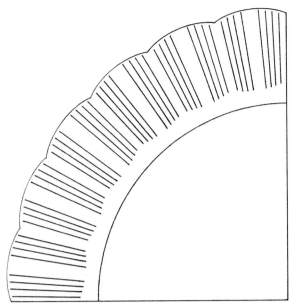

CREMAX

Manufactured by Macbeth-Evans Division of Corning Glass Works, late 1930s to early 1940s.

Pieces are made in Cremax, Cremax with fired-on colors, Delphite, and Robin's Egg Blue. One set is known as Bordette.

Item	Bordette	Cremax	Cremax Fired-on Colors	Delphite	Robin's Egg Blue
Cereal bowl, 5-3/4" d	5.00	6.00	9.00	10.00	10.00
Creamer	6.00	6.50	6.00	11.00	11.00
Cup	5.00	5.00	8.00	7.00	7.00
Demitasse cup	10.00	20.00	24.00	26.00	26.00
Demitasse saucer	6.00	8.00	10.00	12.00	20.00
Eggcup, 2-1/4" h	12.00	—	—	—	—
Plate, 6-1/4" d, bread and butter	4.00	4.00	5.50	7.00	7.00
Plate, 9-3/4" d, dinner	14.00	7.00	11.00	12.00	12.00
Sandwich plate, 11-1/2" d	9.50	10.00	15.00	17.00	17.00
Saucer	3.50	4.00	4.00	6.00	6.00
Sugar, open	6.00	6.50	6.00	11.00	11.00
Vegetable bowl, 9" d	10.00	11.00	10.00	20.00	20.00

Cremax, Bordette dinner plate with blue edge, $14.

CROCHETED CRYSTAL

Manufactured by Imperial Glass Company, Bellaire, Ohio, from 1943 to the early 1950s.

Pieces were made exclusively for Sears, Roebuck, and only in crystal.

Item	Crystal
Basket, 6"	30.00
Basket, 9"	35.00
Basket, 12"	65.00
Buffet set, sauce bowl, ladle, 14" d plate	48.00
Cake stand, 12" d, ftd	42.00
Candlesticks, pr, 4-1/2" h, two-lite	17.50
Candlesticks, pr, 6" w	20.00
Celery tray, 10" l, oval	25.00
Cheese and cracker, 12" d plate, ftd dish	42.00
Cocktail, 3-1/2 oz, 4-1/2" h	15.00
Console bowl, 12" d	30.00
Creamer, flat or footed	25.00
Epergne, 11" h, ftd	140.00
Goblet, 9 oz, 7-1/8" h	15.00
Hors d'oeuvre dish, 10-1/2" d, four parts	30.00
Hurricane lamp, 11" h	48.00
Iced tea tumbler, 12 oz, 7" h, ftd	18.00
Juice tumbler, 6 oz, 6" h, ftd	12.00
Mayonnaise bowl, 5-1/4" d	15.00
Mayonnaise ladle	7.50
Mayonnaise plate, 7-1/2" d	8.00
Narcissus bowl, 7" d	42.00
Plate, 14" d	25.00
Plate, 17" d	40.00
Plate, 8" d, salad	9.50
Plate, 9-1/2" d, luncheon	12.50
Punch bowl, 14" d	70.00
Punch cup, closed handle	5.50
Punch cup, open handle	7.50
Relish, 11-1/2" d, three parts	27.50
Salad bowl, 10-1/2" d	35.00
Salad bowl liner, 13" d plate	25.00
Sherbet, 6 oz, 5" h	12.00
Sugar, flat or footed	25.00
Vase, 5" h, ftd	35.00
Vase, 8" h	35.00
Wine, 4-1/2 oz, 5-1/2" h	24.00

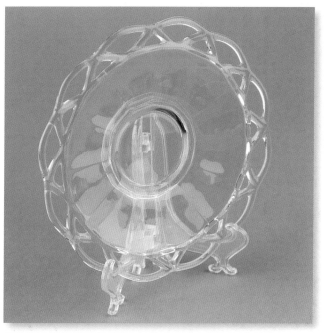

*Crocheted Crystal, luncheon plate **$12.50**.*

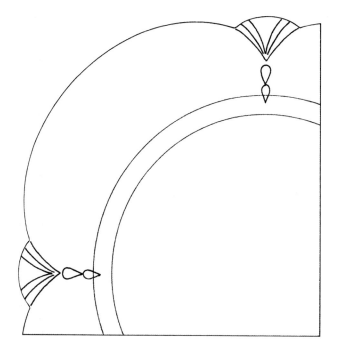

CROW'S FOOT

Line #412 and Line #890

Manufactured by Paden City Glass Company, Paden City, W.V., 1930s. The square-shaped pieces are Line #412, the round line is Line #890.

Pieces are made in amber, amethyst, black, crystal, pink, Ritz blue, ruby red, white, and yellow.

Item	Black or Ritz Blue	Colors	Ruby Red
Bowl, 4-7/8" w, sq	32.00	13.00	25.00
Bowl, 6" d	35.00	15.00	32.00
Bowl, 6-1/2" d, round, 2-1/2" h, 3-1/2" d base	50.00	24.00	45.00
Bowl, 8-1/2" d, sq, two handles	60.00	30.00	50.00
Bowl, 8-3/4" w, sq	55.00	25.00	45.00
Bowl, 10" d, ftd	75.00	35.00	70.00
Bowl, 10" w, sq, two handles	75.00	35.00	89.00
Bowl, 11" l, oval	45.00	20.00	40.00
Bowl, 11" w, sq	72.00	32.00	60.00
Bowl, 11" w, sq, rolled edge	75.00	35.00	70.00
Cake plate, sq, low pedestal foot	95.00	45.00	135.00
Candlesticks, pr, 5-3/4" h	60.00	40.00	90.00
Candlesticks, pr, round base, tall	170.00	75.00	145.00
Candlesticks, pr, sq, mushroom	90.00	45.00	75.00
Candy, 6-1/8" w, 3-1/4" h, three legs, round	195.00	85.00	165.00
Candy, cov, 6-1/2" d, three parts	95.00	25.00	55.00
Cheese stand, 5" h	35.00	40.00	30.00
Comport, 3-1/4" h, 6-1/4" w	35.00	15.00	38.00
Comport, 4-3/4" h, 7-3/8" w	55.00	30.00	45.00
Comport, 6-5/8" h, 7" w	70.00	35.00	80.00
Console bowl, 11-1/2" d, three legs, round	100.00	50.00	150.00
Console bowl, 11-1/2" w, sq	95.00	40.00	80.00
Cracker plate, 11" d	50.00	25.00	45.00
Cream soup bowl, flat	28.00	12.00	22.00
Cream soup bowl, ftd	28.00	12.00	22.00
Creamer, flat	17.50	10.00	15.00
Creamer, footed	17.50	10.00	15.00
Cup, flat	18.50	6.00	15.00
Cup, ftd	15.50	6.00	15.00
Gravy boat, flat	100.00	45.00	85.00
Gravy boat, ftd	215.00	70.00	130.00
Mayonnaise, three legs	60.00	25.00	50.00
Nasturtium bowl, three legs	200.00	100.00	175.00

Item	Black or Ritz Blue	Colors	Ruby Red
Plate, 5-3/4" d	6.00	4.00	10.00
Plate, 8" d, round	12.00	5.00	17.50
Plate, 8-1/2" w, sq	10.00	7.00	8.00
Plate, 9-1/4" d, round, dinner	40.00	20.00	35.00
Plate, 9-1/2" d, two handles	75.00	35.00	65.00
Plate, 10-3/8" d, round, two handles	65.00	30.00	55.00
Plate, 10-3/8" w, sq, two handles	65.00	30.00	55.00
Plate, 10-1/2" d, dinner	100.00	45.00	90.00
Platter, 12" l	50.00	17.50	60.00
Relish, 11" l, three parts	100.00	48.00	85.00
Sandwich server, center handle, round	75.00	50.00	70.00
Sandwich server, center handle, sq	45.00	35.00	50.00
Saucer, 6" d, round	10.00	2.00	5.00
Saucer, 6" w, sq	10.00	2.00	5.00
Sugar, flat	17.50	10.00	15.00
Sugar, ftd	17.50	10.00	22.50
Tumbler, 4-1/4" h	80.00	35.00	75.00
Vase, 4-5/8" h	75.00	45.00	65.00
Vases, 10-1/4" h, cupped	110.00	50.00	90.00
Vases, 10-1/4" h, flared	85.00	35.00	70.00
Vases, 11-3/4" h, flared	185.00	125.00	240.00
Whipped cream bowl, three legs	70.00	30.00	60.00

*Crow's Foot, amber plate, 8-1/2" d, **$7**.*

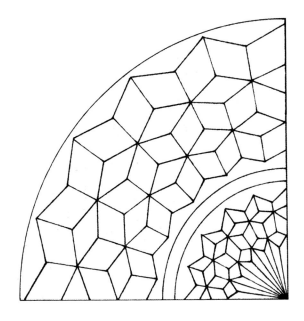

CUBE
Cubist

Manufactured by Jeannette Glass Company, Jeannette, Pa., from 1929 to 1933.

Pieces are made in amber, crystal, green, pink, ultramarine, and white. Production in amber and white is limited to the 2-3/8-inch high sugar bowl, and is valued at $3.

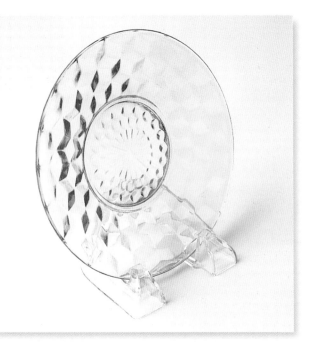

*Cube, pink luncheon plate, **$7.50**.*

Item	Crystal	Green	Pink	Ultramarine
Bowl, 4-1/2" d, deep	—	7.00	10.00	35.00
Butter dish, cov	—	95.00	100.00	—
Candy jar, cov, 6-1/2" h	—	55.00	40.00	—
Coaster, 3-1/4" d	—	10.00	10.00	—
Creamer, 2-5/8" h	5.00	10.00	12.00	70.00
Creamer, 3-9/16" h	—	9.00	9.00	—
Cup	—	7.00	8.00	—
Dessert bowl, 4-1/2" d, pointed rim	4.00	8.50	9.50	—
Pitcher, 8-3/4" h, 45 oz	—	265.00	215.00	—
Plate, 6" d, sherbet	—	11.00	3.50	—
Plate, 8" d, luncheon	—	8.50	7.50	—
Powder jar, cov, three legs	—	30.00	30.00	—
Salad bowl, 6-1/2" d	6.00	15.00	15.00	—
Salt and pepper shakers, pr	—	40.00	36.00	—
Saucer	1.50	3.00	4.50	—
Sherbet, ftd	—	8.50	12.00	—
Sugar, cov, 2-3/8" h	4.00	24.00	6.00	—
Sugar, cov, 3" h	—	35.00	25.00	—
Sugar, open, 3"	5.00	8.00	7.00	—
Tray, 7-1/2" l	8.50	—	5.00	—
Tumbler, 9 oz, 4" h	—	70.00	65.00	—

CUPID

Manufactured by Paden City Glass Company, Paden City, W.V., 1930s.

Pieces are made in amber, black, canary yellow, crystal, green, light blue, peacock blue, and pink. Prices for colors like amber, black, canary yellow, and light blue are still being established as more pieces of this pattern arrive on the secondary market. This expensive pattern is one to keep your eyes open for while searching at flea markets and garage sales.

Cupid, pink low pedestal-foot comport, 6-1/4", $325.

Item	Crystal	Green	Peacock Blue	Pink
Bowl, 8-1/2" l, oval, ftd	—	300.00	—	450.00
Bowl, 9-1/4" d, center handle	—	275.00	—	275.00
Bowl, 10-1/2" d, rolled edge	—	275.00	—	250.00
Cake plate, 11-3/4" h	—	200.00	—	200.00
Cake stand, 2" h, ftd	—	235.00	—	235.00
Candlesticks, pr, 5" h	—	245.00	—	245.00
Candy, cov, three parts	—	385.00	—	385.00
Candy, cov, 5-1/4" h	—	295.00	—	295.00
Champagne, 5-7/8" h	35.00	—	—	—
Cocktail, 5-1/8" h	25.00	—	—	—
Comport, 4-1/2" h, ftd	—	175.00	—	175.00
Comport, 6-1/4" h, ftd	—	185.00	225.00	325.00
Console bowl, 11" d	—	250.00	—	250.00
Creamer, 4-1/2" h, ftd	45.00	150.00	—	150.00
Creamer, 5" h, ftd	—	150.00	—	150.00
Fruit bowl, 9-1/4" d, ftd	—	360.00	—	360.00
Fruit bowl, 10-1/4" d	—	245.00	—	275.00
Ice bucket, 6" h	—	325.00	—	325.00
Ice tub, 4-3/4" h	—	325.00	—	325.00
Mayonnaise, 6" d, spoon, 8" d plate	—	275.00	295.00	275.00
Plate, 10-1/2" d	—	150.00	175.00	150.00
Samovar	—	990.00	—	990.00
Sugar, 4-1/4" h, ftd	—	150.00	—	200.00
Sugar, 5" h, ftd	—	150.00	—	150.00
Tray, 10-3/4" d, center handle	—	225.00	—	200.00
Tray, 10-7/8" l, oval, ftd	—	250.00	—	250.00
Vase, 8-1/4" h, elliptical	—	650.00	—	650.00
Vase, 10" h	—	315.00	—	315.00
Wine, 5-1/8" h	12.50	—	—	—

DAISY

No. 620

Manufactured by Indiana Glass Company, Dunkirk, Ind., from late 1930s to 1980s.

Pieces are made in amber (1940s), crystal (1933-40), dark green (1960s-80s), fired-on red (late 1930s), and milk glass (1960s-80s).

Item	Amber or Fired-On Red	Crystal or Milk White	Dark Green
Berry bowl, 4-1/2" d	12.00	6.00	6.00
Berry bowl, 7-3/8" d	15.50	8.50	12.50
Berry bowl, 9-3/8" d	35.00	26.00	14.00
Cake plate, 11-1/2" d	16.50	12.00	14.00
Cereal bowl, 6" d	25.00	10.00	10.00
Cream soup bowl, 4-1/2" d	12.50	7.50	12.50
Creamer, ftd	10.00	8.00	5.00
Cup	6.00	4.00	6.00
Plate, 6" d, sherbet	3.00	4.50	5.00
Plate, 7-3/8" d, salad	8.50	8.50	9.00
Plate, 8-3/8" d, luncheon	6.00	10.00	12.00
Plate, 9-3/8" d, dinner	9.00	12.00	10.00
Plate, 10-3/8" d, grill	15.00	5.50	18.00
Plate, 10-3/8" d, grill, indent for soup	15.00	8.00	8.00
Platter, 10-3/4" d	16.00	11.00	15.00
Relish dish, 8-3/8" d, three parts	24.00	12.00	12.00
Sandwich plate, 11-1/2" d	16.50	6.00	14.00
Saucer	5.00	6.00	5.00
Sherbet, ftd	10.00	5.00	10.00
Sugar, ftd	10.00	8.00	10.00
Tumbler, 9 oz, ftd	16.00	10.00	10.00
Tumbler, 12 oz, ftd	40.00	15.00	22.00
Vegetable bowl, 10" l, oval	20.00	18.00	18.00

Daisy, amber creamer, **$10**.

Daisy, amber luncheon plate, **$6**.

Daisy, crystal luncheon plate, **$10**.

Daisy, green luncheon plate, **$12**.

DELILAH

Delilah Bird, Peacock Reverse, Line #412

Manufactured by Paden City Glass Company, Paden City, W.V., 1930s.

Pieces are made in amber, black, cobalt blue, crystal, green, pink, red, and yellow.

Delilah Bird, amber candle holders, $90.

Delilah Bird, pink mayonnaise liner, $25.

Item	Colors
Bowl, 4-7/8" w, sq	50.00
Bowl, 8-3/4" w, sq	115.00
Bowl, 8-3/4" w, sq, handles	125.00
Candlesticks, pr, 5-3/4" h, sq base	90.00
Candy dish, 6-1/2" w, sq	200.00
Comport, 3-1/4" h, 6-1/4" w	90.00
Comport, 4-1/4" h, 7-3/8" w	95.00
Console bowl, 11-3/4" d	400.00
Creamer, 2-3/4" h, flat	95.00
Cup	95.00

Item	Colors
Plate, 5-3/4" d, sherbet	25.00
Plate, 8-1/2" d, luncheon	70.00
Plate, 10-3/8" d, two handles	155.00
Saucer	25.00
Server, center handle	85.00
Sherbet, two sizes	75.00
Tumbler, 10 oz, 4" h, flat	95.00
Vase, 6-3/4" h	125.00
Vase, 10" h	100.00

DELLA ROBBIA

#1058

Manufactured by Westmoreland Glass Company, Grapeville, Pa., from late 1920s to 1940s.

Pieces are made in crystal, with applied luster colors and milk glass. Examples of milk white prices are: hand-painted decorated candy jar, $45; creamer, $18; goblet, $20; tumbler, $22.50; and wine, $18.

Della Robbia, crystal salad plate, $22.

Item	Crystal
Basket, 9"	210.00
Basket, 12"	300.00
Bowl, 8" d, bell, handle	48.00
Bowl, 8"d, heart shape, handle	95.00
Bowl, 12" d, ftd	12.00

Item	Crystal
Bowl, 13" d, rolled edge	115.00
Bowl, 14" d, oval, flange	155.00
Bowl, 15" d, bell	175.00
Cake salver, 14" d, ftd	120.00
Candlesticks, pr, 4" h	65.00

Item	Crystal	Item	Crystal
Candlesticks, pr, 4" h, two-lite	350.00	Nappy, 9" d	60.00
Candy jar, cov, scalloped edge	150.00	Pitcher, 32 oz	200.00
Champagne, 6 oz	25.00	Plate, 6" d, finger bowl liner	12.00
Chocolate candy, round, flat	75.00	Plate, 6-1/8" d, bread and butter	14.00
Cocktail, 3-1/4 oz	15.00	Plate, 7-1/4" d, salad	22.00
Comport, 12" d, ftd, bell	115.00	Plate, 9" d, luncheon	35.00
Comport, 13" d, flanged	125.00	Plate, 10-1/2" d, dinner	95.00
Creamer, ftd	18.00	Plate, 18" d	195.00
Cup, coffee	18.50	Platter, 14" l, oval	195.00
Finger bowl, 5" d	30.00	Punch bowl, 14" d	225.00
Ginger ale tumbler, 5 oz	25.00	Punch bowl liner, 18" d plate, upturned edge	200.00
Goblet, 8 oz, 6" h	30.00	Punch cup	15.00
Iced tea tumbler 11 oz, ftd	35.00	Salt and pepper shakers, pr	55.00
Iced tea tumbler 12 oz, 5-3/16" h, straight	40.00	Saucer	10.00
Iced tea tumbler 12 oz, bell	32.00	Sherbet, 5 oz, low foot	22.00
Iced tea tumbler, 12 oz, bell, ftd	32.00	Sherbet, 5 oz, 4-3/4" h, ftd	24.00
Mint comport, 6-1/2" d, 3-5/8" h, ftd	45.00	Sugar, ftd	27.50
Nappy, 7-1/2" d	42.00	Sweetmeat comport, 8" d	115.00
Nappy, 8" d, bell	45.00	Torte plate, 14" d	125.00
Nappy, 4-1/2" d	30.00	Tumbler 8 oz, ftd	30.00
Nappy, 6" d, bell	35.00	Tumbler, 8 oz, water	32.00
Nappy, 6-1/2" d, one handle	32.00	Wine, 3 oz	25.00

Della Robbia, luster-decorated sweetmeat compote, **$115**.

DEWDROP

Manufactured by Jeannette Glass Company, Jeannette, Pa., from 1953 to 1956.

Pieces are made in crystal.

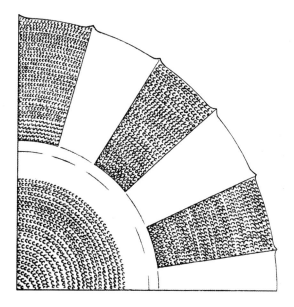

Items	Crystal
Bowl, 4-3/4" d	9.00
Bowl, 8-1/2" d	22.00
Bowl, 10-3/8" d	24.00
Butter, cov.	32.00
Candy dish, cov, 7" d	30.00
Casserole, cov.	27.50
Creamer	8.50
Cup	4.00
Iced tea tumbler, 15 oz	17.50
Lazy Susan, 13" d tray	30.00

Items	Crystal
Pitcher, 1/2 gallon, ftd	48.00
Plate, 11-1/2" d	20.00
Punch cup	4.00
Punch bowl set, bowl, 12 cups	90.00
Snack cup	4.00
Snack plate, indent for cup	8.00
Relish, leaf-shape, handle	9.00
Sugar, cov	14.00
Tray, 10" d	22.00
Tumbler, 9 oz	15.00

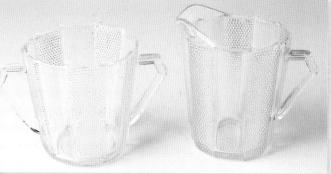

Dewdrop, crystal sugar, $8.50; creamer, $8.50.

Dewdrop, crystal tumbler, $15; iridescent pitcher, $48.

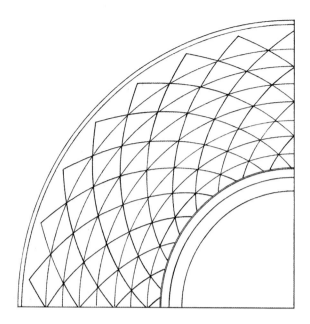

DIAMOND QUILTED

Flat Diamond

Manufactured by Imperial Glass Company, Bellaire, Ohio, from late 1920 to early 1930s.

Pieces are made in amber, black, blue, crystal, green, pink, and red. Amber and red prices would be valued slightly higher than black.

Item	Black	Blue	Crystal
Bowl, 5-1/2" d, one handle	20.00	—	—
Bowl, 7" d, crimped edge	22.00	—	—
Cake salver, 10" d, tall	—	—	—
Candlesticks, pr	60.00	—	50.00
Candy jar, cov, ftd	—	—	25.00
Cereal bowl, 5" d	15.00	—	8.00
Champagne, 9 oz, 6" h	—	—	—
Compote, 6" h, 7-1/4" w	—	—	—
Compote, cov, 11-1/2" d	—	—	—
Console bowl, 10-1/2" d, rolled edge	65.00	60.00	15.00
Cordial, 1 oz	—	—	—
Cream soup bowl, 4-3/4" d	22.00	20.00	20.00
Creamer	18.50	20.00	15.00
Cup	18.00	18.50	7.00
Ice bucket	90.00	90.00	—
Iced tea tumbler, 12 oz	—	—	—
Mayonnaise set, comport, plate, ladle	60.00	65.00	25.00
Pitcher, 64 oz	—	—	—
Plate, 6" d, sherbet	10.00	9.00	7.50
Plate, 7" d, salad	10.00	10.00	8.00
Plate, 8" d, luncheon	12.00	16.00	9.00
Punch bowl and stand	—	—	—
Sandwich plate, 14" d	—	—	—
Sandwich server, center handle	50.00	50.00	20.00
Saucer	5.00	5.00	2.00
Sherbet	16.00	16.00	14.00
Sugar	20.00	25.00	12.00
Tumbler, 6 oz, ftd	—	—	—
Tumbler, 9 oz	—	—	—
Tumbler, 9 oz, ftd	—	—	—
Tumbler, 12 oz, ftd	—	—	—
Vase, fan	80.00	75.00	—
Whiskey, 1-1/2" oz	—	—	—
Wine, 2 oz	—	—	—
Wine, 3 oz	—	—	—

Additional colors

Item	Green	Pink
Bowl, 5-1/2" d, one handle	15.00	18.00
Bowl, 7" d, crimped edge	20.00	25.00
Cake salver, 10" d, tall	60.00	65.00
Candlesticks, pr	30.00	28.00
Candy jar, cov, ftd	65.00	65.00
Cereal bowl, 5" d	9.00	8.50
Champagne, 9 oz, 6" h	12.00	—
Compote, 6" h, 7-1/4" w	45.00	48.00
Compote, cov, 11-1/2" d	80.00	75.00
Console bowl, 10-1/2" d, rolled edge	20.00	40.00
Cordial, 1 oz	12.00	15.00
Cream soup bowl, 4-3/4" d	20.00	14.00
Creamer	12.00	14.00
Cup	10.00	12.00
Ice bucket	50.00	50.00
Iced tea tumbler, 12 oz	10.00	10.00
Mayonnaise set, comport, plate, ladle	37.50	40.00
Pitcher, 64 oz	50.00	55.00
Plate, 6" d, sherbet	7.00	7.50
Plate, 7" d, salad	8.50	8.50
Plate, 8" d, luncheon	6.50	8.50
Punch bowl and stand	450.00	450.00
Sandwich plate, 14" d	15.00	15.00
Sandwich server, center handle	25.00	25.00
Saucer	4.00	4.00
Sherbet	10.00	10.00
Sugar	12.50	12.00
Tumbler, 6 oz, ftd	9.00	10.00
Tumbler, 9 oz	14.00	16.00
Tumbler, 9 oz, ftd	14.00	16.00
Tumbler, 12 oz, ftd	15.00	15.00
Vase, fan	50.00	50.00
Whiskey, 1-1/2" oz	10.00	12.00
Wine, 2 oz	12.50	12.50
Wine, 3 oz	15.00	15.00

*Diamond Quilted, pink sugar, **$12**; creamer, **$14**.*

DIANA

Manufactured by Federal Glass Company, Columbus, Ohio, from 1937 to 1941.

Made in amber, crystal, and pink.

Reproductions: † A 13-1/8-inch diameter scalloped pink bowl has been made, which was not original to the pattern.

*Diana, crystal tumbler, **$18**.*

Item	Amber	Crystal	Pink
Ashtray, 3-1/2" d...	—	4.00	5.00
Bowl, 12" d, scalloped edge..................	20.00	15.00	32.50
Candy jar, cov, round	40.00	18.50	48.00
Cereal bowl, 5" d	15.00	6.50	15.00
Coaster, 3-1/2" d....................................	12.00	4.00	8.00
Console/fruit bowl, 11" d....................	12.00	20.00	44.00
Cream soup bowl, 5-1/2" d..................	18.00	14.00	24.00
Creamer, oval	12.00	5.00	12.50
Cup...	7.00	4.00	19.00
Demitasse cup and saucer, 2 oz,			
4-1/2" d saucer	—	12.50	45.00
Junior set, six cups and saucers, rack........	—	125.00	300.00
Plate, 6" d, bread and butter	3.50	2.00	9.50
Plate, 9-1/2" d, dinner............................	9.00	6.00	18.50
Platter, 12" l, oval..................................	16.50	12.00	28.00
Salad bowl, 9" d	18.00	15.00	30.00
Salt and pepper shakers, pr	100.00	30.00	75.00
Sandwich plate, 11-3/4" d....................	15.00	9.50	28.00
Sandwich plate, 11-3/4" d, advertising in			
center	—	15.00	—
Saucer	2.25	2.00	5.00
Sherbet	12.00	7.00	12.00
Sugar, open, oval....................................	12.00	10.00	16.00
Tumbler, 9 oz, 4-1/8" h........................	30.00	18.00	45.00

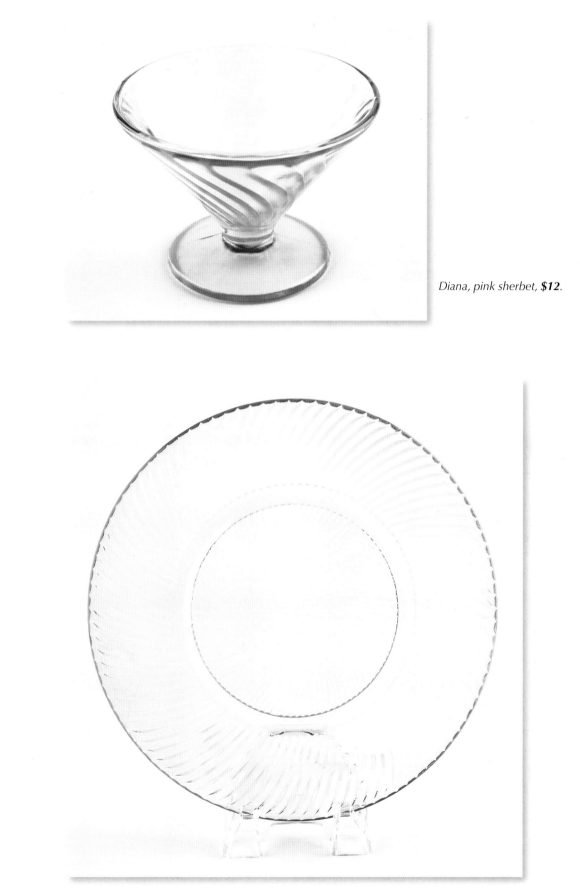

Diana, pink sherbet, **$12**.

Diana, pink dinner plate, **$18.50**.

DOGWOOD
Apple Blossom, Wild Rose

Manufactured by Macbeth-Evans Company, Charleroi, Pa., from 1929 to 1932.

Made in Cremax, crystal, green, Monax, pink and yellow. Yellow is rare; a cereal bowl is known and valued at $95. Crystal items are valued at 50 percent less than green.

*Dogwood,
pink sugar, $20;
creamer, $25;
luncheon plate, $12.*

Item	Cremax or Monax	Green	Pink
Berry bowl, 8-1/2" d	40.00	100.00	65.00
Cake plate, 11" d, heavy solid foot	—	—	650.00
Cake plate, 13" d, heavy solid foot	185.00	135.00	165.00
Cereal bowl, 5-1/2" d	12.00	35.00	35.00
Coaster, 3-1/4" d	—	—	450.00
Creamer, 2-1/2" h, thin	—	48.00	35.00
Creamer, 3-1/4" h, thick	—	—	25.00
Cup, thin	—	32.00	20.00
Cup, thick	36.00	40.00	20.00
Fruit bowl, 10-1/4" d	100.00	250.00	550.00
Pitcher, 8" h, 80 oz, (American Sweetheart style)	—	—	1,250.00
Pitcher, 8" h, 80 oz, decorated	—	550.00	295.00
Plate, 6" d, bread and butter	25.00	10.00	10.00
Plate, 8" d, luncheon	—	12.00	12.00
Plate, 9-1/4" d, dinner	—	—	45.00
Plates, 10-1/2" d, grill, AOP or border design only	—	24.00	35.00
Platter, 12" d, oval	—	—	725.00
Salver, 12" d	175.00	—	45.00
Saucer	20.00	10.00	8.00
Sherbet, low, ftd	—	95.00	42.00
Sugar, 2-1/2" h, thin	—	50.00	30.00
Sugar, 3-1/4" h, thick, ftd	—	—	20.00
Tidbit, 2 tier	—	—	90.00
Tumbler, 10 oz, 4" h, decorated	—	100.00	55.00
Tumbler, 11 oz, 4-3/4" h, decorated	—	95.00	125.00
Tumbler, 12 oz, 5" h, decorated	—	125.00	75.00
Tumbler, molded band	—	—	25.00

DORIC

Manufactured by Jeannette Glass Company, Jeannette, Pa., from 1935 to 1938.

Pieces are made in Delphite, green, pink, and yellow. Yellow is rare.

Doric, green cake plate, **$30**.

Item	Delphite	Green	Pink
Berry bowl, 4-1/2" d	50.00	10.00	12.00
Berry bowl, 8-1/4" d	150.00	38.00	35.00
Bowl, 9" d, two handles	—	45.00	45.00
Butter dish, cov	—	90.00	75.00
Cake plate, 10" d, three legs	—	30.00	30.00
Candy dish, cov, 8" d	—	42.50	45.00
Candy dish, three parts	12.00	20.00	14.50
Cereal bowl, 5-1/2" d	—	65.00	95.00
Coaster, 3" d	—	28.00	20.00
Cream soup, 5" d, two handles	—	385.00	—
Creamer, 4" h	—	17.00	14.00
Cup	—	10.00	10.00
Pitcher, 36 oz, 6" h, flat	1,200.00	75.00	45.00
Pitcher, 48 oz, 7-1/2" h, ftd	—	1,000.00	750.00
Plate, 6" d, sherbet	—	7.50	7.50
Plate, 7" d, salad	—	20.00	18.00

Item	Delphite	Green	Pink
Plate, 9" d, dinner	—	24.00	20.00
Plate, 9" d, grill	—	20.00	30.00
Platter, 12" l, oval	—	32.00	35.00
Relish tray, 4" x 4"	—	12.00	16.00
Relish tray, 4" x 8"	—	20.00	17.50
Salt and pepper shakers, pr	—	40.00	45.00
Saucer	—	7.00	5.00
Sherbet, footed	12.00	17.50	15.00
Sugar, cov	—	35.00	32.00
Tray, 8" x 8", serving	—	30.00	42.50
Tray, 10" l, handle	—	25.00	20.00
Tumbler, 9 oz, 4-1/2" h, flat	—	100.00	75.00
Tumbler, 10 oz, 4" h, ftd	—	90.00	85.00
Tumbler, 12 oz, 5" h, ftd	—	125.00	85.00
Vegetable bowl, 9" l, oval	—	45.00	50.00

DORIC & PANSY

Manufactured by Jeannette Glass Company, Jeannette, Pa., from 1937 to 1938.

Pieces are made in ultramarine, with limited production in pink and crystal.

Item	Crystal	Pink	Ultramarine
Berry bowl, 4-1/2" d	12.00	12.00	25.00
Berry bowl, 8" d	—	24.00	75.00
Bowl, 9" d, handle	15.00	20.00	35.00
Butter dish, cov	—	—	600.00
Candy, cov, three parts	—	—	22.50
Cup	12.00	14.00	20.00
Creamer	72.00	90.00	145.00
Plate, 6" d, sherbet	8.00	12.00	22.00
Plate, 7" d, salad	—	—	40.00
Plate, 9" d, dinner	7.50	8.00	30.00
Salt shaker, orig top	—	—	325.00
Saucer	4.50	4.50	5.50
Sugar, open	80.00	85.00	145.00
Tray, 10" l, handles	45.00	—	35.00
Tumbler, 9 oz, 4-1/2" h	—	—	500.00

Children's

Item	Pink	Ultramarine
Creamer	42.00	50.00
Cup	35.00	48.00
Plate	12.00	12.50
Saucer	7.00	8.50
Sugar	35.00	50.00
14-pc set, orig box	400.00	425.00

*Doric and Pansy, pink dinner plate, **$8**.*

*Doric and Pansy, ultramarine child's sugar, **$50**; child's creamer, **$50**.*

Early American Prescut, crystal cake plate, $25.

EARLY AMERICAN PRESCUT

Manufactured by Anchor Hocking, Lancaster, Ohio, from 1960 and 1999. Pieces are made in crystal, with some limited production in colors.

Item	Crystal
Candy, cov, 7-1/4"	14.50
Chip and dip, 10-1/4" bowl, metal holder	25.00
Coaster	6.00
Cocktail shaker, 30 oz	300.00
Console bowl, 9" d	15.00
Creamer	3.50
Creamer and sugar tray	3.00
Cruet, os	9.50
Dessert bowl, 5-3/8" d	3.00
Deviled egg plate, 11-3/4" d	35.00
Gondola dish, 9-1/2" l	7.50
Hostess tray, 6-1/2" x 12"	14.00
Iced tea tumbler, 15 oz, 6" h	20.00
Juice tumbler, 5 oz, 4" h	5.00
Lamp, oil	335.00
Lazy Susan, nine pcs	60.00
Pitcher, 18 oz	15.00
Pitcher, 40 oz, sq	60.00
Pitcher, 60 oz	20.00
Plate, 6-3/4" d, salad	55.00
Plate, 6-3/4" d, snack, ring for cup	40.00
Plate, 10" d, snack	10.00
Plate, 11" d	15.00
Punch cup	3.00
Punch set, 15 pcs	35.00
Relish, two parts, 10" l, tab handle	7.50
Relish, three parts, 8-1/2" l, oval	6.50
Relish, five parts, 13-1/2" d	30.00
Salad bowl, 10-3/4" d	15.00
Salt and pepper shakers, pr, individual size	75.00
Salt and pepper shakers, pr, metal tops	10.00
Salt and pepper shakers, pr, plastic tops	12.00
Serving plate, 11" d, four parts	90.00
Serving plate, 13-1/2" d	15.00
Sherbet, 6 oz	90.00
Snack cup	3.00
Sugar, cov	4.50
Syrup pitcher, 12 oz	24.00
Tumbler, 10 oz, 4-1/2" h	6.50
Vase, 8-1/2" h	8.00
Vase, 10" h	15.00

Item	Crystal
Ashtray, 4" d	4.00
Ashtray, 5" d	8.00
Ashtray, 7-3/4" d	12.00
Basket, 6" x 4-1/2"	20.00
Bowl, 4-1/4" d, plain rim	20.00
Bowl, 4-1/4" d, scalloped	7.50
Bowl, 5-1/4" d, scalloped	7.50
Bowl, 6-3/4" d, three legs	5.00
Bowl, 7-1/4" d, scalloped	20.00
Bowl, 8-3/4" d	9.00
Bowl, 9" d, oval	8.00
Bowl, 11-3/4" d, paneled	225.00
Bud vase, 5" h, ftd	475.00
Butter dish, cov, 1/4 lb	7.50
Butter dish, cov, metal handle, knife	15.00
Cake plate	25.00
Candlesticks, pr, two-lite	28.50
Candy, cov, 5-1/4"	12.00

ENGLISH HOBNAIL

Line #555

Manufactured by Westmoreland Glass Company, Grapeville, Pa., from the 1920s to 1983.

Pieces are made in amber, cobalt blue, crystal, crystal with various color treatments, green, ice blue, pink, red, and turquoise blue. Values for cobalt blue, red or turquoise blue pieces would be about 25 percent higher than ice blue values. Currently, a turquoise basket is valued at $150; a red basket at $100. Crystal pieces with a color accent would be slightly higher than crystal values.

Reproductions: † A creamer and sugar with a hexagonal foot have been reproduced, as well as a nut bowl and pickle dish.

Item	Amber	Crystal	Green	Ice Blue	Pink
Ashtray, 3" d	20.00	20.00	24.00	—	24.00
Ashtray, 4-1/2" d	9.00	9.00	15.00	24.00	15.00
Ashtray, 4-1/2" sq	9.50	9.50	15.00	—	15.00
Basket, 5" d, handle	20.00	20.00	—	—	—
Basket, 6" d, handle, tall	40.00	40.00	—	—	43.00
Bonbon, 6-1/2" h, handle	15.00	17.50	30.00	40.00	30.00
Bowl, 7" d, six parts	17.50	17.50	—	—	—
Bowl, 7" d, oblong spoon	17.50	17.50	—	—	—
Bowl, 8" d, ftd	30.00	30.00	48.00	—	48.00
Bowl, 8" d, hexagonal foot, two handles	38.00	38.00	75.00	115.00	75.00
Bowl, 8", six pt	24.00	24.00	—	—	—
Bowl, 9-1/2" d, round, crimped	30.00	30.00	—	—	—
Bowl, 10" d, flared	35.00	35.00	40.00	—	40.00
Bowl, 10" l, oval, crimped	40.00	40.00	—	—	—
Bowl, 11" d, bell	35.00	35.00	—	—	—
Bowl, 11" d, rolled edge	35.00	35.00	40.00	85.00	40.00
Bowl, 12" d, flared	32.00	32.00	40.00	—	95.00
Bowl, 12" l, oval crimped	32.00	32.00	—	—	—
Candelabra, two lite	20.00	20.00	—	—	—
Candlesticks, pr, 3-1/2" h, round base	24.00	32.00	36.00	—	60.00
Candlesticks, pr, 5-1/2" h, sq base	30.00	32.00	—	—	—
Candlesticks, pr, 9" h, round base	50.00	40.00	72.00	—	125.00
Candy dish, three feet	45.00	38.00	50.00	—	50.00
Candy dish, cov, 1/2 lb, cone shape	45.00	40.00	55.00	—	90.00
Celery, 12" l, oval	24.00	45.00	36.00	—	36.00
Celery, 9" d	18.00	20.00	32.00	—	32.00
Champagne, two ball, round foot	8.00	7.00	20.00	—	20.00
Chandelier, 17" shade, 200 prisms	425.00	400.00	—	—	—
Cheese, cov, 6" d	40.00	42.00	—	—	—
Cheese, cov, 8-3/4" d	50.00	48.00	—	—	—

Item	Amber	Crystal	Green	Ice Blue	Pink
Cigarette box, cov, 4-1/2 x 2-1/2"	24.50	24.50	30.00	—	55.00
Cigarette jar, cov, round	16.00	18.00	25.00	—	65.00
Claret, 5 oz, round	15.00	17.50	—	—	—
Coaster, 3"	5.00	5.00	—	—	—
Cocktail, 3 oz, round	8.50	12.00	—	—	37.50
Cocktail, 3-1/2 oz, round, ball	15.00	17.50	—	—	—
Compote, 5" d, round, round foot	22.00	20.00	25.00	—	25.00
Compote, 5" d, round, sq foot	24.00	24.00	—	—	—
Compote, 5-1/2" d, bell	12.00	15.00	—	—	—
Compote, 5-1/2" d, bell, sq foot	20.00	20.00	—	—	—
Console bowl, 12" d, flange	30.00	30.00	40.00	—	40.00
Cordial, 1 oz, round, ball	16.50	17.50	—	—	—
Cordial, 1 oz, round, foot	16.50	16.50	—	—	—
Cream soup bowl, 4-5/8" d	15.00	15.00	—	—	—
Cream soup liner, round, 6-1/2" d	5.00	5.00	—	—	—
Creamer, hexagonal foot †	20.00	20.00	25.00	—	48.00
Creamer, low, flat	10.00	10.00	—	—	—
Creamer, sq foot	24.00	24.00	45.00	—	45.00
Cruet, 12 oz	—	25.00	—	—	—
Cup	8.00	12.00	18.00	—	25.00
Decanter, 20 oz	55.00	55.00	—	—	—
Demitasse cup	17.50	17.50	55.00	—	55.00
Dish, 6" d, crimped	15.00	15.00	—	—	—
Eggcup	15.00	15.00	—	—	—
Finger bowl, 4-1/2" d	7.50	7.50	15.00	35.00	15.00
Finger bowl, 4-1/2" sq, foot	9.50	9.50	18.00	40.00	18.00
Finger bowl liner, 6" sq	6.50	7.00	20.00	—	20.00
Finger bowl liner, 6-1/2" d, round	12.00	12.00	10.00	—	10.00
Ginger ale tumbler, 5 oz, flat	10.00	10.00	18.00	—	20.00
Ginger ale tumbler, 5 oz, round foot	10.00	10.00	—	—	—
Ginger ale tumbler, 5 oz, sq foot	8.00	8.00	32.00	—	35.00
Goblet, 8 oz, 6-1/4" h, round, water	12.00	12.00	—	50.00	35.00
Goblet, 8 oz, sq foot, water	10.00	10.00	—	—	50.00
Grapefruit bowl, 6-1/2" d	12.00	12.00	22.00	—	24.00
Hat, high	18.00	18.00	—	—	—
Hat, low	15.00	15.00	—	—	—
Honey compote, 6" d, round foot	18.00	18.00	35.00	—	35.00
Honey compote, 6" d, sq foot	18.00	18.00	—	—	—
Ice tub, 4" h	18.00	18.00	50.00	—	85.00
Ice tub, 5-1/2" h	36.00	36.00	65.00	—	100.00
Iced tea tumbler, 10 oz	14.00	14.00	30.00	—	30.00
Iced tea tumbler, 11 oz, round, ball	12.00	12.00	—	—	—
Iced tea tumbler, 11 oz, sq foot	13.50	13.50	—	—	—
Iced tea tumbler, 12-1/2 oz, round foot	14.00	24.00	—	—	—
Iced tea tumbler, 12 oz, flat	14.00	14.00	32.00	—	32.00
Icer, sq base, patterned insert	45.00	45.00	—	—	—
Ivy bowl, 6-1/2" d, sq foot, crimp top	35.00	45.00	—	—	—
Juice tumbler, 7 oz, round foot	27.50	27.50	—	—	—
Juice tumbler, 7 oz, sq foot	6.50	6.50	—	—	—
Lamp shade, 17" d	175.00	165.00	—	—	—
Lamp, 6-1/2" h, electric	45.00	45.00	50.00	—	50.00
Lamp, 9-1/2" d, electric	45.00	45.00	115.00	—	115.00
Lamp, candlestick	32.00	32.00	—	—	—
Loving cup, two handles, ftd, 8" d, 6" h	—	—	—	95.00	—
Marmalade, cov	40.00	40.00	45.00	—	70.00
Mayonnaise, 6"	12.00	12.00	22.00	—	22.00

English Hobnail, crystal nappy with handle, $22.

English Hobnail, crystal tumbler, $10.

Item	Amber	Crystal	Green	Ice Blue	Pink
Mustard, cov, sq, foot	18.00	18.00	—	—	—
Nappy, 4-1/2" d, round	8.00	8.00	15.00	30.00	15.00
Nappy, 4-1/2" w, sq	8.50	8.50	—	—	—
Nappy, 5" d, round	10.00	10.00	15.00	35.00	15.00
Nappy, 5-1/2" d, bell	12.00	12.00	—	—	—
Nappy, 6" d, round	10.00	10.00	17.50	—	17.50
Nappy, 6" d, sq	10.00	10.00	17.50	—	17.50
Nappy, 6-1/2" d, round	12.50	12.50	20.00	—	20.00
Nappy, 6-1/2" d, sq	14.00	14.00	—	—	—
Nappy, 7" d, round	14.00	14.00	24.00	—	24.00
Nappy, 7-1/2" d, bell	15.00	15.00	—	—	—
Nappy, 8" d, cupped	22.00	22.00	30.00	—	30.00
Nappy, 8" d, round	22.00	22.00	35.00	—	35.00
Nappy, 9" d, bell	25.00	25.00	—	—	—
Nut, individual, ftd †	6.00	8.00	14.50	—	20.00
Oil bottle, 2 oz, handle	25.00	25.00	—	—	—
Oil bottle, 6 oz, handle	27.50	27.50	—	—	—
Old fashioned tumbler, 5 oz	15.00	15.00	—	—	—
Oyster cocktail, 5 oz, sq foot	12.00	12.00	17.50	—	17.50
Parfait, round foot	17.50	17.50	—	—	—
Pickle, 8" d †	15.00	15.00	—	—	—
Pitcher, 23 oz, rounded	48.00	48.00	150.00	—	165.00
Pitcher, 32 oz, straight side	50.00	50.00	175.00	—	175.00
Pitcher, 38 oz, rounded	65.00	65.00	215.00	—	215.00
Pitcher, 60 oz, rounded	70.00	70.00	295.00	—	295.00
Pitcher, 64 oz, straight side	75.00	75.00	310.00	—	310.00
Plate, 5-1/2" d, round	7.00	7.00	10.00	—	10.00
Plate, 6" w, sq	5.00	5.00	—	—	—
Plate, 6-1/2" d, round	6.25	6.25	10.00	—	10.00

Item	Amber	Crystal	Green	Ice Blue	Pink
Plate, 6-1/2" d, round, depressed center	6.00	6.00	—	—	—
Plate, 8" d, round	9.00	9.00	14.00	—	14.00
Plate, 8" d, round, ftd	13.00	13.00	—	—	—
Plate, 8-1/2" d, plain edge	9.00	9.00	—	—	—
Plate, 8-1/2" d, round	7.00	9.00	17.50	—	28.00
Plate, 8-3/4" w, sq	9.25	9.25	—	—	—
Plate, 10" d, round	15.00	15.00	45.00	—	65.00
Plate, 10" w, sq	15.00	15.00	—	—	—
Plate, 10-1/2" d, round, grill	18.00	18.00	—	—	—
Plate, 12" w, sq	20.00	20.00	—	—	—
Plate, 15" w, sq	28.00	28.00	—	—	—
Preserve, 8" d	15.00	15.00	—	—	—
Puff box, cov, 6" d, round	20.00	20.00	47.50	—	80.00
Punch bowl and stand	215.00	215.00	—	—	—
Punch cup	7.00	7.00	—	—	—
Relish, 8" d, three parts	18.00	18.00	—	—	—
Rose bowl, 4" d	17.50	17.50	48.00	—	50.00
Rose bowl, 6" d	20.00	20.00	—	—	—
Salt and pepper shakers, pr, round foot	27.50	27.50	150.00	—	165.00
Salt and pepper shakers, pr, sq, foot	20.00	20.00	—	—	—
Saucer, demitasse, round	10.00	10.00	15.00	—	17.50
Saucer, demitasse, sq	10.00	10.00	—	—	—
Saucer, round	2.00	3.00	6.00	—	6.00
Saucer, sq	2.00	2.00	—	—	—
Sherbet, high, round foot	7.00	10.00	18.00	—	37.50
Sherbet, high, sq foot	8.00	9.50	18.00	—	—
Sherbet, high, two ball, round foot	10.00	10.00	—	—	—
Sherbet, low, one ball, round foot	12.00	10.00	—	—	15.00
Sherbet, low, round foot	12.50	7.00	—	—	—
Sherbet, low, sq foot	6.50	6.00	15.00	—	17.50
Straw jar, 10" h	65.00	60.00	—	—	—
Sundae	9.00	9.00	—	—	—
Sugar, hexagonal, ftd †	9.00	9.00	40.00	—	48.00
Sugar, low, flat	8.00	8.00	45.00	—	—
Sugar, sq foot	9.00	9.00	48.00	—	55.00
Sweetmeat, 5-1/2" d, ball stem	30.00	30.00	—	—	—
Sweetmeat, 8" d, ball stem	40.00	40.00	60.00	—	65.00
Tidbit, two tiers	27.50	24.50	65.00	85.00	80.00
Toilet bottle, 5 oz	25.00	25.00	40.00	65.00	40.00
Torte plate, 14" d, round	35.00	30.00	48.00	—	48.00
Torte plate, 20-1/2" round	55.00	50.00	—	—	—
Tumbler, 8 oz, water	10.00	10.00	24.00	—	24.00
Tumbler, 9 oz, round, ball, water	10.00	10.00	—	—	—
Tumbler, 9 oz, round, ftd water	10.00	10.00	—	—	—
Tumbler, 9 oz, sq foot, water	10.00	10.00	—	—	—
Urn, cov, 11" h	35.00	35.00	350.00	—	350.00
Vase, 6-1/2" h, sq foot	24.00	24.00	—	—	—
Vase, 7-1/2" h, flip	27.50	27.50	70.00	—	70.00
Vase, 7-1/2" h, flip jar with cov	55.00	55.00	85.00	—	85.00
Vase, 8" h, sq foot	35.00	35.00	—	—	—
Vase, 8-1/2" h, flared top	40.00	40.00	120.00	—	235.00
Whiskey, 1-1/2 oz	10.00	10.00	—	—	—
Whiskey, 3 oz	12.00	15.00	—	—	—
Wine, 2 oz, round foot	15.00	12.50	—	—	—
Wine, 2 oz, sq ft	24.00	24.00	35.00	—	65.00
Wine, 2-1/2 oz, ball, foot	20.00	20.00	—	—	—

FAIRFAX

No. 2375

Manufactured by Fostoria Glass Company, Moundsville, Va., from 1927 to 1944. While this pattern is collected as Fairfax by many, the blanks were also used for some Fostoria etchings, such as June, Trojan, and Versailles. The values listed are for the Fairfax pattern; expect to pay more for the etched patterns.

Pieces are made in amber, Azure blue, black, blue, green, orchid, rose, topaz, and wisteria, with limited production in ruby.

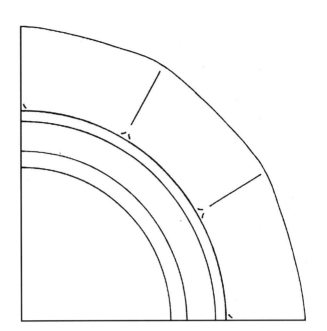

Item	Amber	Azure Blue, Black and Blue	Green	Orchid Rose, Wisteria	Topaz
After dinner cup and saucer	15.00	30.00	18.00	30.00	18.00
Ashtray, 2-1/2" d	9.00	15.00	12.00	15.00	12.00
Ashtray, 4"	10.00	17.50	12.50	17.50	12.50
Ashtray, 5-1/2"	12.00	20.00	15.00	20.00	15.00
Baker, oval, 9" l	17.50	35.00	24.00	35.00	24.00
Baker, oval, 10-1/2" l	20.00	42.00	25.00	42.00	25.00
Bonbon	10.00	12.50	12.00	12.50	12.00
Bouillon, ftd	8.50	14.50	10.00	18.50	10.00
Bowl, 7" d, three ftd	10.00	15.00	14.00	15.00	14.00
Bowl, 12" d	22.00	42.00	24.00	42.00	24.00
Bread plate, 12" d	27.50	45.00	30.00	45.00	30.00
Butter dish, cov	80.00	145.00	125.00	145.00	100.00
Cake plate, 10" d	15.00	24.00	15.00	24.00	15.00
Canapé plate	12.00	20.00	15.00	20.00	15.00
Candlesticks, pr, 3" h	25.00	55.00	35.00	37.50	35.00
Candy, cov, three parts	40.00	65.00	67.50	65.00	50.00
Candy, cov, ftd	45.00	70.00	60.00	70.00	60.00
Celery tray, 11-1/4" l	12.00	25.00	17.50	25.00	17.50
Centerpiece bowl, 12" d	20.00	40.00	25.00	40.00	25.00
Centerpiece bowl, 13" l, oval	24.00	45.00	35.00	45.00	35.00
Centerpiece bowl, 15" d	27.50	48.00	37.50	48.00	40.00
Cereal bowl, 6" d	12.00	24.00	14.50	24.00	18.00
Cheese and cracker set	20.00	45.00	25.00	45.00	25.00
Chop plate, 13" d	15.00	25.00	17.50	25.00	17.50
Cigarette box	20.00	48.00	24.00	48.00	24.00
Claret, 4 oz, 6" h	25.00	40.00	35.00	40.00	35.00
Cocktail, 3 oz, 5-1/4" h	12.00	24.00	20.00	24.00	20.00
Comport, 5"	15.00	30.00	20.00	30.00	20.00
Comport, 7"	20.00	45.00	27.50	32.00	27.50
Cordial, 3/4 oz, 4" h	25.00	65.00	45.00	65.00	45.00
Cream soup, ftd	10.00	20.00	15.00	20.00	15.00
Cream soup underplate	5.00	8.00	5.00	8.00	5.00
Creamer, flat	12.00	—	15.00	—	15.00
Creamer, ftd	10.00	24.00	12.00	15.00	12.00

Item	Amber	Azure Blue, Black and Blue	Green	Orchid Rose, Wisteria	Topaz
Creamer, tea size	9.00	18.50	12.50	35.00	12.50
Cup, flat	4.50	—	7.50	—	6.50
Cup, ftd	7.50	15.00	9.00	10.00	9.00
Dessert bowl, large, handle	15.00	40.00	24.00	40.00	24.00
Flower holder, oval	25.00	85.00	40.00	85.00	40.00
Fruit bowl, 5" d	8.00	15.00	9.00	15.00	9.00
Goblet, 10 oz, 8-1/4" h	17.50	32.00	22.00	35.00	22.00
Grapefruit	17.50	35.00	25.00	35.00	25.00
Grapefruit liner	15.00	32.00	20.00	32.00	22.00
Gravy	—	—	55.00	85.00	—
Ice bowl	12.00	20.00	14.50	20.00	14.50
Ice bowl liner	12.00	22.00	12.00	22.00	14.50
Ice bucket	32.00	50.00	35.00	50.00	35.00
Juice tumbler, 2-1/2 oz, ftd	12.00	32.00	18.50	32.00	18.50
Lemon bowl, two handles, ftd	6.50	12.50	7.50	12.50	7.50
Mayonnaise	10.00	15.00	35.00	20.00	10.00
Mayonnaise ladle	20.00	30.00	24.00	30.00	24.00
Mayonnaise underplate	5.00	8.00	4.00	8.00	5.00
Nappy, 8" d	18.00	40.00	24.00	40.00	24.00
Nut cup	15.00	32.00	20.00	32.00	20.00
Oil bottle, ftd, os	85.00	150.00	110.00	150.00	110.00
Pickle, 8-1/2" l	12.00	27.50	20.00	25.00	15.00
Pitcher	125.00	200.00	155.00	350.00	175.00
Plate, 6" d, bread and butter	2.50	4.50	3.00	4.50	3.00
Plate, 7-1/2" d, salad	5.00	14.00	4.50	5.50	5.00
Plate, 8-3/4" d, salad	4.50	12.00	5.50	7.50	5.50
Plate, 9-1/2" d, luncheon	8.00	12.00	7.50	12.00	7.50
Plate, 10-1/4" d, dinner	18.00	40.00	30.00	40.00	30.00
Plate, 10-1/4" d, grill	17.50	40.00	27.50	40.00	27.50
Platter, 10-1/2" l	18.00	35.00	25.00	35.00	25.00
Platter, 12" l	20.00	40.00	32.00	40.00	32.00
Platter, 15" l	30.00	70.00	42.00	70.00	42.00
Relish, three parts, 8-1/2" l	12.00	22.00	14.00	22.00	14.00
Relish, 11-1/2" l	14.00	24.00	17.50	24.00	17.50
Salad dressing bowl	75.00	180.00	90.00	180.00	90.00
Salt and pepper shakers, pr, ftd	35.00	80.00	45.00	60.00	40.00
Salt and pepper shakers, pr, individual size	20.00	—	25.00	—	25.00
Sauce boat and underplate	30.00	65.00	38.00	65.00	40.00
Saucer	3.00	6.50	3.50	5.00	3.50
Sherbet, 6 oz, 6" h	10.00	20.00	12.50	20.00	12.50
Soup bowl, 7" d	18.00	40.00	24.00	40.00	24.00
Sugar bowl, flat	12.00	—	14.00	—	14.00
Sugar bowl, ftd	8.00	24.00	10.00	12.00	10.00
Sugar bowl, tea size	10.00	20.00	14.50	20.00	14.50
Sugar bowl lid	20.00	35.00	25.00	35.00	25.00
Sugar pail	25.00	60.00	40.00	60.00	40.00
Sweetmeat	12.00	17.50	15.00	17.50	17.50
Tray, 11" d, center handle	15.00	25.00	20.00	25.00	20.00
Tumbler, 5 oz, 4-1/2" h, ftd	10.00	17.50	12.00	17.50	12.00
Tumbler, 9 oz, 5-1/4" h, ftd	14.50	20.00	17.50	20.00	17.50
Tumbler, 12 oz, 6", ftd	17.50	27.50	25.00	27.50	25.00
Vase, 8" h	35.00	50.00	35.00	50.00	35.00
Whipped cream pail	25.00	55.00	40.00	40.00	40.00
Whipped cream underplate	9.00	12.00	10.00	12.00	10.00
Wine, 3 oz, 5-1/2" h	20.00	30.00	25.00	30.00	30.00

FIRE-KING: ALICE

Manufactured by Anchor Hocking Glass Co. Pieces are made in Jade-ite, white with blue trim, and white with red rim, early 1940s.

*Fire King: Alice, Jade-ite cup and saucer, **$16**.*

Item	Jade-ite	White, blue trim	White, red trim
Cup	8.00	12.00	15.00
Cup and saucer	16.00	15.00	20.00
Plate, 9-1/2" d	50.00	20.00	30.00
Saucer	8.00	5.00	5.00

FIRE-KING: CHARM

Made by Anchor Hocking Glass Co. from 1950 to 1954; pieces are in Azure-ite and Jade-ite.

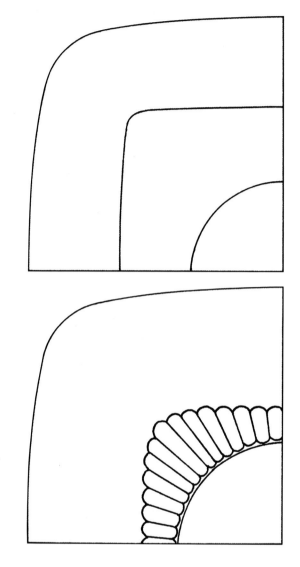

*Fire King: Charm, Azure-ite cup and saucer, **$6**.*

*Fire King: Charm, Azure-ite dinner plate, **$20**; cup, **$4.50**; and saucer, **$2.50**.*

Item	Azure-ite	Jade-ite
Creamer	6.50	17.00
Cup	4.50	15.00
Cup and saucer	7.50	15.00
Dessert bowl, 4-3/4" d	5.00	15.00
Plate, 6-5/8" d, salad	4.00	8.00
Plate, 8-3/4" d, luncheon	12.00	9.50
Plate, 9-1/2" d, dinner	20.00	25.00
Platter, 11" x 8"	15.00	30.00
Salad bowl, 7-3/8" d	15.00	30.00
Saucer, 5-3/8" d	2.50	4.50
Soup bowl, 6" d	20.00	60.00
Sugar	6.00	24.00

FIRE-KING: DINNERWARE

Jade-ite Restaurant Ware

Made by Anchor Hocking from 1950 to 1956.

*Fire-King: Dinnerware, Jade-ite cup, **$12**; saucer, **$5**.*

Item	Jade-ite
Batter bowl	45.00
Bowl, 4-7/8" d	15.00
Bowl, 10 oz deep	18.00
Bowl, 15 oz, deep	40.00
Butter dish, cov	150.00
Cereal bowl, 8 oz, flanged rim	37.50
Chili bowl, 15 oz, 5-5/8" d, rolled rim	24.00
Coffee mug, 7 oz	35.00
Cup, 6 oz, straight	22.00
Cup, 7 oz, extra heavy	12.00
Cup, 7 oz, narrow rim	10.00
Demitasse cup and saucer	85.00
Eggcup, double	65.00

Item	Jade-ite
Fruit bowl, 4-3/4" d	8.50
Plate, 5-1/2" d, bread and butter	15.00
Plate, 6-3/4" d, pie or salad	15.00
Plate, 8" d, luncheon	40.00
Plate, 8-7/8" d, oval, partitioned	28.00
Plate, 9" d, dinner	24.00
Plate, 9-3/4" l, oval, sandwich	30.00
Plate, 9-5/8" d, three sections	35.00
Plate, 9-5/8" d, five sections	30.00
Platter, 9-1/2" d, oval	30.00
Platter, 11-1/2" l, oval	60.00
Saucer, 6" d	5.00
Soup bowl, 9-1/2" d, flat	140.00

FIRE-KING: JANE RAY

Pieces were made by Anchor Hocking from 1945 to 1963 in ivory, Jade-ite, Peach Lustre, white, and white with gold trim.

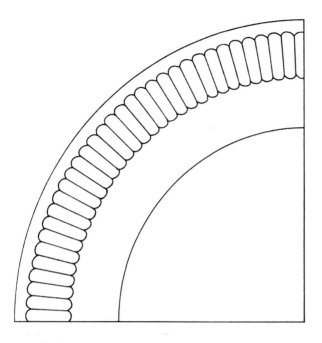

*Fire-King: Jane Ray, Jade-ite dinner plate, **$17.50**.*

Item	Ivory	Jade-ite	Peach Lustre	White
Berry bowl, 4-7/8" d	—	12.00	—	—
Cereal bowl	8.00	35.00	—	8.00
Chili bowl	8.00	6.00	—	8.00
Creamer	9.00	10.00	15.00	9.00
Cup	5.00	8.00	6.00	5.00
Cup, St. Denis	—	7.50	—	—
Demitasse cup	18.00	48.00	30.00	18.00
Demitasse saucer	20.00	45.00	25.00	20.00
Dessert bowl, 4-7/8" d	4.00	18.00	6.00	4.00
Eggcup, double	—	18.50	—	—
Mug	—	8.00	—	—
Oatmeal bowl, 5-7/8" d	8.00	22.00	—	8.00
Plate, 7-3/4" d, salad	12.00	18.00	8.00	12.00
Plate, 9-1/8" d, dinner	15.00	17.50	10.00	15.00
Platter, 9" x 12"	15.00	40.00	—	15.00
Saucer	2.00	4.50	4.00	2.00
Soup bowl	8.00	35.00	—	8.00
Soup plate, 7-5/8" d	12.00	140.00	8.00	12.00
Sugar, cov	15.00	42.00	15.00	15.00
Sugar cover only	5.00	6.00	—	5.00
Sugar, no lid	5.00	5.00	—	5.00
Vegetable bowl, 8-1/4" d	14.00	35.00	—	14.00

FIRE-KING: LAUREL LEAF

Gray Laurel, Peach Lustre

Made by Anchor Hocking from 1952 to 1963.

Reproductions: † Reproductions of the cup and saucer have been found.

Fire-King: Laurel Leaf, Peach Lustre dinner plate, $8.

Fire-King: Laurel Leaf, Peach Lustre sugar, $4; creamer, $4.50.

Item	Gray Laurel	Peach Lustre
Creamer	8.00	4.50
Cup †	4.50	4.00
Dessert bowl, 4-7/8" d	7.00	4.00
Plate, 7-3/8" d, salad	7.00	6.50
Plate, 9-1/8" d, dinner	10.00	8.00
Saucer, 5-3/4" d †	2.00	1.00
Serving plate, 11" d	25.00	18.00
Soup plate, 7-5/8" d	15.00	10.00
Sugar, ftd	10.00	4.00
Vegetable bowl, 8-1/4" d	22.00	15.00

FIRE-KING: PHILBE

Made by Anchor Hocking Glass Co. from 1937 to 1938 in blue, crystal, green and pink.

*Fire-King: Philbe, green creamer, **$135**.*

Item	Blue	Crystal	Green	Pink
Candy jar, cov, 4" d, low	900.00	350.00	850.00	775.00
Cereal bowl, 5-1/2" d	70.00	25.00	45.00	45.00
Cookie jar, cov	1,850.00	650.00	995.00	995.00
Creamer, 3-1/4", ftd	145.00	50.00	135.00	135.00
Cup	160.00	85.00	115.00	115.00
Goblet, 9 oz, 7-1/4" h	225.00	80.00	175.00	175.00
Iced tea tumbler, 15 oz, 6-1/2" h, ftd	85.00	45.00	75.00	75.00
Juice tumbler, 3-1/2" h, ftd	175.00	45.00	150.00	150.00
Pitcher, 36 oz, 6" h	900.00	300.00	625.00	625.00
Pitcher, 56 oz, 8-1/2" h	1,450.00	625.00	1,200.00	1,200.00
Plate, 6" d, sherbet	75.00	35.00	60.00	60.00
Plate, 8" d, luncheon	50.00	22.00	40.00	40.00
Plate, 10-1/2" d, grill	75.00	25.00	65.00	65.00
Platter, 12" l, closed handles	200.00	65.00	175.00	175.00
Refrigerator dish, 4" x 5"	45.00	—	—	—
Refrigerator dish, 5" x 9"	50.00	—	—	—
Salad bowl, 7-1/4" d	85.00	30.00	50.00	50.00
Salver, 10-1/2" d	80.00	25.00	55.00	55.00
Salver, 11-5/8" d	95.00	25.00	65.00	65.00
Sandwich plate, 10" d	150.00	60.00	95.00	95.00
Saucer, 6" d	75.00	35.00	60.00	60.00
Sugar, 3-1/4", ftd	145.00	50.00	135.00	135.00
Tumbler, 9 oz, 4" h, flat	125.00	40.00	100.00	100.00
Tumbler, 10 oz, 5-1/4" h	95.00	35.00	75.00	75.00
Vegetable bowl, 10" l, oval	165.00	75.00	115.00	115.00

FIRE-KING: PRIMROSE

Manufactured by Anchor Hocking Glass Co. from 1960 to 1962.
Pieces are made in white with a red, pink, and black floral decoration.

*Fire-King: Primrose, dinner plate with pink and red floral decoration, **$8**.*

Item	Decorated
Baking pan, 6-1/2" x 10-1/2"	14.00
Baking pan, 8" x 12-1/2"	30.00
Baking pan, cov, 5" x 9"	18.00
Cake pan, 8" d, round	12.50
Cake pan, 8" w, square	12.50
Casserole, cov, one pint	9.50
Casserole, cov, 1/2 quart, oval	12.50
Casserole, cov, one quart	14.00
Casserole, cov, 1-1/2 quart	16.00
Casserole, cov, two quart	18.00
Creamer	5.00
Cup, 8 oz	3.50
Custard cup	3.50
Dessert bowl, 4-5/8" d	3.00

Item	Decorated
Juice tumbler, 5 oz	30.00
Loaf pan, 5" x 9"	15.00
Plate, 7-3/8" d, salad	5.00
Plate, 9-1/8" d, dinner	8.00
Platter, 9" x 12"	15.00
Saucer, 5-3/4" d	1.50
Set, boxed, 19 pcs	150.00
Snack cup, 5 oz	3.00
Snack tray, 11" x 6"	5.00
Soup bowl, 6-5/8" d	9.50
Sugar, cov	10.00
Tumbler, 11 oz	25.00
Vegetable bowl, 8-1/4" d	12.00

FIRE-KING: SWIRL

Made by Anchor Hocking Glass Co. in the 1950s in Azure-ite, ivory, ivory with gold trim, ivory with red trim, Jade-ite (1960s), pink, white, and white with gold trim.

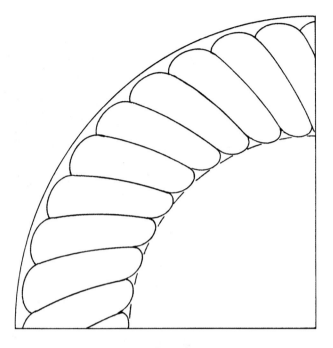

*Fire-King: Swirl, pink dinner plate, **$21**.*

Item	Azure-ite	Ivory	Jade-ite	Pink	White	White/trim
Cereal bowl, 5-3/4" d	25.00	—	—	—	—	—
Cereal bowl, 6-3/8" d	—	—	16.00	—	—	—
Creamer, flat	6.00	4.00	—	9.00	4.50	—
Creamer, ftd	—	5.00	12.00	—	5.00	6.00
Cup	6.50	6.00	6.00	14.00	3.00	3.50
Fruit or dessert bowl, 4-7/8"	4.60	3.00	5.00	4.60	4.00	8.00
Iced tea tumbler, 12 oz	7.00	—	—	7.00	—	—
Juice tumbler, 1 oz	5.00	—	—	5.00	—	—
Mixing bowl, 6" d	—	8.00	12.00	—	9.00	—
Mixing bowl, 7" d	—	15.00	14.00	—	12.00	—
Mixing bowl, 9" d	—	18.00	16.00	—	16.00	—
Plate, 7-1/8" d, salad	12.00	6.50	12.00	8.00	6.50	10.00
Plate, 9-1/8" d, dinner	12.00	6.00	50.00	21.00	5.00	15.00
Platter, 12" x 9"	22.00	7.00	—	18.00	7.00	20.00
Saucer, 5-3/4" d	2.50	3.50	2.00	4.00	2.00	7.50
Serving plate, 11" d	18.00	—	—	25.00	—	—
Soup plate, 7-5/8" d	25.00	12.00	8.50	14.00	5.00	6.50
Sugar lid for flat sugar	6.00	3.00	—	6.00	3.00	—
Sugar lid for ftd sugar	—	3.00	20.00	—	3.00	—
Sugar, flat, tab handles	6.50	4.00	—	6.50	4.00	—
Sugar, ftd, open handles	—	3.50	30.00	—	4.00	6.00
Tumbler, 9 oz, water	15.00	—	—	15.00	—	—
Vegetable bowl, 7-1/4" d	15.00	—	—	15.00	—	—
Vegetable bowl, 8-1/4" d	15.00	—	18.00	15.00	7.50	15.00

FIRE-KING: TURQUOISE BLUE

Made by Anchor Hocking from 1957 to 1958.

Fire King: Turquoise Blue, three-part relish with gold rim, $15. Photo courtesy of Tina Trautman.

Fire-King: Turquoise Blue, snack set in original box, $70.

Fire King: Turquoise Blue, Oven Ware mug, $15. Photo courtesy of Tina Trautman.

Item	Turquoise Blue
Ashtray, 3-1/2" d	7.50
Ashtray, 4-5/8" d	8.50
Ashtray, 5-3/4" d	12.00
Batter bowl, spout	200.00
Berry bowl, 4-1/2" d	10.00
Cereal bowl, 5" d	15.00
Creamer	18.00
Cup	5.00
Egg plate, 9-3/4" d	18.00
Mixing bowl, one pt, tear	15.00
Mixing bowl, one qt, round	18.00
Mixing bowl, one qt, tear	20.00
Mixing bowl, two-qt, round, splash proof	45.00
Mixing bowl, two-qt, tear	28.00

Item	Turquoise Blue
Mixing bowl, three-qt, round, splash proof	40.00
Mixing bowl, three-qt, tear	30.00
Mixing bowl, four-qt, round	35.00
Mug, 8 oz	15.00
Plate, 6-1/8" d	12.50
Plate, 7" d	12.00
Plate, 9" d	20.00
Plate, 9" d, cup indent	7.50
Plate, 10" d, dinner	30.00
Relish, 11-1/8" l, three parts	15.00
Saucer	10.00
Soup/salad bowl, 6-5/8" ftd	50.00
Sugar	18.00
Vegetable bowl, 8" d	18.00

FLORAGOLD

Louisa

Manufactured by Jeannette Glass Company, Jeannette, Pa., 1950s.

Pieces are made in iridescent. Some large comports were later made in ice blue, crystal, red-yellow, and shell pink.

Floragold, iridescent dinner plate, **$48**; ruffled berry bowl, 5-1/4" d, **$15**.

Floragold, four-footed bonbon, **$12**. Photo courtesy of Tina Trautman.

Item	Iridescent
Ashtray, 4" d	7.00
Bowl, 4-1/2" sq	5.00
Bowl, 5-1/4" d, ruffled	15.00
Bowl, 8-1/2" d, sq	20.00
Bowl, 8-1/2" d, ruffled	10.00
Bowl, 12" d, ruffled	8.00
Butter dish, cov, 1/4 pound, oblong	30.00
Butter dish, cov, round, 5-1/2" w sq base	800.00
Butter dish, cov, round, 6-1/4" w sq base	55.00
Candlesticks, pr, double branch	60.00
Candy dish, one handle	12.50
Candy or cheese dish, cov, 6-3/4" d	130.00
Candy, 5-3/4" l, four feet	12.00
Celery vase	420.00
Cereal bowl, 5-1/2" d, round	40.00
Coaster, 4" d	10.00
Comport, 5-1/4", plain top	750.00
Comport, 5-1/4", ruffled top	850.00
Creamer	15.00
Cup	8.00

Item	Iridescent
Fruit bowl, 5-1/2" d, ruffled	8.50
Fruit bowl, 12" d, ruffled, large	12.00
Nappy, 5" d, one handle	12.00
Pitcher, 64 oz	55.00
Plate, 5-1/4" d, sherbet	12.00
Plate, 8-1/2" d, dinner	48.00
Platter, 11-1/4" d	28.00
Salad bowl, 9-1/2" d, deep	50.00
Salt and pepper shakers, pr, plastic tops	60.00
Saucer, 5-1/4" d	15.00
Sherbet, low, ftd	15.00
Sugar	15.00
Sugar lid	15.00
Tidbit, wooden post	35.00
Tray, 13-1/2" d	50.00
Tray, 13-1/2" d, with indent	65.00
Tumbler, 11 oz, ftd	20.00
Tumbler, 10 oz, ftd	20.00
Tumbler, 15 oz, ftd	110.00
Vase	420.00

FLORAL

Poinsettia

Manufactured by Jeannette Glass Company, Jeannette, Pa., from 1931 to 1935.

Pieces are made in amber, crystal, Delphite, green, Jade-ite, pink, red, and yellow. Production in amber, crystal, red, and yellow was limited. A crystal vase that is 6-7/8-inch high is valued at $295.

Reproductions: † Reproduction salt and pepper shakers have been made in cobalt blue, dark green, green, pink and red.

Item	Delphite	Green	Jade-ite	Pink
Berry bowl, 4" d	50.00	25.00	—	25.00
Berry bowl, large	—	—	—	45.00
Butter dish, cov	—	95.00	—	100.00
Candlesticks, pr, 4" h	—	90.00	—	95.00
Candy jar, cov	80.00	50.00	—	48.00
Canister set	—	—	60.00	—
Casserole, cov	—	45.00	—	28.00
Coaster, 3-1/4" d	—	15.50	—	12.50
Comport, 9"	—	875.00	—	795.00
Cream soup, 5-1/2" d	—	735.00	—	735.00
Creamer, flat	—	18.00	—	25.00
Cup	—	15.00	—	15.00
Dresser set	—	1,350.00	—	—
Dresser tray, 9-1/4" l, oval	—	200.00	—	—
Flower frog	—	695.00	—	—
Ice tub, 3-1/2" h, oval	—	850.00	—	825.00
Juice tumbler, ftd	—	20.00	—	22.00
Juice tumbler, 5 oz, 4" h, flat	—	35.00	—	35.00
Lamp	—	295.00	—	260.00
Lemonade pitcher, 48 oz, 10-1/4" h	—	295.00	—	350.00
Lemonade tumbler, 9 oz, 5-1/4" h, ftd	—	60.00	—	60.00
Pitcher, 23 or 24 oz, 5-1/2" h	—	595.00	—	45.00
Pitcher, 32 oz, ftd, cone, 8" h	—	45.00	—	60.00
Plate, 6" d, sherbet	—	12.00	—	10.00
Plate, 8" d, salad	—	15.00	—	20.00
Plate, 9" d, dinner	145.00	30.00	—	25.00
Plate, 9" d, grill	—	185.00	—	—
Plate, 10-3/4" l, oval	—	20.00	—	17.50
Platter, 11" l	150.00	25.00	—	24.00
Refrigerator dish, cov, 5" sq	—	—	15.00	—
Relish, two parts, oval	165.00	32.00	—	32.00
Rose bowl, three legs	—	500.00	—	—

Item	Delphite	Green	Jade-ite	Pink
Salad bowl, 7-1/2" d	—	40.00	—	40.00
Salad bowl, 7-1/2" d, ruffled	65.00	125.00	—	120.00
Salt and pepper shakers, pr, 4" h, ftd †	—	60.00	—	50.00
Salt and pepper shakers, pr, 6" flat	—	—	—	60.00
Saucer	—	12.50	—	12.50
Sherbet	90.00	30.00	—	20.00
Sugar, cov	—	32.00	—	30.00
Sugar, open	75.00	—	—	—
Tray, 6" sq, closed handles	—	195.00	—	—
Tumbler, 3 oz, 3-1/2" h, ftd	—	18.00	—	25.00
Tumbler, 7 oz, 4-1/2", ftd	175.00	25.00	—	22.00
Tumbler, 5-1/4" h, ftd	—	60.00	—	55.00
Vase, flared, three legs	—	485.00	—	—
Vase, 6-7/8" h	—	475.00	—	—
Vegetable bowl, 8" d, cov	—	50.00	—	65.00
Vegetable bowl, 8" d, open	80.00	—	—	40.00
Vegetable bowl, 9" l, oval	—	35.00	—	40.00

*Floral, pink dinner plate, **$25**.*

FLORAL AND DIAMOND BAND

Manufactured by U.S. Glass Company, Pittsburgh, Pa., in the late 1920s.
Pieces are made in pink and green, with limited production in black, crystal, and iridescent.

Floral and Diamond Band, green luncheon plate, $55.

Item	Green	Pink
Berry bowl, 4-1/2" d	12.00	15.00
Berry bowl, 8" d	15.00	18.00
Butter dish, cov	140.00	150.00
Compote, 5-1/2" h	18.00	17.50
Creamer, 4-3/4"	20.00	17.50
Iced tea tumbler, 5" h	45.00	65.00
Nappy, 5-3/4" d, handle	12.00	11.00
Pitcher, 42 oz, 8" h	95.00	90.00
Plate, 8" d, luncheon	55.00	45.00
Sherbet	10.00	9.50
Sugar, cov, 5-1/4"	70.00	55.00
Tumbler, 4" h, water	25.00	25.00

FLORENTINE NO. 1

Old Florentine, Poppy No. 1

Manufactured by Hazel Atlas Glass Company, Clarksburg, W.V., and Zanesville, Ohio, from 1932 to 1935.

Pieces are made in crystal, green, pink, yellow, and limited production in cobalt blue.

Reproductions: † Salt and pepper shakers have been reproduced in cobalt blue, pink, and red.

*Florentine No. 1, green creamer, **$15**; covered sugar, **$12.50**.*

Item	Cobalt Blue	Crystal	Green	Pink	Yellow
Ashtray, 5-1/2" d	—	24.00	24.00	28.00	28.00
Berry bowl, 5" d	24.00	15.00	40.00	40.00	15.00
Berry bowl, 8-1/2" d	—	24.00	25.00	28.00	28.00
Butter dish, cov	—	110.00	140.00	165.00	160.00
Cereal bowl, 6" d	—	32.00	32.00	35.00	35.00
Coaster/ashtray, 3-3/4" d	—	18.00	20.00	25.00	25.00
Comport, 3-1/2" h, ruffled	60.00	25.00	25.00	15.00	—
Cream soup, 5" d, ruffled	50.00	15.00	18.00	20.00	—
Creamer	—	9.00	15.00	20.00	20.00
Creamer, ruffled	65.00	45.00	35.00	37.00	—
Cup	85.00	5.00	10.00	18.00	13.50
Iced tea tumbler, 12 oz, 5-1/4" h, ftd	—	28.00	28.00	30.00	24.00
Juice tumbler, 5 oz, 3-3/4" h, ftd	—	16.00	16.00	20.00	22.00
Lemonade tumbler, 9 oz, 5-1/4" h	—	—	—	100.00	—
Pitcher, 36 oz, 6-1/2", ftd	850.00	45.00	45.00	65.00	50.00
Pitcher, 48 oz, 7-1/2", flat, with or without ice lip	—	75.00	75.00	135.00	195.00
Plate, 6" d, sherbet	—	7.50	9.00	7.50	9.00
Plate, 8-1/2" d, salad	—	9.00	12.50	14.00	14.50
Plate, 10" d, dinner	—	16.00	20.00	22.00	24.00
Plate, 10" d, grill	—	12.00	12.50	20.00	22.00
Platter, 11-1/2" l, oval	—	19.00	10.00	22.00	35.00
Salt and pepper shakers, pr, ftd †	—	22.00	60.00	55.00	60.00
Saucer	18.00	3.00	4.50	6.00	3.00
Sherbet, 3 oz, ftd	—	8.00	10.00	15.00	14.00
Sugar, cov	—	10.00	12.50	25.00	12.00
Sugar, ruffled	55.00	35.00	30.00	42.50	—
Tumbler, 4 oz, 3-1/4" h, ftd	—	15.00	16.00	—	—
Tumbler, 9 oz, 4" h, ribbed	—	12.00	14.00	22.00	—
Tumbler, 10 oz, 4-3/4" h, ftd	—	22.00	20.00	22.00	24.00
Vegetable bowl, cov, 9-1/2" l, oval	—	45.00	45.00	60.00	60.00

FLORENTINE NO. 2

Poppy No. 2

Manufactured by Hazel Atlas Glass Company, Clarksburg, W.V., and Zanesville, Ohio, from 1932 to 1935.

Pieces are made in amber, cobalt blue, crystal, green, ice blue, pink, and yellow. Ice blue production is limited to a 7-1/2-inch high pitcher valued at $525. Amber production is limited to 9-ounce and 12-ounce tumblers, both currently valued at $80; a cup and saucer valued at $75; and a sherbet valued at $45. Cobalt blue production is limited to a 3-1/2-inch comport valued at $60, and a 9-ounce tumbler valued at $80.

Reproductions: † A cone-shaped pitcher that is 7-1/2-inch high and a 4-inch high footed tumbler. Reproductions are found in amber, cobalt blue, crystal, deep green, and pink.

Item	Crystal	Green	Pink	Yellow
Ashtray, 3-1/2" d	18.50	18.50	—	25.00
Ashtray, 5-1/2" d	20.00	25.00	—	32.00
Berry bowl, 4-1/2" d	12.50	16.50	17.50	27.50
Berry bowl, 8" d	24.00	26.00	30.00	35.00
Bowl, 5-1/2" d	32.00	35.00	—	42.00
Bowl, 7-1/2" d, shallow	—	—	—	85.00
Bowl, 9" d, flat	27.50	27.50	—	—
Butter dish, cov	115.00	125.00	—	165.00
Candlesticks, pr, 2-3/4" h	45.00	48.00	—	70.00
Candy dish, cov	120.00	115.00	150.00	170.00
Cereal bowl, 6" d	28.00	28.00	—	40.00
Coaster, 3-1/4" d	—	—	—	25.00
Coaster, 3-3/4" d	18.50	18.50	—	25.00
Coaster, 5-1/2" d	20.00	25.00	—	35.00
Cocktail, 3-1/4" h, ftd	—	—	—	14.50
Comport, 3-1/2" d, ruffled	25.00	25.00	25.00	—
Condiment tray, round	—	—	—	65.00
Cream soup, 4-3/4" d, two handles	12.50	16.00	18.50	20.00
Creamer	5.00	12.00	—	14.50
Cup	5.50	10.00	—	10.00
Custard cup	60.00	60.00	—	140.00
Gravy boat	—	—	—	65.00
Gravy boat underplate, 11-1/2" l	—	—	—	95.00
Iced tea tumbler, 12 oz, 5" h	35.00	35.00	—	45.00
Juice tumbler, 5 oz, 3-1/8" h, flat	14.50	14.50	16.00	22.00
Juice tumbler, 5 oz, 3-1/8" h, ftd	13.00	15.00	—	22.00
Parfait, 6" h	30.00	32.00	—	65.00

Item	Crystal	Green	Pink	Yellow
Pitcher, 24 oz, cone, ftd, 6-1/4" h................................ —		—	—	35.00
Pitcher, 28 oz, cone ftd, 7-1/2" h †.........................60.00		40.00	—	50.00
Pitcher, 48 oz, 7-1/2" h...60.00		70.00	120.00	32.00
Pitcher, 76 oz, 8-1/4" h...90.00		95.00	225.00	400.00
Plate, 6" d, sherbet..6.00		6.00	—	9.50
Plate, 6-1/2" d, indent...16.00		17.50	—	30.00
Plate, 8-1/2" d, salad...8.50		9.50	9.00	10.00
Plate, 10" d, dinner...16.50		16.00	—	15.00
Plate, 10-1/4" d, grill..15.00		15.00	—	18.50
Plate, 10-1/4" d, grill, cream soup ring......................35.00		35.00	—	—
Platter, 11" oval..15.00		20.00	18.50	25.00
Relish, 10" d, divided, three parts.............................22.50		24.00	26.00	35.00
Relish, 10" d, plain...22.50		24.00	26.00	32.00
Salt and pepper shakers, pr.....................................48.00		50.00	—	60.00
Saucer...5.00		6.00	—	5.00
Sherbet, ftd..10.00		12.50	—	12.50
Sugar, cov...6.50		9.00	—	38.00
Tumbler, 5 oz, 3-1/4" h, ftd.....................................18.00		15.00	15.00	—
Tumbler, 5 oz, 4" h, ftd †..13.50		15.00	18.00	20.00
Tumbler, 5 oz, 3-5/16" h, blown...............................18.50		18.50	—	—
Tumbler, 6 oz, 3-9/16" h, blown...............................16.00		18.50	—	—
Tumbler, 9 oz, 4" h...12.50		18.50	16.00	22.50
Tumbler, 9 oz, 4-1/2" h, ftd.....................................25.00		25.00	—	38.00
Tumbler, 10 oz, 4-11/16, blown................................19.00		19.00	—	—
Tumbler, 12 oz, 5" h, blown.....................................20.00		20.00	—	20.00
Vase, 6" h...30.00		32.00	—	65.00
Vegetable bowl, cov, 9" l, oval..................................55.00		60.00	—	85.00

Florentine No. 2, yellow cup, **$10**.

FLOWER GARDEN WITH BUTTERFLIES

Butterflies and Roses

Manufactured by U.S. Glass Company, Pittsburgh, Pa., in the late 1920s.

Pieces are made in amber, black, blue, blue-green, canary yellow, crystal, green, and pink.

Item	Amber or Crystal	Black	Blue-Green, Green or Pink	Blue or Canary Yellow
Ashtray	175.00	—	185.00	225.00
Bonbon, cov, 6-5/8" d	—	265.00	—	—
Bowl, 9" d, rolled edge	—	225.00	—	—
Candlesticks, pr, 4" h	50.00	—	60.00	100.00
Candlesticks, pr, 8" h	90.00	325.00	145.00	145.00
Candy, cov, 6" d, flat	135.00	—	165.00	—
Candy, cov, 7-1/2" cone shape	90.00	100.00	165.00	175.00
Candy, cov, heart shape	—	—	1,250.00	1,500.00
Cologne bottle, 7-1/2" h	—	—	225.00	365.00
Comport, 2-7/8" h	—	250.00	40.00	45.00
Comport, 3" h	25.00	—	30.00	35.00
Comport, 4-1/4" h, 4-3/4" w	—	—	—	65.00
Comport, 4-3/4" h, 10-1/4" w	50.00	250.00	70.00	90.00
Comport, 5-7/8" h, 11" w	60.00	—	—	95.00
Comport, 7-1/4" h, 8-1/4" w	65.00	175.00	85.00	—
Creamer	—	—	75.00	—
Cup	—	—	70.00	—
Mayonnaise, ftd, 4-3/4" h, 6-1/4" w, 7" d plate, ladle	70.00	—	95.00	145.00
Orange bowl, 11" d, ftd	—	250.00	—	—
Plate, 7" d	20.00	—	25.00	30.00
Plate, 8" d	17.50	—	20.00	27.50
Plate, 10" d	—	—	45.00	50.00
Plate, 10" d, indent	35.00	150.00	45.00	50.00

Item	Amber or Crystal	Black	Blue-Green, Green or Pink Yellow	Blue or Canary
Powder jar, 3-1/2", flat	—	—	75.00	—
Powder jar, 6-1/4" h, ftd	225.00	—	130.00	175.00
Powder jar, 7-1/2" h, ftd	85.00	—	135.00	195.00
Sandwich server, center handle	55.00	135.00	75.00	100.00
Saucer	—	—	30.00	—
Tray, 5-1/2" x 10", oval	50.00	—	75.00	9.00
Tray, 11-3/4" x 7-3/4", rect	50.00	—	75.00	90.00
Tumbler, 7-1/2 oz	175.00	—	—	—
Vase, 6-1/4" h	75.00	145.00	135.00	145.00
Vase, 8" h, Dahlia, cupped	—	275.00	—	—
Vase, 10" h, two handles	—	250.00	—	—
Vase, 10-1/2" h	—	—	150.00	225.00
Wall pocket, 9" l	—	365.00	—	—

Flower Garden with Butterflies, blue comport, 5-7/8" h, 11" w, **$95**.

FOREST GREEN

Manufactured by Anchor Hocking Glass Company, Lancaster, Ohio, and Long Island City, N.Y., from 1950 to 1957.

Pieces are made only in forest green.

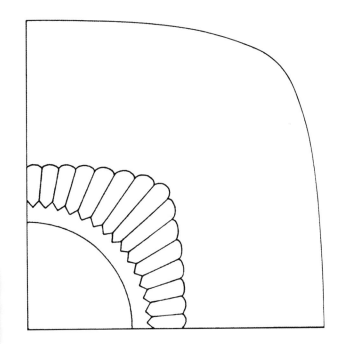

Forest Green, vase with original foil label, $15.

Forest Green, cup, $7; saucer, $3.

Item	Forest Green
Ashtray, 3-1/4" round	12.00
Ashtray, 3-1/2" sq	5.00
Ashtray, 4-5/8" sq	6.00
Ashtray, 5-3/4" hexagon	8.00
Ashtray, 5-3/4" sq	7.50
Batter bowl, spout	25.00
Berry bowl, large	15.00
Berry bowl, small	7.50
Bonbon, 6-1/4" w, tricorn	12.00
Bowl, 4-1/2" w, sq	7.00
Bowl, 5-1/4" deep	10.00
Bowl, 6" w, sq	18.00
Bowl, 6-1/2" d, scalloped	10.00
Bowl, 6-3/8" d, three toes	15.00
Bowl, 7-3/8" w, sq	30.00
Bowl, 7-1/2" d, crimped	10.00
Cocktail, 3-1/2 oz	12.00
Cocktail, 4-1/2 oz	14.00
Creamer, flat	7.50
Cup, sq	7.00
Dessert bowl, 4-3/4" d	7.00
Goblet, 9 oz	10.00
Goblet, 9-1/2 oz	14.00
Iced tea tumbler, 13 oz	8.00
Iced tea tumbler, 14 oz, Boopie	8.00
Iced tea tumbler, 15 oz, tall	10.00
Iced tea tumbler, 32 oz, giant	18.00
Ivy ball, 4" h	5.00
Juice tumbler, 4 oz	10.00
Juice tumbler, 5-1/2 oz	12.50
Juice Roly Poly tumbler, 3-3/8" h	6.00
Ladle, all green glass	80.00
Mixing bowl, 4-3/4" d, ribbed, crystal lid	22.00
Mixing bowl, 6" d	12.00

Item	Forest Green
Pitcher, 22 oz	22.50
Pitcher, 36 oz	25.00
Pitcher, 86 oz, round	45.00
Plate, 6-3/4" d, salad	7.50
Plate, 7" w, sq	6.75
Plate, 8-3/8" d, luncheon	9.00
Plate, 9-1/4" d, dinner	33.50
Platter, 11" l, rect	22.00
Popcorn bowl, 5-1/4" d	10.00
Punch bowl	25.00
Punch bowl and stand	60.00
Punch cup	3.00
Relish tray, 4-3/4" x 6-3/4" l, two handles	25.00
Roly Poly tumbler, 5 1/8" h	7.50
Salad bowl, 7-3/8" d	15.00
Sandwich plate, 13-3/4" d	45.00
Saucer, 5-3/8" w	3.00
Sherbet, 6 oz	9.00
Sherbet, 6 oz, Boopie	7.00
Sherbet, flat	7.50
Soup bowl, 6" d	17.00
Sugar, flat	7.00
Tray, 6" x 10", two handles	30.00
Tumbler, 5 oz, 3-1/2" h	4.00
Tumbler, 7 oz	4.50
Tumbler, 5-1/4" h	7.00
Tumbler, 9-1/2 oz, tall	8.00
Tumbler, 9 oz, fancy	7.00

Item	Forest Green
Tumbler, 9 oz, table	5.00
Tumbler, 10 oz, 4-1/2" h, ftd	8.50
Tumbler, 11 oz	7.00
Tumbler, 14 oz, 5" h	8.00
Tumbler, 15 oz, long boy	10.00
Tumbler, 20 oz, 6-1/4" h	22.00
Vase, 3-1/2" h, ruffled	6.00
Vase, 6-3/8" h, Harding	7.50
Vase, 7" h, crimped	15.00
Vase, 9" h	22.00
Vegetable bowl, 8-1/2" l, oval	30.00

Forest Green, deep bowl, 5" d, 4-1/4" deep, $10. Photos courtesy of Tina Trautman.

Forest Green, sherbet, Boopie, $7.

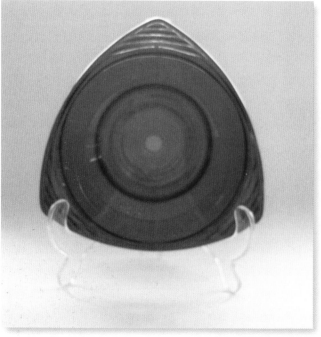

Forest Green, tricorn bonbon, $12.

FORTUNE

Manufactured by Hocking Glass Company, Lancaster, Ohio, from 1937 to 1938.

Pieces are made in crystal and pink.

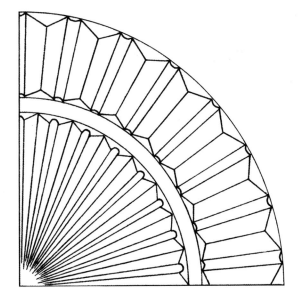

Item	Crystal	Pink
Berry bowl, 4" d	10.00	12.00
Berry bowl, 7-3/4" d	25.00	28.00
Bowl, 4-1/2" d, handle	12.00	15.00
Bowl, 5-1/4" d, rolled edge	20.00	22.00
Candy dish, cov, flat	28.00	30.00
Cup	12.00	15.00
Dessert bowl, 4-1/2" d	12.00	12.00
Juice tumbler, 5 oz, 3-1/2" h	12.00	13.50
Plate, 6" d, sherbet	8.00	15.00
Plate, 8" d, luncheon	25.00	25.00
Salad bowl, 7-3/4" d	25.00	25.00
Saucer	5.00	8.50
Tumbler, 9 oz, 4" h	15.00	16.50

*Fortune, pink berry bowl, 7-3/4", **$28**.*

FRUITS

Manufactured by Hazel Atlas Company, and several other small glass companies, from 1931 to 1935.

Pieces are made in crystal, green, iridized, and pink. Iridized production includes only a 4-inch tumbler, valued at $10.

Item	Crystal	Green	Pink
Berry bowl, 5" d	17.50	32.00	28.00
Berry bowl, 8" d	40.00	85.00	45.00
Console bowl, 7-1/4" d	—	325.00	—
Cup	5.00	12.00	7.00
Juice tumbler, 5 oz, 3-1/2" h	20.00	60.00	22.00
Pitcher, 7" h	50.00	95.00	—
Plate, 8" d, luncheon	12.00	15.00	12.00
Saucer	2.50	6.00	4.50
Sherbet	10.00	15.00	12.00
Tumbler, 4" h, multiple fruits	15.00	24.00	22.00
Tumbler, 4" h, single fruit	20.00	30.00	25.00
Tumbler, 12 oz, 5" h	70.00	200.00	95.00

*Fruits, green luncheon plate, **$15**.*

*Fruits, green cup, **$12**; saucer, **$6**.*

GEORGIAN

Lovebirds

Manufactured by Federal Glass Company, Columbus, Ohio, from 1931 to 1936.

Pieces are made in green. A crystal hot plate is valued at $25.

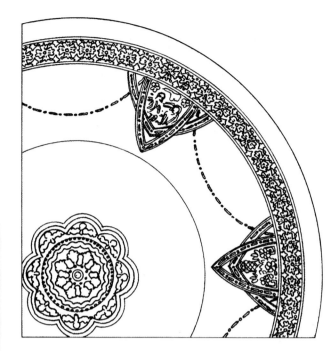

Georgian, green luncheon plate, **$12**.

Georgian, green sherbet, **$12**.

Item	Green
Berry bowl, 4-1/2" d	15.00
Berry bowl, 7-1/2" d, large	65.00
Bowl, 6-1/2" d, deep	65.00
Butter dish, cov	85.00
Cereal bowl, 5-3/4" d	28.50
Cold cuts server, 18-1/2" d, wood, seven openings for 5" d coasters	875.00
Creamer, 3" d, ftd	40.00
Creamer, 4" d, ftd	20.00
Cup	10.00
Hot plate, 5" d, center design	48.00
Plate, 6" d, sherbet	7.50
Plate, 8" d, luncheon	12.00
Plate, 9-1/4" d, center design only	25.00
Plate, 9-1/4" d, dinner	36.00
Platter, 11-1/2" l, closed handle	70.00
Saucer	4.00
Sherbet, ftd	12.00
Sugar cover, 3" d	15.00
Sugar cover, 4" d	15.00
Sugar, 3" d, ftd	35.00
Sugar, 4" d, ftd	35.00
Tumbler, 9 oz, 4" h, flat	65.00
Tumbler 12 oz, 5-1/4" h, flat	125.00
Vegetable bowl, 9" l, oval	65.00

GOLF BALL

#7643

Manufactured by Morgantown Glass, Morgantown, W.V., from 1928 to 1971.

Pieces are made in Anna Rose (Pink Champagne), Azure (Gloria Blue), Caramel, Cobalt, Copen Blue, crystal, 14K Topaz (Topaz Mist), India Black, Light Amethyst, Meadow Green (crystal ball and foot), Mission Gold, Old Amethyst, Peach (non-opaque), Ritz Blue, Ruby, Smoke, Spanish Red, Stiegel Green, and Venetian Green (Shamrock). There was some production in all-Alabaster (opalescent milk glass) in stemware and vases during the late 1920s and early 1930s.

Decorations include gold and platinum #769 Sparta etching, Berne (platinum #12 border) on Spanish Red; Vernay (platinum #12 border) on Ritz Blue; Avon, Chateau, Eton, Gorton and Toland cuttings; special crest, logo and slogan cuttings, Lotus Decorating Co. silver overlay Hunt Scene. To calculate values for etched pieces, increase crystal by 35 percent and colors as much as 100 percent higher. For values for pieces with cuttings, increase the value of crystal by 25 percent and colored wares about 50 percent higher.

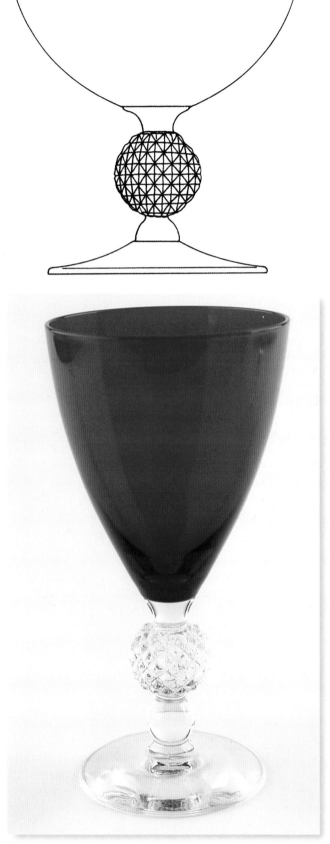

Golf Ball, Spanish Red goblet, **$55**.

Item	Crystal	India Black	Pastels	Ritz Blue	Spanish Red	Stiegel Green
Bell, 5-1/2" h	—	—	—	225.00	—	—
Bonbon, #2938, Helga, 5-1/4" d	—	375.00	500.00	415.00	415.00	375.00
Bonbon, #7758, Leora, 5" d	—	360.00	—	495.00	495.00	360.00
Bonbon, #9074, Maureen, 4-1/2" d	—	365.00	365.00	495.00	495.00	365.00
Box, cov, #1212, Michael, 7" d	—	—	—	375.00	375.00	—
Brandy snifter, 21 oz, 6-1/2" h	—	—	—	165.00	185.00	145.00
Cafe parfait, 5 oz, 6-1/4" h	50.00	—	50.00	72.00	65.00	60.00
Candleholder, 4" h, Jacobi, price for pr	—	255.00	235.00	265.00	265.00	255.00
Candleholder, 4-5/8" h, Dupont, price for pr	—	—	285.00	—	—	—
Candleholder, 6" h, torch, single	—	—	—	280.00	225.00	200.00
Candy jar, cov, Fairway, 22 oz, #14-1/2	—	325.00	—	345.00	325.00	325.00
Champagne, 5-1/2 oz, 5" h	45.00	—	50.00	60.00	55.00	52.00
Claret, 4-1/2 oz, 5-1/4" h	48.00	—	52.00	68.00	55.00	55.00
Compote, cov, Celeste, 6" d	—	285.00	285.00	285.00	285.00	260.00
Compote, open, Celeste, 6" d	—	190.00	175.00	21.00	190.00	175.00
Cordial, 1-1/2 oz, 3-1/2" h	40.00	—	55.00	58.00	55.00	55.00
Creamer and sugar	—	—	255.00	285.00	285.00	285.00
Goblet, 9 oz, 6-3/4" h	38.00	—	55.00	58.00	55.00	55.00
Iced tea tumbler, 12 oz, 6-3/4" h, ftd	35.00	—	45.00	50.00	55.00	45.00
Irish coffee, 6 oz, 5-1/4" h	—	—	—	95.00	—	—
Ivy ball, #7643, Kennon, 4" d	—	—	—	85.00	85.00	85.00
Ivy ball, #7643, Kimball, 4" d	—	—	—	85.00	85.00	85.00
Juice tumbler, 5 oz, 5" h, ftd	32.00	—	45.00	45.00	45.00	42.00
Lamp, Amherst water	—	—	—	—	—	625.00
Liquor cocktail, 3-1/2 oz, 4-1/8" h	35.00	—	42.00	42.00	42.00	42.00
Luncheon tumbler/goblet, 9 oz, 6-1/8" h, ftd	30.00	—	42.00	55.00	48.00	45.00
Oyster cocktail, 4 oz, 4-1/4" h, flared	40.00	—	—	55.00	50.00	48.00
Oyster cocktail, 4-1/2 oz, 4-3/8" h, cupped	40.00	—	—	55.00	50.00	48.00
Pilsner, 11 oz, 9-1/8" h	100.00	—	—	125.00	—	—
Schooner, 32 oz	245.00	—	—	—	—	—
Sherbet/sundae, 5-1/2 oz, 4-1/8" h	30.00	—	40.00	45.00	40.00	40.00
Sherry, 2-1/2 oz, 4-5/8" h	40.00	—	35.00	50.00	50.00	45.00
Vase, 6-1/2" h, #7643, Urn	—	—	—	125.00	125.00	110.00
Vase, 6-1/2" h, #7643-1/2, urn, Stephanie	—	—	—	150.00	150.00	125.00
Vase, 8" h, #7643, Charlotte	—	—	175.00	165.00	165.00	165.00
Vase, 9-1/2" h, #79, Montague	—	—	—	255.00	255.00	240.00
Vase, 10-1/2" h, #78, Lancaster	—	—	—	245.00	245.00	245.00
Wine tumbler, 2-1/2 oz, 4-3/8" h, ftd	35.00	—	48.00	48.00	45.00	45.00
Wine, 3 oz, 4-3/4" h	45.00	—	55.00	65.00	60.00	55.00

HARP

Manufactured by Jeannette Glass Company, Jeannette, Pa., from 1954 to 1957.

Pieces are made in crystal and crystal with gold trim; limited pieces are made in ice blue, iridescent white, pink, and shell pink.

Item	Crystal	Ice Blue	Shell Pink
Ashtray	10.00	—	—
Cake stand, 9" d	30.00	45.00	50.00
Coaster	6.00	—	—
Cup	30.00	—	—
Parfait	20.00	—	—
Plate, 7" d	25.00	25.00	—
Saucer	14.00	—	—
Snack set, cup, saucer, 7" plate	48.00	—	—
Tray, two handles, rectangular	35.00	35.00	65.00
Vase, 7-1/2" h	30.00	—	—

Harp, crystal gold-edge plate, $25; cake stand, $30.

HERITAGE

Manufactured by Federal Glass Company, Columbus, Ohio, from 1940 to 1955.

Pieces are made in blue, crystal, green, and pink.

Reproductions: † Bowls have been reproduced in amber, crystal, and green. Some are marked with an N or MC.

Item	Blue	Crystal	Green	Pink
Berry bowl, 5" d †	80.00	8.00	75.00	75.00
Berry bowl, 8-1/2" d †	250.00	40.00	200.00	195.00
Creamer, ftd	—	25.00	—	—
Cup	—	7.50	—	—
Fruit bowl, 10-1/2" d	—	15.00	—	—
Plate, 8" d, luncheon	—	9.00	—	—
Plate, 9-1/4" d, dinner	—	12.00	—	—
Sandwich plate, 12" d	—	18.00	—	—
Saucer	—	4.00	—	—
Sugar, open, ftd	—	25.00	—	—

Heritage, crystal cup, **$7.50**; *saucer,* **$4**.

Heritage, crystal dinner plate, **$12**.

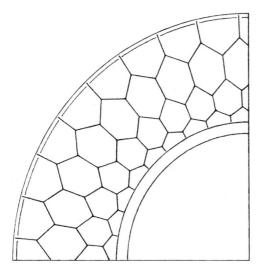

HEX OPTIC

Honeycomb

Manufactured by Jeannette Glass Company, Jeannette, Pa., from 1928 to 1932.

Pieces are made in green and pink. Ultramarine tumblers have been found. Iridescent tumblers and pitchers were made about 1960 and it is assumed they were made by Jeannette.

Item	Green	Pink
Berry bowl, 4-1/4" d, ruffled	9.50	8.50
Berry bowl, 7-1/2" d	15.00	12.00
Bucket reamer	65.00	60.00
Butter dish, cov, rect, 1-lb size	90.00	90.00
Creamer, two style handles	8.00	7.00
Cup, two style handles	5.00	5.00
Ice bucket, metal handle	30.00	35.00
Mixing bowl, 7-1/4" d	15.00	15.00
Mixing bowl, 8-1/4" d	18.00	18.00
Mixing bowl, 9" d	20.00	20.00
Mixing bowl, 10" d	20.00	20.00
Pitcher, 32 oz, 5" h	25.00	25.00
Pitcher, 48 oz, 9" h, ftd	48.00	50.00
Pitcher, 96 oz, 8" h	225.00	235.00
Plate, 6" d, sherbet	3.00	3.00

Item	Green	Pink
Plate, 8" d, luncheon	6.00	6.00
Platter, 11" d, round	14.00	16.00
Refrigerator dish, 4" x 4"	20.00	18.00
Refrigerator stack set, four pcs	75.00	75.00
Salt and pepper shakers, pr	30.00	50.00
Saucer	4.00	4.00
Sherbet, 5 oz, ftd	5.00	5.00
Sugar, two styles of handles	6.00	6.00
Sugar shaker	225.00	225.00
Tumbler, 12 oz, 5" h	8.00	8.00
Tumbler, 5-3/4" h, ftd	10.00	10.00
Tumbler, 7" h, ftd	15.00	12.00
Tumbler, 7 oz, 4-3/4" h, ftd	8.00	8.00
Tumbler, 9 oz, 3-3/4" h	5.00	5.00
Whiskey, 1 oz, 2" h	8.50	8.50

Hex Optic, green luncheon plate, $6; bucket reamer, $65.

HOBNAIL

Manufactured by Hocking Glass Company, Lancaster, Ohio, from 1934 to 1936.

Pieces are made in crystal, crystal with red trim, and pink.

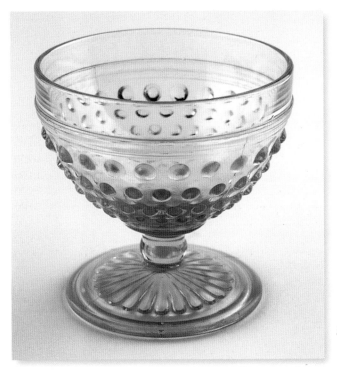

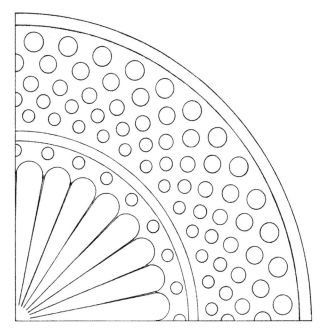

*Hobnail, pink sherbet, **$10**.*

Item	Crystal	Crystal, red trim	Pink
Cereal bowl, 5-1/2" d	4.25	4.25	—
Cordial, 5 oz, ftd	6.00	6.00	—
Creamer, ftd	10.00	4.00	—
Cup	5.00	5.00	10.00
Decanter and stopper, 32 oz	27.50	60.00	—
Goblet, 10 oz	7.50	7.50	—
Iced tea goblet, 13 oz	8.50	8.50	—
Iced tea tumbler, 15 oz	8.50	8.50	—
Juice tumbler, 5 oz	4.00	4.00	—
Milk pitcher, 18 oz	32.50	30.00	—
Pitcher, 67 oz	25.00	25.00	—
Plate, 6" d, sherbet	2.50	2.50	7.50
Plate, 8-1/2" d, luncheon	5.00	5.00	7.50
Salad bowl, 7" d	5.00	5.00	—
Saucer	4.00	4.00	6.00
Sherbet	4.00	4.00	10.00
Sugar, ftd	10.00	8.00	—
Tumbler, 9 oz, 4-3/4" h, flat	5.00	5.00	—
Whiskey, 1-1/2 oz	5.00	5.00	—
Wine, 3 oz, ftd	6.50	6.50	—

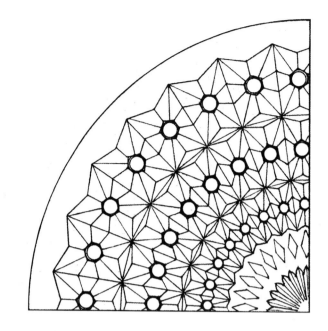

HOLIDAY

Button and Bows

Manufactured by Jeannette Glass Company, Jeannette, Pa., from 1947 to the 1950s.

Pieces are made in crystal, iridescent, pink, and shell pink. Shell pink production was limited to the console bowl, valued at $48.

Item	Crystal	Iridescent	Pink
Berry bowl, 5-1/8" d	—	—	18.00
Berry bowl, 8-1/2" d	—	—	55.00
Butter dish, cov	—	—	75.00
Cake plate, 10-1/2" d, three legs	—	—	150.00
Candlesticks, pr, 3" h	—	—	150.00
Chop plate, 13-3/4" d	—	—	140.00
Console bowl, 10-1/4" d	—	—	225.00
Creamer, ftd	—	—	18.00
Cup, plain	—	—	10.00
Cup, rayed bottom, 2" d base	—	—	10.00
Cup, rayed bottom, 2-3/8" d base	—	—	16.00
Juice tumbler, 5 oz, 4" h, ftd	—	—	60.00
Pitcher, 16 oz, 4-3/4" h	17.50	35.00	85.00
Pitcher, 52 oz, 6-3/4" h	—	—	45.00
Plate, 6" d, sherbet	—	—	10.00
Plate, 9" d, dinner	—	—	20.00
Platter, 11-3/8" l, oval	—	17.50	35.00
Sandwich tray, 10-1/2" l	—	20.00	28.00
Saucer, plain center	—	—	5.00
Saucer, rayed center, 2-1/8" d ring	—	—	7.50
Saucer, rayed center, 2-1/2" d ring	—	—	7.50
Sherbet	—	—	10.00
Soup bowl, 7-3/4" d	—	—	65.00
Sugar, cov	—	—	12.00
Sugar lid	—	—	20.00
Tumbler, 5 oz, 4" h, ftd	—	15.00	35.00
Tumbler, 5-1/4 oz, 4-1/4" h, ftd	8.00	—	45.00
Tumbler, 6" h, ftd	—	—	195.00
Tumbler, 9 oz, 4" h, ftd	—	—	55.00
Tumbler, 10 oz, 4" h, flat	—	—	25.00
Vegetable bowl, 9-1/2" l, oval	—	—	36.00

*Holiday, pink pitcher, 16 oz, **$85**.*

HOMESPUN

Fine Rib

Manufactured by Jeannette Glass Company, Jeannette, Pa., from 1939 to 1949.

Pieces are made in crystal and pink.

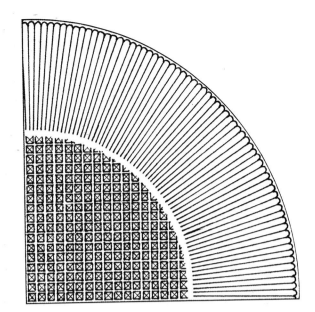

Item	Crystal	Pink
Ashtray	6.00	6.00
Berry bowl, 4-1/2" d, closed handles	15.00	20.00
Berry bowl, 8-1/4" d	20.00	20.00
Butter dish, cov	55.00	90.00
Cereal bowl, 5" d, closed handles	30.00	30.00
Coaster	6.00	6.00
Creamer, ftd	12.50	12.50
Cup	12.00	15.00
Iced tea tumbler, 13 oz, 5-1/4" h	32.00	32.00
Plate, 6" d, sherbet	7.50	12.50
Plate, 9-1/4" d, dinner	18.00	18.00
Platter, 13" d, closed handles	20.00	20.00
Saucer	5.50	10.00
Sherbet, low, flat	17.50	19.00
Sugar, ftd	12.50	12.50
Tumbler, 5 oz, 4" h, ftd	8.00	10.00
Tumbler, 6 oz, 3-7/8" h, straight	7.00	7.50
Tumbler, 9 oz, 4" h, flared top	17.50	17.50
Tumbler, 9 oz, 4-1/4" h, top band	17.50	17.50
Tumbler, 15 oz, 6-1/4" h, ftd	38.00	38.00
Tumbler, 15 oz, 6-3/8" h, ftd	36.00	36.00

Children's

Item	Crystal	Pink
Cup	25.00	35.00
Plate	10.00	185.00
Saucer	9.00	12.00
Teapot	—	125.00

*Homespun, pink sugar, **$12.50**; look-alike tumbler.*

HORSESHOE

No. 612

Manufactured by the Indiana Glass Company, Dunkirk, Ind., from 1930 to 1933.

Pieces are made in crystal, green, pink, and yellow. There is limited collector interest in crystal and pink at the current time.

Horseshoe, yellow cup, $17.50.

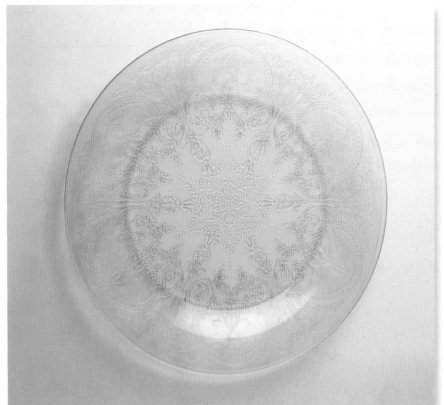

Horseshoe, yellow luncheon plate, $20.

Item	Green	Yellow
Berry bowl, 4-1/2" d	30.00	25.00
Berry bowl, 9-1/2" d	40.00	35.00
Butter dish, cov	995.00	—
Candy dish, metal holder	175.00	—
Cereal bowl, 6-1/2" d	50.0	35.00
Creamer, ftd	30.00	30.00
Cup and saucer	20.00	28.00
Pitcher, 64 oz, 8-1/2" h	295.00	350.00
Plate, 6" d, sherbet	9.00	10.00
Plate, 8-3/8" d, salad	10.00	18.00
Plate, 9-3/8" d, luncheon	15.00	20.00
Plate, 10-3/8" d, grill	175.00	165.00
Platter, 10-3/4" l, oval	25.00	25.00
Relish, three parts, ftd	40.00	42.50
Salad bowl, 7-1/2" d	24.00	24.00
Sandwich plate, 11-1/2" d	24.00	27.50
Saucer	10.00	10.00
Sherbet	16.00	18.50
Sugar, open	25.00	27.50
Tumbler, 9 oz, ftd	25.00	30.00
Tumbler, 9 oz, 4-1/4" h	150.00	—
Tumbler, 12 oz, ftd	140.00	150.00
Tumbler, 12 oz, 4-3/4" h	150.00	—
Vegetable bowl, 8-1/2" d	30.00	30.00
Vegetable bowl, 10-1/2" d, oval	25.00	50.00

INDIANA CUSTARD

Flower and Leaf Band

Manufactured by Indiana Glass Company, Dunkirk, Ind., in the 1930s and in the 1950s.

Pieces are made in a custard color, which is known as French Ivory.

*Indiana Custard, covered sugar, **$30**.*

Item	French Ivory
Berry bowl, 5-1/2" d	20.00
Berry bowl, 9" d, 1-3/4" deep	36.00
Butter dish, cov	70.00
Cereal bowl, 6-1/2" d	32.00
Creamer	22.00
Cup	38.00
Plate, 5-3/4" d, bread and butter	7.50
Plate, 7-1/2" d, salad	16.00
Plate, 8-7/8" d, luncheon	18.00
Plate, 9-3/4" d, dinner	28.00
Platter, 11-1/2" l, oval	30.00
Saucer	8.00
Sherbet	90.00
Soup bowl, 7-1/2" d, flat	32.00
Sugar, cov	30.00

IRIS

Iris and Herringbone

Manufactured by Jeannette Glass Company, Jeannette, Pa., from 1928 to 1932 and in the 1950s and 1970s.

Pieces are made in crystal, iridescent, some green, and pink. Recent color combinations of yellow and red and blue and green and white have been made. A record price of $495 is noted for a rare amethyst demitasse cup and saucer.

Reproductions: † Some collectors and dealers feel strongly that the newer re-issues of this pattern are actually reproductions. Forms that have the potential to fool buyers are the 4-1/2-inch berry bowl, covered candy jar, 10-inch diameter dinner plate, 6-1/2-inch high footed tumbler, and vase. Careful examination of the object, plus careful consideration of the color, should help determine age.

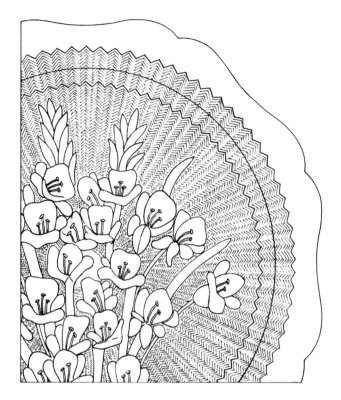

Item	Crystal	Green	Iridescent	Pink
Berry bowl, 4-1/2" d, beaded edge †	60.00	—	32.00	—
Berry bowl, 8" d, beaded edge	125.00	—	30.00	—
Bowl, 5-1/2" d, scalloped	12.00	—	25.00	—
Bowl, 9-1/2" d, scalloped	20.00	—	15.00	—
Bread plate, 11-3/4" d	20.00	—	38.00	—
Butter dish, cov	60.00	—	65.00	—
Candlesticks, pr	45.00	—	50.00	—
Candy jar, cov †	235.00	—	—	—
Cereal bowl, 5" d	140.00	—	—	—
Coaster †	115.00	—	—	—
Cocktail, 4 oz, 4-1/4" h	25.00	—	—	—
Creamer, ftd	12.00	135.00	15.00	150.00
Cup	20.00	—	18.00	—
Demitasse cup and saucer	225.00	—	350.00	—
Fruit bowl, 11" d, straight edge	70.00	—	—	—
Fruit bowl, 11-1/2" d, ruffled	20.00	—	25.00	—
Fruit set	75.00	—	—	—
Goblet, 4 oz, 5-3/4" h	30.00	—	135.00	—
Goblet, 8 oz, 5-3/4" h	30.00	—	175.00	—
Iced tea tumbler, 6-1/2" h, ftd	35.00	—	—	—
Lamp shade, 11-1/2"	100.00	—	—	—
Nut set	115.00	—	—	—
Pitcher, 9-1/2" h, ftd	40.00	—	60.00	—
Plate, 5-1/2" d, sherbet	20.00	—	17.50	—

Item	Crystal	Green	Iridescent	Pink
Plate, 7" d	95.00	—	—	—
Plate, 8" d, luncheon	160.00	—	115.00	—
Plate, 9" d, dinner †	70.00	—	50.00	—
Salad bowl, 9-1/2" d, ruffled	25.00	150.00	20.00	135.00
Sandwich plate, 11-3/4" d	48.00	—	35.00	—
Sauce, 5" d, ruffled	12.50	—	30.00	—
Saucer	18.00	—	12.00	—
Sherbet, 2-1/2" h, ftd	30.00	—	20.00	—
Sherbet, 4" h, ftd	32.00	—	15.50	—
Soup bowl, 7-1/2" d	195.00	—	90.00	—
Sugar, cov	40.00	150.00	25.00	150.00
Tumbler, 4" h, flat †	150.00	—	18.00	—
Tumbler, 6" h, ftd †	25.00	—	22.00	—
Tumbler, 6-1/2" h, ftd †	30.00	—	—	—
Tumbler, flat, water †	165.00	—	—	—
Vase, 9" h †	32.00	—	30.00	225.00
Wine, 4" h	20.00	—	33.50	—
Wine, 4-1/4" h, 3 oz	25.00	—	28.00	—
Wine, 5-1/2" h	25.00	—	—	—

*Iris, crystal candlesticks, **$45**; and iridescent plate, **$50**.*

JAMESTOWN

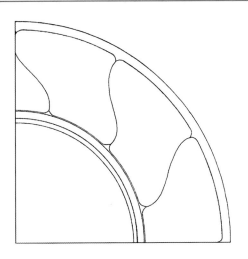

Manufactured by Fostoria Glass Company, Moundsville, Va., from 1958 to 1982.

Pieces are made in amber, amethyst, blue, brown, crystal, green, pink, and red.

*Jamestown, crystal goblet, **$20**, brown goblet, **$12**.*

*Jamestown, pink goblet, **$22**; blue goblet, **$20**.*

Item	Amber or Brown	Amethyst	Blue or Red	Crystal or Green	Pink
Butter, cov	25.00	48.00	60.00	48.00	60.00
Cake plate	25.00	45.00	60.00	45.00	60.00
Celery	20.00	35.00	40.00	35.00	40.00
Creamer, ftd	12.00	20.00	25.00	20.00	25.00
Dessert bowl, 4-1/2" d	8.50	14.00	17.50	13.50	15.00
Goblet, 9 oz or 10 oz	12.00	17.50	20.00	20.00	22.00
Iced tea tumbler, 11 or 12 oz	12.00	20.00	24.00	22.00	24.00
Jelly, cov	35.00	60.00	80.00	60.00	80.00
Juice tumbler, 5 oz	12.00	24.00	30.00	24.00	30.00
Muffin tray	30.00	45.00	55.00	45.00	55.00
Pickle	20.00	40.00	48.00	40.00	48.00
Pitcher, 48 oz, ice lip	48.00	95.00	145.00	95.00	145.00
Plate, 8" d	9.50	17.50	25.00	17.50	25.00
Relish, two parts	18.00	35.00	40.00	35.00	40.00
Salad bowl, 10" d	24.00	40.00	50.00	40.00	50.00
Salt and pepper shakers, pr, chrome top	30.00	42.00	55.00	42.00	55.00
Salver, 10" d, 7" h	60.00	120.00	125.00	135.00	125.00
Sauce dish, cov	20.00	35.00	42.00	35.00	42.00
Serving bowl, two handles, 10" d	22.00	45.00	60.00	45.00	60.00
Sherbet, 6 oz or 7 oz	8.50	15.00	17.00	15.00	17.50
Sugar, ftd	12.00	17.50	25.00	17.50	25.00
Torte plate, 14" d	30.00	45.00	60.00	45.00	60.00
Tumbler, 9 oz	7.50	18.00	25.00	18.00	25.00
Tumbler, 12 oz	7.50	20.00	25.00	20.00	25.00
Wine, 4 oz	12.00	25.00	30.00	35.00	33.50

JUBILEE

Manufactured by Lancaster Glass Company, Lancaster, Ohio, early 1930s.

Pieces are made in pink and yellow.

Item	Pink	Yellow
Bowl, 8" d, 5-1/8" h, three legs	275.00	225.00
Bowl, 11-1/2" d, three legs	265.00	250.00
Bowl, 11-1/2" d, three legs, curved in	—	250.00
Bowl, 13" d, three legs	250.00	245.00
Cake tray, 11" d, two handles	75.00	85.00
Candlesticks, pr	190.00	195.00
Candy jar, cov, three legs	325.00	325.00
Cheese and cracker set	265.00	255.00
Cordial, 1 oz, 4" h	—	245.00
Creamer	45.00	30.00
Cup	40.00	17.50
Fruit bowl, 9" d, handle	—	125.00
Fruit bowl, 11-1/2" h, flat	200.00	165.00
Goblet, 3 oz, 4-7/8" h	—	150.00
Goblet, 11 oz, 7-1/2" h	—	75.00
Iced tea tumbler, 12-1/2 oz, 6-1/8" h	—	135.00
Juice tumbler, 6 oz, 5" h, ftd	—	100.00
Mayonnaise, plate, orig ladle	315.00	285.00
Mayonnaise underplate	125.00	110.00
Plate, 7" d, salad	25.00	16.50
Plate, 8-3/4" d, luncheon	30.00	16.50
Plate, 14" d, three legs	—	210.00
Sandwich plate, 13-1/2" d	95.00	85.00
Sandwich tray, 11" d, center handle	215.00	250.00
Saucer	15.00	6.00
Sherbet, 8 oz, 3" h	—	75.00
Sherbet/champagne, 7 oz, 5-1/2" h	—	75.00
Sugar	40.00	24.00
Tumbler, 10 oz, 6" h, ftd	75.00	40.00
Vase, 12" h	—	385.00

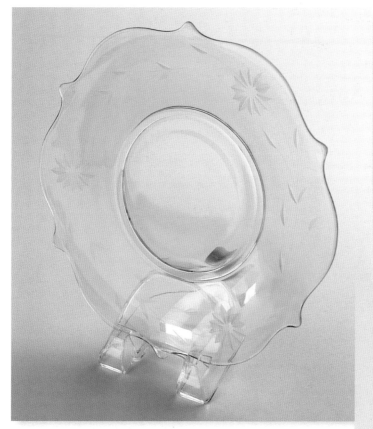

*Jubilee, yellow luncheon plate, **$16.50**.*

*Jubilee, yellow goblet, **$75**.*

*Jubilee, yellow saucer, **$6**; cup, **$17.50**.*

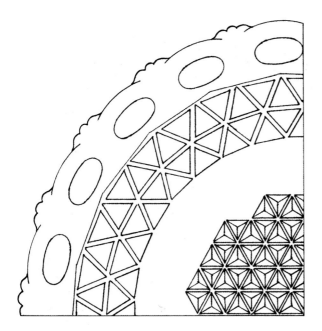

LACED EDGE

Katy Blue

Manufactured by Imperial Glass Company, Bellaire, Ohio, early 1930s.

Pieces are made in blue and green and have opalescent edges.

*Laced Edge, blue bowl, 5-1/2" d, **$42**.*

Item	Blue	Green
Basket, 9" d	265.00	—
Bowl, 5" d	40.00	40.00
Bowl, 5-1/2" d	42.00	42.00
Bowl, 5-7/8" d	42.00	42.00
Bowl, 10-1/2" d	60.00	60.00
Bowl, 11" l, oval	295.00	285.00
Bowl, 11" l, oval, divided	165.00	165.00
Candlesticks, pr, double lite	175.00	180.00
Creamer	45.00	40.00
Cup	35.00	35.00
Fruit bowl, 4-1/2" d	32.00	30.00
Mayonnaise, three pieces	100.00	125.00
Plate, 6-1/2" d, bread and butter	24.00	24.00
Plate, 8" d, salad	35.00	35.00
Plate, 10" d, dinner	95.00	95.00
Plate, 12" d, luncheon	90.00	90.00
Platter, 13" l	185.00	165.00
Saucer	18.00	15.00
Soup bowl, 7" d	85.00	80.00
Sugar	45.00	40.00
Tidbit, two tiers, 8" and 10" plates	110.00	100.00
Tumbler, 9 oz	60.00	60.00
Tumbler, 10 oz	62.50	—
Vase, 4-1/2" h	45.00	—
Vase, 5-1/2" h	45.00	—
Vegetable bowl, 9" d	110.00	95.00

LAKE COMO

Manufactured by Hocking Glass Company, Lancaster, Ohio, from 1934 to 1937.

Pieces are made in opaque white with a blue scene.

Item	White
Cereal bowl, 6" d	30.00
Creamer, ftd	35.00
Cup, regular	35.00
Cup, St. Denis	35.00
Plate, 7-1/4" d, salad	24.00
Plate, 9-1/4" d, dinner	35.00
Platter, 11" d	75.00

Item	White
Salt and pepper shakers, pr	50.00
Saucer	12.00
Saucer, St. Denis	12.00
Soup bowl, flat	100.00
Sugar, ftd	37.50
Vegetable bowl, 9-3/4" l	45.00

Lake Como, blue and white salad plate, $24.

LAUREL

Manufactured by McKee Glass Company, Pittsburgh, Pa., 1930s.

Pieces are made in French Ivory, Jade Green, Poudre Blue, and White Opal.

Item	French Ivory	Jade Green	Poudre Blue	White Opal
Berry bowl, 4-3/4" d	9.00	15.00	16.00	14.00
Berry bowl, 9" d	30.00	65.00	60.00	30.00
Bowl, 6" d, three legs	15.00	25.00	—	15.00
Bowl, 10-1/2" d, three legs	37.50	50.00	68.00	45.00
Bowl, 11" d	40.00	55.00	85.00	37.50
Candlesticks, pr, 4" h	50.00	65.00	—	45.00
Cereal bowl, 6" d	12.00	25.00	28.00	20.00
Cheese dish, cov	60.00	95.00	—	75.00
Creamer, short	12.00	25.00	—	18.00
Creamer, tall	15.00	30.00	40.00	24.00
Cup	9.50	15.00	20.00	12.00
Plate, 6" d, sherbet	6.00	15.00	10.00	8.00
Plate, 7-1/2" d, salad	10.00	20.00	17.50	12.00
Plate, 9-1/8" d, dinner	15.00	25.00	30.00	18.50
Plate, 9-1/8" d, grill, round	15.00	25.00	—	18.50
Plate, 9-1/8" d, grill, scalloped	15.00	25.00	—	18.50
Platter, 10-3/4" l, oval	32.00	80.00	45.00	30.00
Salt and pepper shakers, pr	60.00	85.00	—	65.00
Saucer	3.25	4.50	7.50	3.50
Sherbet	12.50	20.00	—	18.00
Sherbet/champagne, 5"	50.00	72.00	—	60.00
Soup bowl, 7-7/8" d	35.00	40.00	—	40.00
Sugar, short	12.00	25.00	—	18.00
Sugar, tall	15.00	28.00	40.00	24.00
Tumbler, 9 oz, 4-1/2" h, flat	40.00	60.00	—	60.00
Tumbler, 12 oz, 5" h, flat	60.00	—	—	—
Vegetable bowl, 9-3/4" l, oval	18.50	480.00	45.00	20.00

Children's

Item	Plain	Green or Decorated	Scotty Dog Green	Scotty Dog Ivory
Creamer	30.00	100.00	250.00	125.00
Cup	25.00	50.00	100.00	50.00
Plate	15.00	20.00	75.00	40.00
Saucer	12.00	14.00	75.00	40.00
Sugar	30.00	100.00	250.00	125.00

Laurel, jade green dinner plate, $25.

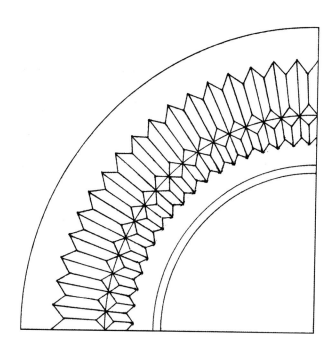

LINCOLN INN

Manufactured by Fenton Art Glass Company, Williamstown, W.V., late 1920s.

Pieces are made in amber, amethyst, black, cobalt blue, crystal, green, green opalescent, light blue, opaque jade, pink, and red. Production in black was limited to salt and pepper shakers, valued at $325. Some rare pieces have been identified in several other colors.

Item	Cobalt Blue	Crystal	Other Colors	Red
Ashtray	17.50	12.00	12.00	17.50
Bonbon, oval, handle	17.50	12.00	14.00	18.00
Bonbon, sq, handle	15.00	12.00	14.00	15.00
Bowl, 6" d, crimped	14.50	7.50	10.00	14.50
Bowl, 9" d, shallow	—	9.00	—	—
Bowl, 9-1/4" d, ftd	42.00	18.00	20.00	45.00
Bowl, 10-1/2" d, ftd	50.00	28.00	30.00	50.00
Candy dish, ftd, oval	24.00	14.50	14.50	24.00
Cereal bowl, 6" d	12.50	7.50	9.50	12.50
Comport	25.00	14.00	15.00	25.00
Creamer	24.00	12.00	15.00	24.00
Cup	17.50	8.50	9.50	18.00
Finger bowl	20.00	14.00	14.50	20.00
Fruit bowl, 5" d	14.00	7.00	9.00	14.00
Goblet, 6" h	30.00	12.50	16.00	30.00
Iced tea tumbler, 12 oz, ftd	50.00	24.00	28.00	40.00
Juice tumbler, 4 oz, flat	35.00	12.00	18.00	30.00
Nut dish, ftd	20.00	14.50	16.00	20.00
Olive bowl, handle	15.00	8.50	12.00	15.00
Pitcher, 46 oz, 7-1/4" h	820.00	700.00	715.00	820.00
Plate, 6" d	19.50	12.00	12.50	19.50
Plate, 8" d	27.50	15.00	14.00	27.50
Plate, 9-1/4" d	30.00	15.00	16.50	30.00
Plate, 12" d	35.00	16.00	18.00	35.00
Salt and pepper shakers, pr	265.00	175.00	175.00	265.00
Sandwich server, center handle	175.00	110.00	110.00	175.00
Saucer	5.00	4.00	4.50	5.00
Sherbet, 4-1/2" h, cone shape	18.00	12.00	14.00	18.00
Sherbet, 4-3/4" h	10.00	14.00	20.00	20.00
Sugar	18.00	12.00	15.00	24.00

Item	Cobalt Blue	Crystal	Other Colors	Red
Tumbler, 5 oz, ftd	24.00	14.00	14.50	24.00
Tumbler, 9 oz, flat	—	14.00	15.00	15.00
Tumbler, 9 oz, ftd	28.00	32.00	35.00	30.00
Vase, 9-3/4" h	160.00	85.00	95.00	145.00
Vase, 12" h, ftd	225.00	115.00	125.00	175.00
Wine	35.00	20.00	24.00	40.00

*Lincoln Inn, cobalt blue goblet, **$30**.*

*Lincoln Inn, pink plate, 8" d, **$14**.*

LORAIN

Basket, No. 615

Manufactured by Indiana Glass Company, Dunkirk, Ind., from 1929 to 1939.

Pieces are made in crystal, green, and yellow.

Reproductions: † A fantasy sherbet has been reported in both milk white and avocado green.

*Lorain, yellow luncheon plate, **$32.50**; tumbler, **$35**.*

Item	Crystal	Green	Yellow
Berry bowl, 8" d	125.00	190.00	250.00
Cereal bowl, 6" d	55.00	65.00	135.00
Creamer, ftd	20.00	20.00	30.00
Cup and saucer	32.00	32.00	25.00
Plate, 5-1/2" d, sherbet	10.00	12.00	15.00
Plate, 7-3/4" d, salad	15.00	18.00	20.00
Plate, 8-3/4" d, luncheon	20.00	24.00	32.50
Plate, 10-1/4" d, dinner	30.00	40.00	90.00
Platter, 11-1/2" l	32.50	32.50	48.00
Relish, 8" d, four parts	20.00	32.00	40.00
Salad bowl, 7-3/4" d	40.00	40.00	75.00
Saucer	6.00	6.00	8.00
Sherbet, ftd †	32.00	20.00	40.00
Snack tray, crystal trim	32.00	37.50	—
Sugar, ftd	20.00	24.00	30.00
Tumbler, 9 oz, 4-3/4" h, ftd	32.00	35.00	35.00
Vegetable bowl, 9-3/4" l, oval	50.00	60.00	65.00

MADRID

Manufactured by Federal Glass Company, Lancaster, Ohio, from 1932 to 1939.

Pieces are made in amber, blue, crystal, green, iridescent, and pink. Iridized pieces are limited to a console set, consisting of a low bowl and pair of candlesticks, valued at $40.

Reproductions: † Reproductions include candlesticks, cups, saucers and a vegetable bowl. Reproductions are found in amber, blue, crystal, and pink. Federal Glass Company reissued this pattern under the name "Recollection." Some of these pieces were dated 1976. When Federal went bankrupt, the molds were sold to Indiana Glass, which removed the date and began production of crystal, then pink. Several pieces were made recently that were not part of the original production and include a footed cake stand, goblet, two-section grill plate, preserves stand, squatty salt and pepper shakers, and 11-ounce tumbler and vase.

Madrid, amber sugar, $20; creamer, $30.

Item	Amber	Blue	Crystal	Green	Pink
Ashtray, 6" sq	300.00	—	—	295.00	—
Berry bowl, small	10.00	—	6.50	—	—
Berry bowl, 9-3/8" d	25.00	—	25.00	—	25.00
Bowl, 7" d	17.50	—	12.00	17.50	—
Butter dish, cov	85.00	—	65.00	90.00	—
Cake plate, 11-1/4" d	24.00	—	20.00	—	20.00
Candlesticks, 2-1/4" h, pr †	18.50	—	14.50	—	28.00
Coaster, 5" d	40.00	—	40.00	35.00	—
Console bowl, 11" d	15.00	—	18.00	—	36.00
Cookie jar	50.00	—	45.00	—	40.00
Creamer	30.00	18.00	7.00	20.00	—
Cream soup, 4 3/4" d	25.00	—	15.50	—	—
Cup †	10.00	20.00	6.50	12.00	8.50
Gelatin mold, 2-1/2" h	25.00	—	20.00	—	—
Gravy boat	1,950.00	—	900.00	—	—
Gravy boat platter	900.00	—	900.00	—	—
Hot dish coaster, 3-1/2" d	195.00	—	40.00	45.00	—
Iced tea tumbler, round	25.00	—	24.00	22.00	—
Jam dish, 7" d	24.00	35.00	12.00	25.00	—

Item	Amber	Blue	Crystal	Green	Pink
Jello, 2" h	18.00	—	—	—	—
Juice pitcher	50.00	—	45.00	—	—
Juice tumbler, 5 oz, 3-7/8" h, ftd	18.00	45.00	40.00	35.00	—
Pitcher, jug-type	60.00	—	24.00	190.00	—
Pitcher, 60 oz, 8" h, sq	55.00	225.00	150.00	145.00	50.00
Pitcher, 80 oz, 8-1/2" h, ice lip	75.00	—	30.00	225.00	—
Plate, 6" d, sherbet	5.50	12.00	4.00	4.50	4.00
Plate, 7-1/2" d, salad	15.00	17.00	12.00	9.00	9.00
Plate, 8-7/8" d, luncheon	10.00	20.00	7.50	12.00	10.00
Plate, 10-1/2" d, dinner	48.00	60.00	24.00	45.00	—
Plate, 10-1/2" d, grill	12.00	—	10.00	18.50	—
Platter, 11-1/2" oval	20.00	32.00	20.00	18.00	18.00
Relish dish, 10-1/2" d	14.50	—	7.00	16.00	20.00
Salad bowl, 8" d	17.00	—	9.50	15.50	—
Salad bowl, 9-1/2" d	32.00	—	30.00	—	—
Salt and pepper shakers, 3-1/2" h	135.00	145.00	95.00	110.00	—
Sauce bowl, 5" d	12.00	—	7.50	8.50	11.00
Saucer †	5.00	8.00	4.00	7.00	5.00
Sherbet, cone	5.50	18.00	6.50	14.00	—
Sherbet, ftd	10.00	15.00	6.00	12.00	—
Soup bowl, 7" d †	20.00	20.00	6.00	15.50	—
Sugar, cov †	65.00	175.00	32.50	80.00	—
Sugar, open †	20.00	15.00	8.00	20.00	—
Tumbler, 9 oz, 4-1/2" h	18.00	40.00	17.50	25.00	22.50
Tumbler, 12 oz, 5-1/4" h, ftd or flat	30.00	—	30.00	45.00	—
Vegetable bowl, 10" l, oval †	30.00	35.00	25.00	25.00	30.00

*Madrid, amber grill plate, **$12**; berry bowl, **$10**; cup, **$10**.*

*Madrid, amber bowl, **$17.50**.*

MANHATTAN
Horizontal Ribbed

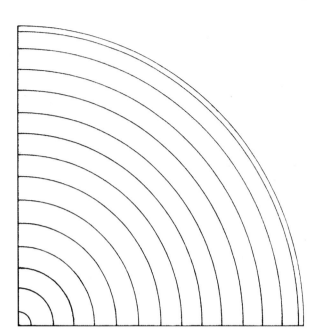

Manufactured by Anchor Hocking Glass Company, from 1938 to 1943.

Pieces are made in crystal, green, iridized, pink, and ruby. Ruby pieces are limited to relish tray inserts, currently valued at $8 each. Green and iridized production was limited to footed tumblers, currently valued at $17.50.

Anchor Hocking introduced a similar pattern, Park Avenue, in 1987. Anchor Hocking was careful to preserve the Manhattan pattern. Collectors should pay careful attention to measurements if they are uncertain of the pattern.

Manhattan, relish tray with ruby inserts and crystal base, **$110**; and crystal comport, **$35**; vase, **$25**; and fruit bowl with open handles, **$40**.

Item	Crystal	Pink
Ashtray, 4" d, round	15.00	10.00
Ashtray, 4-1/2" w, sq	20.00	—
Berry bowl, 5-3/8" d, handles	24.00	25.00
Berry bowl, 7-1/2" d	28.00	—
Bowl, 4-1/2" d	12.50	—
Bowl, 8" d, closed handles	28.00	25.00
Bowl, 8" d, metal handle	35.00	—
Bowl, 9-1/2" d, handle	—	45.00
Candlesticks, pr, 4-1/2" h	20.00	—
Candy dish, three legs	—	18.00

Item	Crystal	Pink
Candy dish, cov	40.00	—
Cereal bowl, 5-1/4" d, no handles	120.00	—
Coaster, 3-1/2"	30.00	—
Cocktail	18.00	—
Comport, 5-3/4" h	35.00	60.00
Creamer, oval	9.00	20.00
Cup	22.00	160.00
Fruit bowl, 9-1/2" d, two open handles	40.00	50.00
Juice pitcher, 24 oz	55.00	—
Pitcher, 80 oz, tilted	55.00	85.00
Plate, 6" d, sherbet	12.00	50.00
Plate, 8-1/2" d, salad	20.00	—
Plate, 10-1/4" d, dinner	25.00	120.00
Relish tray insert	2.50	10.00
Relish tray, 14" d, inserts	110.00	50.00
Relish tray, 14" d, four parts	85.00	—
Salad bowl, 9" d	20.00	—
Salt and pepper shakers, pr, 2" h, sq	30.00	60.00
Sandwich plate, 14" d	22.00	—
Sauce bowl, 4-1/2" d, handles	10.00	—
Saucer	7.00	50.00
Sherbet	12.50	20.00
Sugar, oval	15.00	17.50
Tumbler, 10 oz, 5-1/4" h, ftd	20.00	27.50
Vase, 8" h	25.00	—
Wine, 3-1/2" h	8.00	—

*Manhattan, small crystal bowl (on pedestal), **$9**; pink creamer, **$20**, and sugar, **$17.50**; crystal salt and pepper shakers, **$30**; crystal iced tea tumbler, **$20**; crystal pitcher, **$55**; relish with metal stand, **$30**; and pink footed candy dish, **$18**.*

MAYFAIR

Federal

Manufactured by Federal Glass Company, Columbus, Ohio, 1934.

Pieces are made in amber, crystal, and green.

*Mayfair Federal, amber dinner plate, **$16.50**.*

Item	Amber	Crystal	Green
Cereal bowl, 6" d	18.50	15.00	22.00
Cream soup, 5" d	22.00	12.00	20.00
Creamer, ftd	17.50	14.00	16.00
Cup	8.50	5.00	8.50
Plate, 6-3/4" d, salad	7.00	4.50	8.50
Plate, 9-1/2" d, dinner	16.50	12.00	14.50
Plate, 9-1/2" d, grill	17.50	15.00	17.50
Platter, 12" l, oval	27.50	22.00	30.00
Sauce bowl, 5" d	8.50	7.00	12.00
Saucer	4.50	2.50	4.50
Sugar, ftd	12.00	10.00	12.00
Tumbler, 9 oz, 4-1/2" h	27.50	16.50	32.00
Vegetable, 10" l, oval	32.00	32.00	32.00

MAYFAIR

Open Rose

Manufactured by Hocking Glass Company, Lancaster, Ohio, from 1931 to 1937.

Pieces are made in crystal, green, ice blue, pink, and yellow.

Reproductions: † This pattern has been plagued with reproductions since 1977. Items reproduced include cookie jars, salt and pepper shakers, juice pitchers, and whiskey glasses. Reproductions are found in amethyst, blue, cobalt blue, green, pink, and red.

*Mayfair Open Rose, pink tumbler, 11 oz, **$225**; pink satin-finish covered cookie jar, **$37**.*

Item	Crystal	Green	Ice Blue	Pink	Pink Satin	Yellow
Bowl, 11-3/4" l, flat..	—	35.00	75.00	85.00	70.00	195.00
Butter dish, cov..	—	1,295.00	350.00	80.00	95.00	1,295.00
Cake plate, 10" d, ftd..	—	115.00	90.00	40.00	45.00	—
Cake plate, 12" d, handles...	—	40.00	95.00	50.00	50.00	—
Candy dish, cov..	—	575.00	325.00	70.00	85.00	475.00
Celery dish, 9" l, divided..	—	155.00	75.00	—	—	150.00
Celery dish, 10" l, divided..	—	—	90.00	295.00	—	—
Celery dish, 10" l, not divided......................................	—	115.00	80.00	65.00	50.00	115.00
Cereal bowl, 5-1/2" d...	—	24.00	48.00	35.00	35.00	75.00
Claret, 4-1/2 oz, 5-1/4" h...	—	950.00	—	1,150.00	—	—
Cocktail, 3 oz, 4" h..	—	975.00	—	130.00	—	—
Console bowl, 9" d, 3-1/8" h, three legs	—	5,000.00	—	5,000.00	—	—
Cookie jar, cov †...	—	575.00	295.00	75.00	37.00	860.00
Cordial, 1 oz, 3-3/4" h..	—	950.00	—	1,100.00	—	—
Cream soup, 5" d..	—	—	—	65.00	68.00	—
Creamer, ftd..	—			40.00	30.00	
Cup...	—	150.00	55.00	20.00	27.50	150.00
Decanter, stopper, 32 oz...	—	—	—	275.00	—	—
Fruit bowl, 12" d, scalloped...	—	50.00	125.00	95.00	75.00	215.00
Goblet, 2-1/2 oz, 4-1/8"...	—	950.00	—	950.00	—	—
Goblet, 9 oz, 5-3/4" h..	—	465.00	—	80.00	—	—
Goblet, 9 oz, 7-1/4" h, thin...	—	—	225.00	475.00	—	—
Iced tea tumbler, 13-1/2 oz, 5-1/4" h............................	—	—	225.00	80.00	—	—
Iced tea tumbler, 15 oz, 6-1/2" h, ftd...........................	—	250.00	285.00	45.00	65.00	—
Juice pitcher, 37 oz, 6" h †...	24.50	525.00	150.00	85.00	65.00	525.00
Juice tumbler, 3 oz, 3-1/4" h, ftd..................................	—	—	—	80.00	—	—
Juice tumbler, 5 oz, 3-1/2"..	—	—	225.00	85.00	—	—
Pitcher, 60 oz, 8" h..	—	475.00	195.00	85.00	100.00	425.00
Pitcher, 80 oz, 8-1/2" h...	—	725.00	225.00	135.00	135.00	725.00
Plate, 5-3/4" d..	—	90.00	25.00	20.00	15.00	90.00
Plate, 6-1/2" d, off-center indent...................................	—	115.00	44.00	30.00	35.00	—
Plate, 6-1/2" d, sherbet..	—	—	24.00	20.00	—	—
Plate, 8-1/2" d, luncheon..	—	85.00	70.00	35.00	35.00	80.00
Plate, 9-1/2" d, dinner...	—	150.00	100.00	70.00	65.00	150.00
Plate, 9-1/2" d, grill...	—	75.00	70.00	50.00	35.00	80.00
Plate, 11-1/2" d, grill, handles.......................................	—	—	—	—	—	100.00
Platter, 12" l, oval, open handles...................................	17.50	175.00	60.00	35.00	35.00	115.00

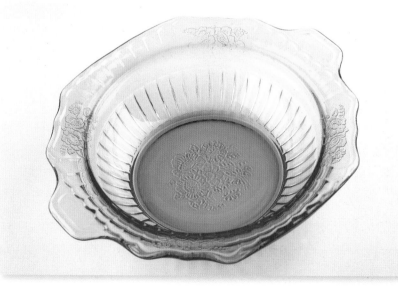

Mayfair Open Rose, blue handled vegetable bowl, $60.

Item	Crystal	Green	Ice Blue	Pink	Pink Satin	Yellow
Platter, 12-1/2" oval, 8" wide, closed handles	—	245.00	—	—	—	245.00
Relish, 8-3/8" d, four parts	—	160.00	65.00	37.50	37.50	160.00
Relish, 8-3/8" d, non-partitioned	—	275.00	—	200.00	—	275.00
Salt and pepper shakers, pr, flat †	20.00	1,000.00	175.00	65.00	70.00	800.00
Sandwich server, center handle	—	40.00	85.00	50.00	50.00	130.00
Saucer	—	90.00	30.00	45.00	35.00	140.00
Sherbet, 2-1/4" flat	—	—	135.00	185.00	—	—
Sherbet, 3" ftd	—	—	—	20.00	—	—
Sherbet, 4-3/4" ftd	—	150.00	75.00	185.00	75.00	150.00
Sugar, ftd	—	195.00	85.00	38.00	40.00	185.00
Sweet pea vase	—	285.00	150.00	250.00	145.00	—
Tumbler, 9 oz, 4-1/4" h	—	—	100.00	30.00	—	—
Tumbler, 10 oz, 5-1/4" h	—	—	145.00	65.00	—	185.00
Tumbler, 11 oz, 4-3/4" h	—	200.00	250.00	225.00	225.00	215.00
Vase	—	—	175.00	295.00	—	—
Vegetable bowl, 7" d, two handles	—	33.00	75.00	60.00	70.00	195.00
Vegetable bowl, 9-1/2" l, oval	—	110.00	70.00	45.00	30.00	125.00
Vegetable bowl, 10" d cov	—	—	120.00	150.00	120.00	900.00
Vegetable bowl, 10" d open	—	—	85.00	48.50	20.00	200.00
Whiskey, 1-1/2 oz, 2-1/4" h †	—	—	—	58.00	—	—
Wine, 3 oz, 4-1/2" h	—	450.00	—	120.00	—	—

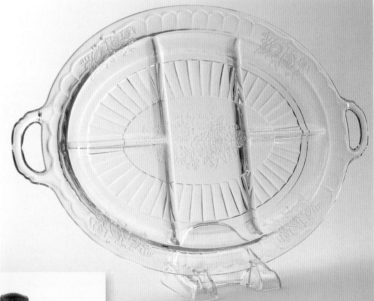

*Mayfair Open Rose, crystal platter, open handles, **$17.50**.*

REPRODUCTION! Mayfair Open Rose, green and blue cookie jars.

MELBA
Line #707

Manufactured by L.E. Smith Glass Company, Mount Pleasant, Pa., in the early 1930s.

Pieces are made in amethyst, black, green, and pink.

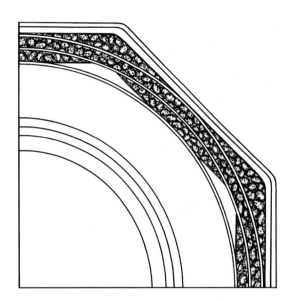

Melba, amethyst luncheon plate, $9.

Items	Amethyst	Black	Green	Pink
Baker, oval	20.00	22.00	18.00	18.00
Bowl, 10-1/2" d, ruffled	18.00	20.00	15.00	15.00
Candleholder	15.00	17.00	12.00	12.00
Creamer	15.00	18.00	12.00	12.00
Cup	6.50	8.50	5.00	5.00
Dessert bowl	4.50	5.00	3.50	3.50
Plate, 6" d, bread and butter	5.00	7.50	4.00	4.00
Plate, 7" d, salad	7.00	9.50	6.00	6.00
Plate, 9" d, luncheon	9.00	12.00	8.00	8.00
Platter	15.00	18.00	12.00	12.00
Salad bowl	18.00	20.00	15.00	15.00
Saucer	3.50	4.50	3.00	3.00
Serving plate, 9" d, handles	15.00	18.00	12.00	12.00
Sugar	15.00	18.00	12.00	12.00
Vegetable bowl, 9-1/2" l	18.00	20.00	15.00	15.00

MISS AMERICA
Diamond Pattern

Manufactured by Hocking Glass Company, Lancaster, Ohio, from 1935 to 1938.

Pieces are made in crystal, green, ice blue, jade-ite, pink, and royal ruby.

Reproductions: † Reproductions include the butter dish (including a new importer), creamer, 8-inch pitcher, salt and pepper shakers, sugar, and tumbler. Reproductions are found in amberina, blue, cobalt blue, crystal, green, pink, and red.

Item	Crystal	Green	Ice Blue	Pink	Royal Ruby
Berry bowl, 4-1/2" d	—	25.00	—	—	—
Bowl, 8" d, curved at top	48.00	—	—	95.00	—
Bowl, 8" d, straight sides	—	—	—	110.00	—
Bowl, 11" d, shallow	—	—	—	—	850.00
Butter dish, cov †	300.00	—	—	575.00	—
Cake plate, 12" d, ftd	40.00	—	—	45.00	—
Candy jar, cov, 11-1/2"	125.00	—	—	200.00	—
Celery dish, 10-1/2" l, oval	19.50	—	160.00	45.00	—
Cereal bowl, 6-1/4" d	15.00	18.00	—	35.00	—
Coaster, 5-3/4" d	19.50	—	—	45.00	—
Comport, 5" d	18.00	—	—	50.00	—
Creamer, ftd †	12.50	—	—	24.00	215.00
Cup	11.00	20.00	14.00	30.00	235.00
Fruit bowl, 8-3/4" d	40.00	—	—	60.00	450.00
Goblet, 10 oz, 5-1/2" h	30.00	—	—	75.00	250.00
Iced tea tumbler, 14 oz, 5-3/4" h	25.00	—	—	85.00	—
Juice goblet, 5 oz, 4-3/4" h	35.00	—	—	115.00	250.00
Juice tumbler, 5 oz, 4" h	27.50	—	150.00	60.00	200.00
Pitcher, 65 oz, 8" h †	45.00	—	—	175.00	—
Pitcher, 65 oz, 8-1/2" h, ice lip	75.00	—	—	295.00	50.00
Plate, 5-3/4" d, sherbet	10.00	9.00	55.00	16.00	—
Plate, 6-3/4" d	—	12.00	—	—	—
Plate, 8-1/2" d, salad	15.00	14.00	—	60.00	150.00
Plate, 10-1/4" d, dinner	25.00	—	150.00	45.00	—
Plate, 10-1/4" d, grill	12.00	—	—	50.00	—
Platter, 12-1/4" l, oval	18.00	—	—	95.00	—
Relish, 8-3/4" l, 4 part	30.00	—	—	30.00	—
Relish, 11-3/4" d, divided	50.00	—	—	40.00	—
Salt and pepper shakers, pr †	40.00	300.00	—	95.00	—

Item	Crystal	Green	Ice Blue	Pink	Royal Ruby
Saucer	4.00	—	—	10.00	60.00
Sherbet	12.50	—	60.00	35.00	175.00
Sugar †	12.00	—	—	40.00	225.00
Tumbler, 10 oz, 4-1/2" h, flat †	25.00	35.00	—	80.00	—
Tumbler, 14 oz, 5-3/4" h	28.00	—	—	—	—
Vegetable bowl, 10" l, oval	20.00	—	—	70.00	—
Whiskey	24.00	—	—	—	—
Wine, 3 oz, 3-3/4" h	25.00	—	—	85.00	250.00

Miss America, green salad plate, **$14**; *berry bowl,* **$25**.

Miss America, pink goblet, **$75**; *comport,* **$50**; *and 10-oz tumbler with original label,* **$80**.

Close-up view of original Miss America label on the pink tumbler.

MODERNTONE

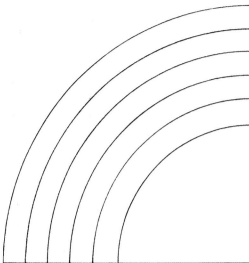

Manufactured by Hazel Atlas Glass Company, Clarksburg, W.V., and Zanesville, Ohio, from 1934 to 1942; also, in the late 1940s to early 1950s.

Pieces are made in amethyst, cobalt blue, crystal, pink, and Platonite fired-on colors. Later period production saw plain white, as well as white with blue or red stripes, a Willow-type design in blue or red on white. Collector interest in crystal is limited and prices remain low, less than 50 percent of Platonite.

*Moderntone, cobalt blue dinner plate, **$20**; salad plate, **$12.50**; sherbet (on pedestal), **$15**; cup, **$18**, and saucer, **$5**; cream soup, **$25**.*

Item	Amethyst	Cobalt Blue	Platonite, Darker Shades	Platonite, Pastel Shades	White or White with Dec	Willow-Type Dec
Ashtray, 7-3/4" d, match holder center	—	185.00	—	—	—	—
Berry bowl, 5" d, rim	25.00	35.00	—	7.00	5.00	15.00
Berry bowl, 5" d, without rim	—	—	12.50	25.00	—	—
Berry bowl, 8-3/4" d	42.00	50.00	—	—	7.50	28.00
Bowl, 8" d, no rim	—	—	40.00	50.00	—	—
Bowl, 8" d, rim	—	—	—	15.00	6.00	28.00
Butter dish, metal cov	—	95.00	—	—	—	—
Cereal bowl, 5" d, deep, no white	—	—	17.50	10.00	—	—
Cereal bowl, 5" deep, with white	—	—	—	9.00	4.50	—
Cereal bowl, 6-1/2" d	70.00	70.00	—	—	—	—
Cheese dish, 7" d, metal cov	—	475.00	—	—	—	—
Cream soup, 4-3/4" d	25.00	25.00	—	12.00	9.00	25.00
Cream soup, 5" d, ruffled	25.00	85.00	—	—	—	—
Creamer	18.00	13.50	12.00	5.50	4.50	20.00
Cup	12.00	18.00	10.00	6.00	2.50	22.00
Custard cup	18.00	20.00	—	—	—	—
Mug, 4" h, 8 oz	—	—	—	—	8.50	—
Mustard, metal lid	—	25.00	—	—	—	—
Plate, 5-7/8" d, sherbet	5.50	10.00	—	—	—	—
Plate, 6-3/4" d, salad	12.50	12.50	12.00	10.00	6.00	10.00

Item	Amethyst	Cobalt Blue Shades	Platonite, Darker Shades	Platonite, Pastel with Dec	White or White Dec	Willow-Type Dec
Plate, 7-3/4" d, luncheon	10.00	18.00	—	—	—	—
Plate, 8-7/8" d, dinner	12.00	20.00	20.00	12.00	4.00	20.00
Platter, 11" l, oval	40.00	55.00	—	—	14.00	30.00
Platter, 12" l, oval	48.00	165.00	32.00	15.00	10.00	35.00
Salt and pepper shakers, pr	45.00	50.00	—	10.00	12.00	—
Sandwich plate, 10-1/2" d	35.00	75.00	—	20.00	12.50	—
Saucer	4.50	5.00	7.50	3.50	3.50	4.50
Sherbet	13.00	15.00	12.00	8.00	4.50	14.00
Soup bowl, 7-1/2" d	95.00	195.00	—	—	—	—
Sugar	18.00	15.00	12.00	6.00	4.50	20.00
Tumbler, 5 oz	40.00	55.00	—	—	—	—
Tumbler, 9 oz	30.00	40.00	45.00	12.00	—	—
Tumbler, 12 oz	85.00	95.00	—	—	—	—
Tumbler, cone, ftd	—	—	—	—	4.00	—
Whiskey, 1-1/2 oz	—	45.00	—	18.50	—	—

Children's

Hazel Atlas also manufactured children's sets in the early 1950s, known as Little Hostess Party Dishes. The original box adds to the value. Colorful combinations were found.

Item	Gray/ Rust/ Gold	Green/ Gray/ Chartreuse	Lemon/ Beige/ Pink/Aqua	Pastel Pink/ Green/Blue/ Yellow	Pink/ Black/ White
Creamer, 1-3/4"	12.50	16.00	15.00	15.00	15.00
Cup, 3/4"	15.00	12.00	12.00	13.50	15.00
Plate, 5-1/4" d	15.00	10.00	12.00	10.00	12.00
Saucer, 3-7/8" d	8.00	7.00	12.50	7.00	7.00
Sugar, 1-3/4"	12.00	15.00	20.00	15.00	18.00
Teapot, 3-1/2" d	125.00	115.00	95.00	—	95.00

*Moderntone, darker shades of Platonite saucers, **$7.50** each. Photo courtesy of Tina Trautman.*

MONTICELLO

Waffle, #698

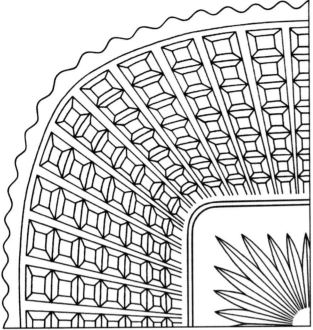

Manufactured by Imperial Glass Company, c1920 to 1950s.

Pieces are made in crystal, Rubigold (Imperial's trademarked name for marigold carnival glass), teal, and white milk glass. Some other colors are known in very limited production runs, such as a basket in Rose Marie. Collector interest is highest for crystal.

Item	Crystal
Cake plate, 12" d	35.00
Celery tray, 9" l	20.00
Cheese dish, cov	75.00
Coaster, 3-1/4" d	7.50
Cocktail	15.00
Compote, 5-1/4" d	12.50
Compote, 5-3/4" d, belled rim	15.00
Cream soup bowl, 5-1/2" d	12.50
Creamer	18.00
Cup	10.00
Finger bowl, 4-1/2" d	10.00
Fruit bowl, 4-1/2" d or 5" d	10.00
Goblet	15.00
Iced tea tumbler, 12 oz	15.00
Lily bowl, 5" d	20.00
Lily bowl, 6" d	25.00
Lily bowl, 7" d	30.00
Lily bowl, 8" d, cupped	35.00
Mayonnaise, three pcs	32.50
Nappy, 7" d	15.00
Pickle dish, 6" l, oval	15.00
Pitcher, 52 oz, ice lip	60.00
Plate, 6" d, bread and butter	5.00
Plate, 8" d, salad	8.00
Plate, 9" d, dinner	18.00
Plate, 10-1/2" w, sq	25.00
Punch bowl	65.00
Punch cup	8.50
Relish, 8-1/4" l, divided	18.00
Salad bowl, 7-1/2" sq	30.00
Salt and pepper shakers, pr, glass tops	24.00
Saucer	4.50
Serving plate, 16" d, cupped	50.00
Sherbet	13.00
Sugar	18.00
Tidbit, two tiers	45.00
Tumbler, 9 oz	12.00
Vase, 6" h	25.00
Vase, 10-1/2" h	35.00
Vegetable bowl, 8" d	25.00

*Monticello, crystal compote, stemmed, **$15**.*

Item	Crystal
Basket, 10" h	25.00
Bonbon, 5-1/2" d, handle	15.00
Bowl, 6" d	10.00
Bowl, 6-1/2" d or 7-1/2" d, belled	15.00
Bowl, 8-1/2" d or 10" d, belled	18.00
Bowl, 9" d	18.00
Bowl, 10" d	20.00
Butter tub, 5-1/2" d	35.00

MOONDROPS

Manufactured by New Martinsville Glass Company, New Martinsville, W.V., from 1932 to 1940.

Pieces are made in amber, amethyst, black, cobalt blue, crystal, dark green, green, ice blue, jade-ite, light green, pink, red, and smoke.

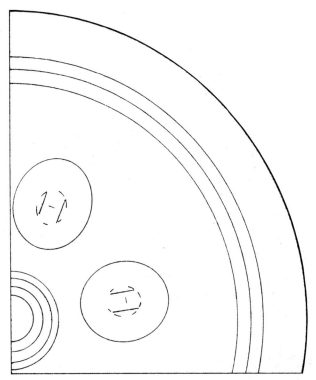

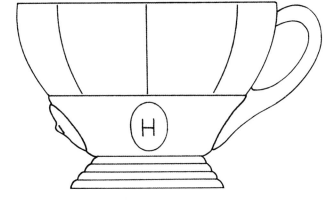

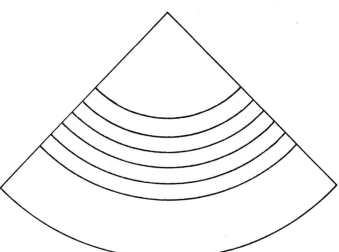

Item	Cobalt Blue	Crystal	Other Colors	Red
Ashtray	30.00	—	18.00	35.00
Berry bowl, 5-1/4" d	20.00	—	12.00	20.00
Bowl, 8-1/2" d, ftd, concave top	40.00	—	25.00	40.00
Bowl, 9-1/2" d, three legs, ruffled	60.00	—	—	60.00
Bowl, 9-3/4" l, oval, handles	50.00	—	30.00	50.00
Butter dish, cov	425.00	—	275.00	295.00
Candlesticks, pr, 2" h, ruffled	40.00	—	25.00	40.00
Candlesticks, pr, 4" h, sherbet style	30.00	—	18.00	30.00
Candlesticks, pr, 5" h, ruffled	32.00	—	22.00	32.00
Candlesticks, pr, 5" h, wings	90.00	—	60.00	90.00

Item	Cobalt Blue	Crystal	Other Colors	Red
Candlesticks, pr, 5-1/4" h, triple light	100.00	65.00	65.00	100.00
Candlesticks, pr, 8-1/2" h, metal stem	40.00	—	32.00	40.00
Candy dish, 8" d, ruffled	40.00	—	20.00	40.00
Casserole, cov, 9-3/4" d	185.00	—	100.00	185.00
Celery bowl, 11" l, boat-shape	30.00	—	24.00	30.00
Cocktail shaker, metal top	60.00	—	35.00	60.00
Comport, 4" d	25.00	—	15.00	25.00
Comport, 11-1/2" d	60.00	—	30.00	60.00
Console bowl, 12" d, round, three ftd	—	—	40.00	—
Console bowl, 13" d, wings	—	—	80.00	120.00
Cordial, 3/4 oz, 2-7/8" h	55.00	—	25.00	48.00
Cream soup, 4-1/4" d	90.00	—	35.00	90.00
Creamer, 2-3/4" h	15.00	—	10.00	25.00
Creamer, 3-3/4" h	12.00	—	12.00	16.00
Cup	16.00	8.00	10.00	16.00
Decanter, 7-3/4" h	70.00	—	40.00	70.00
Decanter, 8-1/2" h	72.00	—	45.00	72.00
Decanter, 10-1/4" h, rocket-shape	425.00	—	375.00	425.00
Decanter, 11-1/4" h	100.00	—	50.00	110.00
Goblet, 5 oz, 4-3/4" h	25.00	—	15.00	22.00
Goblet, 8 oz, 5-3/4" h	35.00	—	20.00	33.00
Goblet, 9 oz, 6-1/4" h, metal stem	15.00	—	17.50	15.00
Gravy boat	120.00	—	90.00	125.00
Juice tumbler, 3 oz, 3-1/4" h, ftd	15.00	—	10.00	18.00
Mayonnaise, 5-1/4" h	32.50	—	30.00	32.50
Mug, 12 oz, 5-1/8" h	40.00	—	24.00	42.00
Perfume bottle, rocket-shape	200.00	—	150.00	210.00
Pickle, 7-1/2" d	25.00	—	15.00	25.00
Pitcher, 22 oz, 6-7/8" h	175.00	—	90.00	175.00
Pitcher, 32 oz, 8-1/8" h	195.00	—	110.00	195.00
Pitcher, 50 oz, 8" h, lip	200.00	—	115.00	200.00
Pitcher, 53 oz, 8-1/8" h	195.00	—	120.00	195.00
Plate, 5-7/8" d	12.00	—	7.50	12.00

*Moondrops, red sugar, **$20**; creamer, **$16**.*

Item	Cobalt Blue	Crystal	Other Colors	Red
Plate, 6" d, round, off center indent	12.50	—	10.00	12.50
Plate, 6-1/8" d, sherbet	8.00	—	6.00	8.00
Plate, 7-1/8" d, salad	12.00	—	10.00	12.00
Plate, 8-1/2" d, luncheon	20.00	—	12.00	15.00
Plate, 9-1/2" d, dinner	25.00	—	15.00	25.00
Platter, 12" l, oval	35.00	—	20.00	35.00
Powder jar, three ftd	175.00	—	100.00	185.00
Relish, 8-1/2" d, 3 ftd, divided	30.00	—	20.00	30.00
Sandwich plate, 14" d	40.00	—	20.00	40.00
Sandwich plate, 14" d, with handles	44.00	—	24.00	45.00
Saucer	6.00	2.00	4.00	8.50
Sherbet, 2-5/8" h	15.00	10.00	11.00	20.00
Sherbet, 3-1/2" h	35.00	—	15.00	25.00
Shot glass, 2 oz, 2-3/4" h	17.50	—	12.00	24.50
Shot glass, 2 oz, 2-3/4" h, handle	17.50	—	12.00	17.50
Soup bowl, 6-3/4" d	80.00	—	—	80.00
Sugar, 2-3/4" h	12.00	—	12.00	20.00
Tray, 7-1/2" l	15.00	—	20.00	16.00
Tumbler, 5 oz, 3-5/8" h	15.00	—	10.00	15.00
Tumbler, 7 oz, 4-3/8" h	17.50	—	10.00	18.00
Tumbler, 8 oz, 4-3/8" h	17.50	—	12.00	22.00
Tumbler, 9 oz, 4-7/8" h, handle	30.00	—	15.00	28.00
Tumbler, 9 oz, 4-7/8" h	20.00	—	15.00	22.00
Tumbler, 12 oz, 5-1/8" h	30.00	—	15.00	35.00
Vase, 7-1/4" h, flat, ruffled	60.00	—	60.00	60.00
Vase, 8-1/2" h, bud, rocket-shape	245.00	—	185.00	245.00
Vase, 9-1/4" h, rocket-shape	240.00	—	125.00	240.00
Vegetable bowl, 9-3/4" l, oval	48.00	—	24.00	48.00
Wine, 3 oz, 5-1/2" h, metal stem	17.50	—	12.00	16.00
Wine, 4-3/4" h, rocket-shape	27.50	—	30.00	85.00
Wine, 4 oz, 4" h	24.00	—	12.00	27.50
Wine, 4 oz, 5-1/2" h, metal stem	20.00	—	12.00	20.00

*Moondrops, pink saucer, **$4**; cup, **$10**.*

MOONSTONE

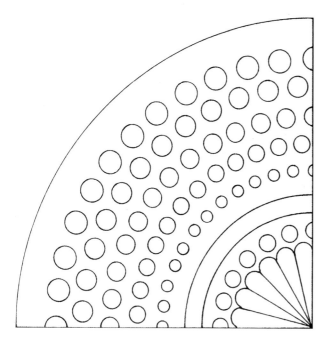

Manufactured by Anchor Hocking Glass Company, Lancaster, Ohio, from 1941 to 1946.

Pieces are made in crystal with opalescent hobnails and Ocean Green with opalescent hobnails.

Moonstone, crystal luncheon plate, with opalescent hobnails, $17.50.

Moonstone, crystal sandwich plate, 10-3/4", $45. Photo courtesy of James Hintz.

Item	Crystal	Ocean Green
Berry bowl, 5-1/2" d	25.00	—
Bonbon, heart shape, handle	15.00	—
Bowl, 5-1/2" d, ruffled	10.00	—
Bowl, 6-1/2" d, crimped, handle	20.00	—
Bowl, 9-1/2" d, crimped	25.00	—
Bud vase, 5-1/2" h	18.00	—
Candleholder, pr	20.00	—
Candy jar, cov, 6" h	30.00	—
Cigarette box, cov	25.00	—
Creamer	10.00	9.50
Cup	8.00	10.00
Dessert bowl, 5-1/2" d, crimped	12.50	—
Goblet, 10 oz	20.00	24.00
Plate, 6-1/4" d, sherbet	7.00	9.00
Plate, 8-3/8" d, luncheon	17.50	17.50
Puff box, cov, 4-3/4" d, round	25.00	—
Relish, 7-3/4" d, divided	12.00	—
Relish, cloverleaf	14.00	—
Sandwich plate, 10-3/4" d	45.00	—
Saucer	6.00	6.00
Sherbet, ftd	7.50	7.00
Sugar, ftd	10.00	12.50
Vase, 5-1/2" h	24.00	—

Moonstone, crystal goblet, **$20**; cup and saucer, **$14**; luncheon plate, 8-1/4", **$17.50**. Photos on this page are courtesy of James Hintz.

Moonstone, crystal sugar, **$10**; and creamer, **$10**.

Moonstone, crystal puff box, covered, 4-3/4", **$25**; cigarette box, covered, **$25**.

Moonstone, crystal bud vase, 5-1/2", **$18**; candleholders, pair, **$20**.

MOROCCAN AMETHYST

Manufactured by Hazel Ware, division of Continental Can, 1960s.

Pieces are made in amethyst.

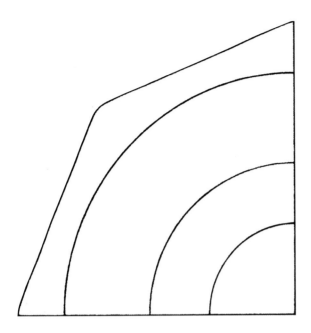

*Moroccan Amethyst, cup, **$7.50**; saucer, **$3**.*

Item	Amethyst
Ashtray, 3-1/4" d, round	5.75
Ashtray, 3-1/4" w, triangular	5.75
Ashtray, 5-3/8" w, triangular	15.00
Ashtray, 6-7/8" w, triangular	12.50
Ashtray, 8" w, square	14.00
Bowl, 5-3/4" w, deep, square	12.00
Bowl, 6" d, round	12.50
Bowl, 7-3/4" l, oval	168.00
Bowl, 7-3/4" l, rectangular	15.00
Bowl, 7-3/4" l, rectangular, metal handle	17.50
Bowl, 9-1/2" x 4-1/4", rectangular	18.00
Bowl, 10-3/4" d	30.00
Candy, cov, short	35.00
Candy, cov, tall	32.00
Chip and dip, 10-3/4" and 5-3/4" bowls in metal frame	40.00
Cocktail shaker, chrome lid	30.00
Cocktail, stirrer, 16 oz, 6-1/4" h, lip	30.00
Cup	7.50
Fruit bowl, 4-3/4" d, octagonal	9.00
Goblet, 9 oz, 5-1/2" h	12.50
Ice bucket, 6" h	50.00
Iced tea tumbler, 16 oz, 6-1/2" h	18.50

Item	Amethyst
Juice goblet, 5-1/2 oz, 4-3/8" h	12.00
Juice tumbler, 4 oz, 2-1/2" h	12.00
Old fashioned tumbler, 8 oz, 3-1/4" h	12.50
Plate, 5-3/4" d, sherbet	4.50
Plate, 7-1/4" d, salad	7.00
Plate, 9-3/4" d, dinner	9.00
Punch bowl	85.00
Punch cup	6.00
Relish, 7-3/4" l	14.00
Salad fork and spoon	12.00
Sandwich plate, 12" d, metal handle	15.00
Saucer	3.00
Sherbet, 7-1/2 oz, 4-1/4" h	7.50
Snack plate, 10" l, fan shaped, cup rest	8.00
Snack set, square plate, cup	12.00
Tidbit, three tiers	75.00
Tumbler, 9 oz	10.00
Tumbler, 11 oz, 4-1/4" h, crinkled bottom	12.00
Tumbler, 11 oz, 4-5/8" h	12.00
Vase, 8-1/2" h, ruffled	40.00
Wine, 4-1/2 oz, 4" h	10.00

MT. PLEASANT

Manufactured by L.E. Smith, Mt. Pleasant, Pa., from the 1920s to 1934.

Pieces are made in amethyst, black, cobalt blue, crystal, green, pink, and white.

*Mt. Pleasant, black scalloped fruit bowl, **$40**.*

Item	Amethyst	Black	Cobalt Blue	Green	Pink
Bonbon, 7" d, rolled edge	24.00	24.50	24.00	16.00	16.00
Bowl, 6" d, three legs	—	25.00	—	—	—
Bowl, 6" w, sq, two handles	27.50	18.00	24.00	15.00	15.00
Bowl, 7" d, three ftd, rolled out edge	18.50	24.50	18.50	17.50	17.50
Bowl, 8" d, scalloped, two handles	37.50	35.00	37.50	20.00	20.00
Bowl, 8" d, sq, two handles	38.00	40.00	38.00	20.00	20.00
Bowl, 9" d, scalloped, 1-3/4" deep, ftd	28.00	32.00	30.00	—	—
Bowl, 10" d, two handles, turned-up edge	30.00	34.00	32.00	—	—
Cake plate, 10-1/2" d, 1-1/4" h, ftd	45.00	47.00	40.00	—	—
Cake plate, 10-1/2" d, two handles	26.00	40.00	28.00	17.50	17.50
Candlesticks, pr, single lite	28.00	42.50	30.00	24.00	28.00
Candlesticks, pr, two lite	50.00	50.00	60.00	30.00	32.00
Creamer	21.00	20.00	22.50	20.00	24.00
Cup	15.00	15.00	14.00	12.50	12.50
Fruit bowl, 4-7/8" sq	16.00	20.00	18.00	12.00	12.50
Fruit bowl, 9-1/4" sq	30.00	50.00	35.00	20.00	20.00
Fruit bowl, 10" d, scalloped	40.00	40.00	40.00	—	—
Leaf, 8" l	12.50	17.50	16.00	—	—
Leaf, 11-1/4" l	25.00	30.00	28.00	—	—
Mayonnaise, 5-1/2" h, three ftd	25.00	30.00	35.00	17.50	17.50
Mint, 6" d, center handle	25.00	27.50	30.00	16.00	16.00
Plate, 7" h, two handles, scalloped	15.00	16.00	18.00	12.50	12.50
Plate, 8" d, scalloped	16.00	15.00	16.00	12.50	12.50

Item	Amethyst	Black	Cobalt Blue	Green	Pink
Plate, 8" d, scalloped, three ftd	17.50	27.00	17.50	12.50	12.50
Plate, 8" w, sq	17.50	25.00	17.50	12.50	12.50
Plate, 8-1/4" w, sq, indent for cup	17.50	19.00	17.50	—	—
Plate, 9" d, grill	20.00	20.00	20.00	—	—
Plate, 12" d, two handles	35.00	35.00	35.00	20.00	20.00
Rose bowl, 4" d	25.00	30.00	27.50	20.00	20.00
Salt and pepper shakers, pr	50.00	50.00	45.00	25.00	25.00
Sandwich server, center handle	40.00	37.50	40.00	—	—
Saucer	5.00	5.00	5.00	3.50	3.50
Sherbet	15.00	15.00	18.00	12.50	12.50
Sugar	9.00	22.50	22.00	20.00	20.00
Tumbler, ftd	25.00	27.50	32.50	—	—
Vase, 7-1/4" h	30.00	35.00	40.00	—	35.00

*Mt. Pleasant, black creamer, **$20**; sugar (on pedestal), **$22.50**; scalloped bowl with two handles, **$35**; cup, **$15**.*

NATIONAL

Manufactured by Jeannette Glass Company, Jeannette, Pa., from the late 1940s to the mid-1950s.

Pieces are made in crystal, pink, and shell pink. Collector interest is primarily with crystal. Prices for pink and shell pink are not yet firmly established, but usually command slightly higher than crystal.

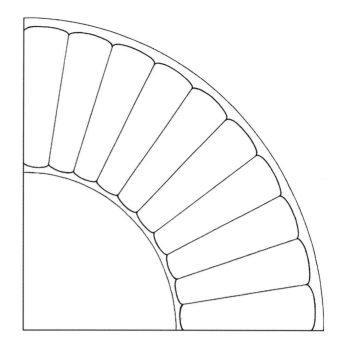

Item	Crystal
Ashtray	4.50
Berry bowl, 4-1/2" d	4.00
Berry bowl, 8-1/2" d	8.00
Bowl, 12" d	15.00
Candleholders, pr	30.00
Candy dish, cov, ftd	20.00
Cigarette box	15.00
Creamer	5.00
Creamer and sugar tray	6.00
Cup	4.00
Jar, cov	15.00
Lazy Susan	40.00
Milk pitcher, 20 oz	20.00
Plate, 8" d	6.50
Punch bowl stand	10.00
Punch bowl, 12" d	25.00
Punch cup	3.50
Relish, three parts	15.00
Salt and pepper shakers, pr	10.00
Saucer	1.00
Sherbet, 3-1/4" h, ftd	10.00
Sugar, open	6.50
Serving plate, 15" d	17.50
Tray, two handles	17.50
Tumbler, ftd	8.50
Vase, 9"	20.00
Water pitcher, 64 oz	30.00

*National, crystal candleholders, **$30**.*

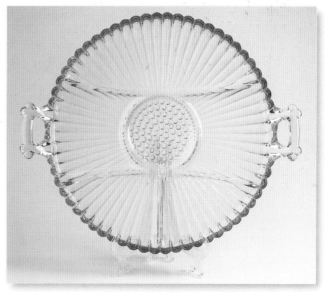

*National, crystal tray with two handles, **$17.50**.*

NEW CENTURY

Manufactured by Hazel Atlas Company, Clarksburg, W.V., and Zanesville, Ohio, from 1930 to 1935.

Pieces are made in crystal and green, with limited production in amethyst, cobalt blue, and pink.

Item	Amethyst	Cobalt Blue	Crystal	Green	Pink
Ashtray/coaster, 5-3/8" d	—	—	30.00	30.00	—
Berry bowl, 4-1/2" d	—	—	35.00	35.00	—
Berry bowl, 8" d	—	—	30.00	30.00	—
Butter dish, cov	—	—	75.00	75.00	—
Casserole, cov, 9" d	—	—	115.00	115.00	—
Cocktail, 3-1/4 oz	—	—	42.00	42.00	—
Cream soup, 4-3/4" d	—	—	25.00	25.00	—
Creamer	—	—	12.00	14.00	—
Cup	20.00	20.00	10.00	12.00	20.00
Decanter, stopper	—	—	90.00	90.00	—
Pitcher, with or without ice lip, 60 oz	55.00	55.00	45.00	48.00	50.00
Pitcher, with or without ice lip, 80 oz	55.00	55.00	45.00	48.00	50.00
Plate, 6" d, sherbet	—	—	6.00	6.50	—
Plate, 7-1/8" d, breakfast	—	—	12.00	12.00	—
Plate, 8-1/2" d, salad	—	—	10.00	12.00	—
Plate, 10" d, dinner	—	—	24.00	24.00	—
Plate, 10" d, grill	—	—	15.00	18.00	—
Platter, 11" l, oval	—	—	30.00	30.00	—
Salt and pepper shakers, pr	—	—	45.00	45.00	—
Saucer	7.50	7.50	5.00	6.50	8.00
Sherbet, 3" h	—	—	9.00	9.00	—
Sugar, cov	—	—	40.00	45.00	—
Tumbler, 5 oz, 3-1/2" h	12.00	16.50	15.00	18.00	18.00
Tumbler, 5 oz, 4" h, ftd	—	—	30.00	32.50	—
Tumbler, 8 oz, 3-1/2" h	—	—	25.00	27.50	—
Tumbler, 9 oz, 4-1/4" h	15.00	20.00	24.00	18.00	15.00
Tumbler, 9 oz, 4-7/8" h, ftd	—	—	25.00	25.00	—
Tumbler, 10 oz, 5" h	16.00	30.00	20.00	17.50	16.00
Tumbler, 12 oz, 5-1/4" h	25.00	40.00	30.00	32.50	20.00
Whiskey, 2-1/2" h, 1-1/2 oz	—	—	18.00	20.00	—
Wine, 2-1/2 oz	—	—	35.00	40.00	—

New Century, green dinner plate, $24.

New Century, green salt and pepper shakers, $45.

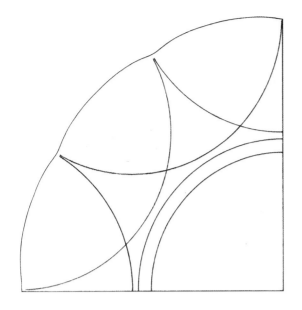

NEWPORT

Hairpin

Manufactured by Hazel Atlas Glass Company, Clarksburg, W.V., and Zanesville, Ohio, from 1936 to the early 1950s.

Pieces are made in amethyst, cobalt blue, pink (from 1936 to 1940), Platonite white, and fired-on colors (from the 1940s to early 1950s).

Item	Amethyst	Cobalt Blue	Fired-On Color	Pink	Platonite
Berry bowl, 4-3/4" d	18.00	25.00	8.00	12.00	5.00
Berry bowl, 8-1/4" d	50.00	50.00	16.00	25.00	10.00
Cereal bowl, 5-1/4" d	42.00	45.00	—	20.00	—
Cream soup, 4-3/4" d	25.00	25.00	10.00	17.50	8.50
Creamer	20.00	20.00	8.50	10.00	6.00
Cup	12.00	15.00	9.50	9.00	6.50
Plate, 6" d, sherbet	7.50	10.00	5.00	3.50	2.00
Plate, 8-1/2" d, luncheon	15.00	22.00	8.00	8.00	6.50
Plate, 8-13/16" d, dinner	32.00	35.00	15.00	15.00	12.00
Platter, 11-3/4" l, oval	42.00	55.00	18.00	20.00	12.00
Salt and pepper shakers, pr	60.00	65.00	32.00	30.00	15.00
Sandwich plate, 11-1/2" d	48.00	50.00	15.00	24.00	16.00
Saucer	5.25	6.00	3.00	2.50	2.00
Sherbet	15.00	16.50	10.00	8.00	4.00
Sugar	20.00	20.00	9.50	10.00	8.00
Tumbler, 9 oz, 4-1/2" h	42.00	50.00	18.50	20.00	—

*Newport,
amethyst dinner plate, **$32**;
cream soup bowl, **$25**;
creamer, **$20**;
and sugar, **$20**.*

NORA BIRD

Line #300

Manufactured by Paden City Glass Company, Paden City, W.V., from 1929 to 1930s.

Pieces are made in amber, crystal, green and pink. Amber production is limited; a pair of candlesticks is valued at $150.

Item	Green	Pink
Candlesticks, pr	220.00	155.00
Candy dish, cov, 5-1/4" h, ftd	325.00	325.00
Candy dish, cov, 6-1/2" d, three parts	350.00	350.00
Creamer, 4-1/2" h, round handle	75.00	85.00
Creamer, 5" h, pointed handle	75.00	85.00
Cup	60.00	60.00
Ice tub, 6" d	125.00	125.00
Mayonnaise and liner	150.00	165.00
Plate, 8" d	45.00	50.00
Saucer	15.00	15.00
Sugar, 4-1/2" h, round handle	75.00	85.00
Sugar, 5" h, pointed handle	75.00	85.00
Tumbler, 2-1/4" h, 3 oz	45.00	45.00
Tumbler, 3" h	42.00	42.00
Tumbler, 4" h	50.00	50.00
Tumbler, 4-3/4" h, ftd	60.00	60.00
Tumbler, 5-1/4" h, 10 oz	65.00	65.00

NORMANDIE

Bouquet and Lattice

Manufactured by Federal Glass Company, Columbus, Ohio, from 1933 to 1940.

Pieces are made in amber, crystal, iridescent, and pink.

Item	Amber	Crystal	Iridescent	Pink
Berry bowl, 5" d	9.50	6.00	7.50	14.00
Berry bowl, 8-1/2" d	35.00	24.00	30.00	80.00
Cereal bowl, 6-1/2" d	30.00	20.00	12.00	35.00
Creamer, ftd	20.00	10.00	10.00	15.00
Cup	7.50	4.00	10.00	12.50
Iced tea tumbler, 12 oz, 5" h	45.00	—	—	—
Juice tumbler, 5 oz, 4" h	40.00	—	—	—
Pitcher, 80 oz, 8" h	115.00	—	—	245.00
Plate, 6" d, sherbet	4.50	2.00	3.00	10.00
Plate, 7-3/4" d, salad	13.00	5.00	55.00	14.00
Plate, 9-1/4" d, luncheon	25.00	6.00	16.50	100.00
Plate, 11" d, dinner	55.00	15.00	12.00	18.00
Plate, 11" d, grill	15.00	8.00	8.00	25.00
Platter, 11-3/4" l	24.00	10.00	12.00	80.00
Salt and pepper shakers, pr	50.00	20.00	—	4.00
Saucer	4.00	1.50	2.50	10.00
Sherbet	7.50	6.00	7.50	9.50
Sugar	10.00	6.00	9.50	12.00
Tumbler, 9 oz, 4-1/4" h	25.00	10.00	—	50.00
Vegetable bowl, 10" l, oval	27.50	12.00	25.00	45.00

Normandie, iridescent cup, $10.

Normandie, iridescent dinner plate, $12.

OLD CAFÉ

Manufactured by Hocking Glass Company, Lancaster, Ohio, from 1936 to 1940.

Pieces are made in crystal, pink, and royal ruby.

Old Café, royal ruby berry bowl, $9.

Item	Crystal	Pink	Royal Ruby
Berry bowl, 3-3/4" d	9.50	10.00	9.00
Bowl, 4-1/2" d, handle	—	18.00	—
Bowl, 6-1/2" d	15.00	18.00	—
Bowl, 9" d, closed handles	12.00	10.00	15.00
Candy dish, 8" d, low	12.50	18.50	20.00
Candy jar, 5-1/2" d, crystal with ruby cover	—	—	30.00
Cereal bowl, 5-1/2" d	30.00	30.00	30.00
Cup	12.00	16.00	12.00
Juice tumbler, 3" h	18.00	25.00	20.00
Lamp	100.00	100.00	150.00
Mint tray, 8" l	—	—	20.00
Olive dish, 6" l, oblong	7.50	10.00	—
Pitcher, 36 oz, 6" h	125.00	145.00	—
Pitcher, 80 oz	150.00	165.00	—
Plate, 6" d, sherbet	5.00	5.00	—
Plate, 10" d, dinner	60.00	65.00	—
Saucer	5.00	5.00	—
Sherbet, low, ftd	7.50	18.00	12.00
Tumbler, 4" h	18.00	20.00	18.00
Vase, 7-1/4" h	25.00	45.00	50.00

*Old Café, crystal vase, **$25**; and bowl, 9-1/2" d, plain, **$40**.*

*Old Café, royal ruby bowl with handles and original label, **$15**.*

Close-up view of original Old Café label on the ruby bowl with handles.

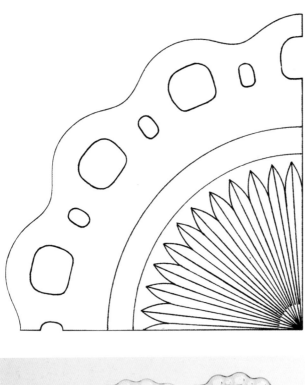

OLD COLONY

Lace Edge, Open Lace

Manufactured by Hocking Glass Company, Lancaster, Ohio, from 1935 to 1938.

Pieces are made in crystal and pink. Crystal Old Colony pieces are valued at about 50 percent of pink, as are frosted or satin finish prices. Many other companies made a look-alike to Old Colony, so care must be exercised. Some Old Colony plates have solid, flatter loops. Pieces hard to find are candlesticks, the 9-inch comport, tumblers and vase.

*Old Colony, pink luncheon plate, **$30**; platter, **$48**; divided relish, **$75**.*

*Old Colony, pink satin-finish candlestick, **$350** for pair.*

Item	Pink
Bonbon, cov	65.00
Bowl, 9-1/2" d, plain	32.50
Bowl, 9-1/2" d, ribbed	35.00
Butter dish, cov	100.00
Candlesticks, pr	350.00
Candy jar, cov, ribbed	65.00
Cereal bowl, 6-3/8" d	30.00
Comport, 7" d, cov	60.00
Comport, 9" d	950.00
Console bowl, 10-1/2" d, three legs	325.00
Cookie jar, cov	110.00
Creamer	40.00
Cup	40.00
Flower bowl, crystal frog	50.00
Plate, 7-1/4" d, salad	35.00
Plate, 8-1/4" d, luncheon	30.00
Plate, 10-1/2" d, dinner	40.00
Plate, 10-1/2" d, grill	28.50
Plate, 13" d, four parts, solid lace	65.00
Plate, 13" d, solid lace	65.00
Platter, 12-3/4" l	48.00
Platter, 12-3/4" l, five parts	42.00
Relish, 7-1/2" d, three parts, deep	60.00
Relish, 10-1/2" d, three parts	35.00
Relish, 13" l, divided	75.00
Salad bowl, 7-3/4" d, ribbed	60.00
Saucer	12.00
Sherbet, ftd	175.00
Sugar	25.00
Tumbler, 5 oz, 3-1/2" h, flat	120.00
Tumbler, 9 oz, 4-1/2" h, flat	32.50
Tumbler, 10-1/2 oz, 5" h, ftd	95.00
Vase, 7" h	650.00

*Old Colony, pink bowls, 9-1/2" d, ribbed, **$35**; 9-1/2" d, plain, **$40**. Photos on this page are courtesy of James Hintz.*

*Old Colony, pink platter, 12-3/4" l, divided, **$42**; plain, **$48**.*

*Old Colony, pink flower bowl with crystal frog, **$50**; butter dish, covered, **$100**.*

OLD ENGLISH

Threading

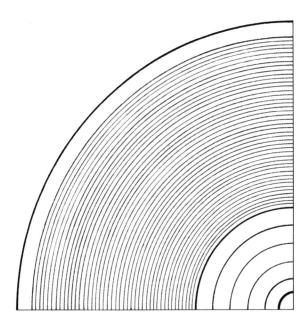

Manufactured by Indiana Glass Company, Dunkirk, Ind., late 1920s.

Pieces are made in amber, crystal, green, and pink.

Old English, green compote, $24.

Item	Amber	Crystal	Green	Pink
Bowl, 4" d, flat	20.00	18.00	22.00	20.00
Bowl, 9-1/2" d, flat	35.00	25.00	35.00	35.00
Candlesticks, pr, 4" h	35.00	25.00	45.00	35.00
Candy dish, cov, flat	50.00	40.00	50.00	50.00
Candy jar, cov	55.00	45.00	55.00	55.00
Cheese compote, 3-1/2" h	17.50	12.00	17.50	17.50
Cheese plate, indent	20.00	10.00	20.00	20.00
Compote, 3-1/2" h, 6-3/8" w, two handles	24.00	12.00	24.00	24.00
Compote, 3-1/2" h, 7" w	24.00	12.00	24.00	24.00
Creamer	18.00	10.00	18.00	18.00
Eggcup	—	10.00	—	—
Fruit bowl, 9" d, ftd	30.00	20.00	30.00	30.00
Fruit stand, 11" h, ftd	50.00	18.00	40.00	40.00
Goblet, 8 oz, 5-3/4" h	30.00	15.00	30.00	30.00
Pitcher	70.00	35.00	70.00	70.00
Pitcher, cov	125.00	55.00	125.00	125.00
Sandwich server, center handle	60.00	—	60.00	60.00
Sherbet	20.00	10.00	20.00	20.00
Sugar, cov	38.00	14.00	38.00	38.00
Tumbler, 4-1/2" h, ftd	24.00	12.00	32.50	28.00
Tumbler, 5-1/2" h, ftd	40.00	20.00	40.00	65.00
Vase, 5-3/8" h, 7" w, fan-shape	48.00	24.00	48.00	48.00
Vase, 8" h, 4-1/2" w, ftd	45.00	20.00	45.00	45.00
Vase, 8-1/4" h, 4-1/4" w, ftd	45.00	20.00	45.00	45.00
Vase, 12" h, ftd	72.00	35.00	72.00	72.00

ORANGE BLOSSOM

Manufactured by Indiana Glass Company, Dunkirk, Ind., in 1957. This pattern was originally made in a custard color in the 1930s. That pattern is known as Indiana Custard.

Pieces are made in milk white. Some plates have a decaled Currier and Ives type scene in the center.

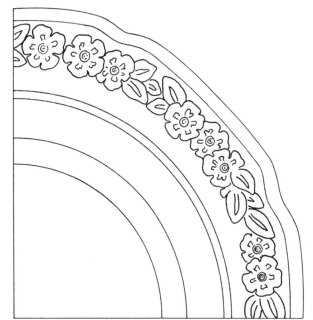

Item	Milk White
Creamer, ftd	10.00
Cup	6.50
Dessert bowl, 5-1/2" d	5.00
Plate, 5-3/8" d, sherbet	3.50
Plate, 8-7/8" d, lunch	8.50
Saucer	2.00
Sugar, ftd	10.00

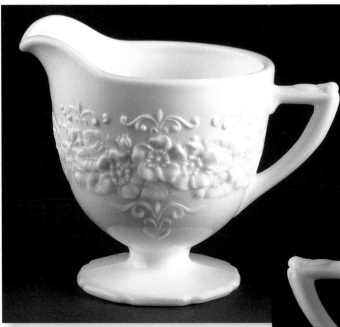

*Orange Blossom, milk white creamer, **$10**.*

*Orange Blossom, milk white open sugar, **$10**.*

ORCHID

Manufactured by Paden City Glass Company, Paden City, W.V., early 1930s.

Pieces are made in amber, black, cobalt blue, green, pink, red, and yellow.

Item	Amber	Black Blue	Cobalt	Green	Pink	Red	Yellow
Bowl, 4-1/2" sq	40.00	50.00	50.00	40.00	55.00	50.00	55.00
Bowl, 8-1/2" d, two handles	60.00	95.00	95.00	60.00	100.00	95.00	100.00
Bowl, 8-3/4" w, sq	50.00	85.00	85.00	50.00	90.00	85.00	90.00
Bowl, 10" d, ftd	85.00	165.00	165.00	75.00	150.00	165.00	150.00
Bowl, 11" d, sq	60.00	115.00	115.00	60.00	120.00	115.00	120.00
Candlesticks, pr, 5-3/4" h	110.00	195.00	195.00	95.00	225.00	195.00	215.00
Candy, cov, 6-1/2" w, sq, three parts	70.00	145.00	145.00	70.00	150.00	145.00	150.00
Comport, 3-1/4" h, 6-1/4" w	30.00	48.00	48.00	30.00	50.00	48.00	50.00
Comport, 6-5/8" h, 7" w	42.00	95.00	95.00	42.00	115.00	95.00	100.00
Creamer	60.00	95.00	95.00	60.00	75.00	95.00	75.00
Ice bucket, 6" h	95.00	195.00	195.00	95.00	185.00	195.00	200.00
Mayonnaise, three pcs	85.00	165.00	165.00	85.00	150.00	150.00	165.00
Plate, 8-1/2" w, sq	—	135.00	135.00	—	—	135.00	—
Sandwich server, center handle	85.00	125.00	125.00	125.00	125.00	125.00	135.00
Sugar	48.00	95.00	95.00	50.00	95.00	95.00	95.00
Vase, 8" h	95.00	275.00	275.00	95.00	95.00	275.00	95.00
Vase, 10" h	125.00	295.00	295.00	125.00	145.00	295.00	150.00

*Orchid, yellow comport, 6-5/8" h, 7" w, **$100**.*

OVIDE

Manufactured by Hazel Atlas Glass Company, Clarksburg, W.V., and Zanesville, Ohio, 1930-35 and in the 1950s.

Pieces are made in black, green, and white Platonite with fired-on colors in the 1950s.

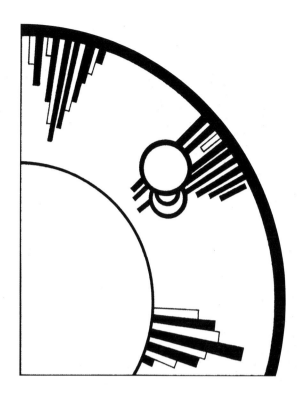

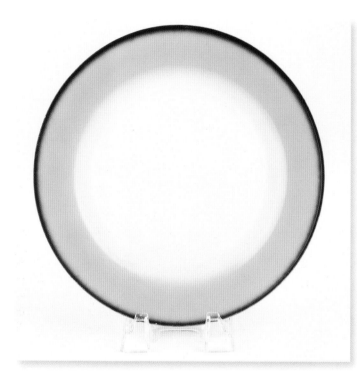

Ovide, pink and gray platonite luncheon plate, **$15**.

Item	Black	Green	Platonite
Berry bowl, 4-3/4" d	—	5.50	6.00
Berry bowl, 8" d	—	—	22.00
Bowl, 6" d	—	—	9.00
Candy dish, cov	50.00	24.00	35.00
Cereal bowl, 5-1/2" d	10.00	—	12.50
Creamer	10.00	6.00	18.00
Cup	8.00	4.50	5.00
Eggcup	—	—	22.00
Fruit cocktail, ftd	5.00	4.50	—
Plate, 6" d, sherbet	—	2.50	6.00
Plate, 7" d, salad	—	4.50	4.50
Plate, 8" d, luncheon	8.00	3.50	15.00
Plate, 9" d, dinner	—	8.00	10.00
Platter, 11" d	—	—	24.00
Salt and pepper shakers, pr	32.00	28.00	25.00
Saucer	4.50	2.50	3.00
Sherbet	6.50	3.50	5.00
Soup bowl, 8" d	—	20.00	20.00
Sugar, open	10.00	7.00	20.00
Tumbler	18.00	—	14.00
Vase, 6" h, sterling silver trim	35.00	—	—

OYSTER & PEARL

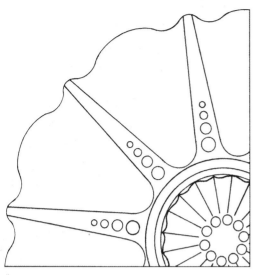

Manufactured by Anchor Hocking Glass Corporation, from 1938 to 1940.

Pieces are made in crystal, pink, royal ruby, and white with fired-on green or pink.

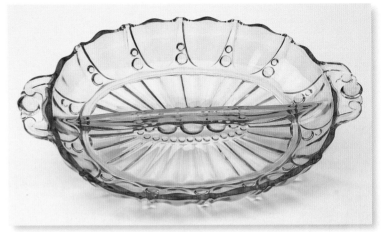

Oyster and Pearl, pink relish dish, $35.

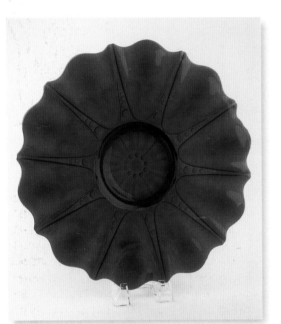

Oyster and Pearl, royal ruby sandwich plate, $50.

Oyster and Pearl, royal ruby bowl with handles, $20.

Item	Crystal	Pink	Royal Ruby	White, Fired-On Green	White, Fired-On Pink
Bowl, 5-1/2" d, handle	8.00	15.00	20.00	—	—
Bowl, 5-1/4" w, handle, heart-shape	15.00	21.00	—	20.00	15.00
Bowl, 6-1/2" d, handle	12.00	15.00	28.00	—	—
Candle holders, pr, 3-1/2" h	35.00	45.00	65.00	25.00	25.00
Fruit bowl, 10-1/2" d, deep	20.00	25.00	50.00	30.00	30.00
Relish dish, 10-1/4" l, divided	10.00	35.00	—	—	—
Sandwich plate, 13-1/2" d	20.00	40.00	50.00	—	—

PANELED GRAPE

Pattern #188

Manufactured by Westmoreland Glass Company, from 1950 to the 1970s.

Pieces are made in milk white glass. Some pieces were decorated. A limited production in mint green occurred in 1979. Decorated pieces are usually valued the same as the white pieces, providing the painted decoration is in very good condition. The re-sale market on green is very limited at the present time.

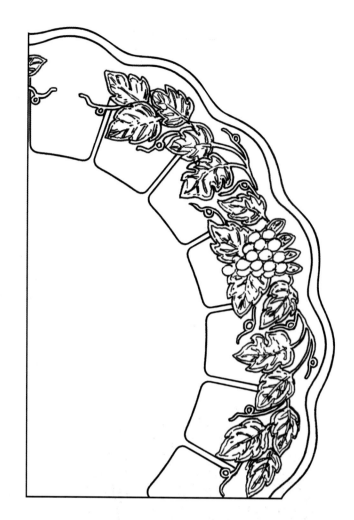

Item	Milk White
Appetizer set, three pcs	95.00
Banana bowl, 12" d, ftd	175.00
Basket, 5-1/2", ruffled	50.00
Basket, 6-1/2", oval	30.00
Basket, 8"	70.00
Bowl, 4" d, crimped	22.00
Bowl, 6" d, crimped, stemmed	30.00
Bowl, 6" d, ruffled, stemmed	30.00
Bowl, 6-1/2" d, oval	30.00
Bowl, 8" d, cupped	35.00
Bowl, 9" d, ftd, skirted base	50.00
Bowl, 9-1/2" d, bell shape	45.00
Bowl, 9-1/2" d, bell shape, ftd	125.00
Bowl, 10-1/2" d	70.00
Bowl, 11" l, oval, ftd	125.00
Bowl, 12" d, flat	120.00
Bowl, 12" d, ftd	125.00
Bowl, cov, 9" d, ftd	75.00
Bowl, cov, 9" w, sq	85.00
Bud vase, 10" h	24.00
Butter, cov, 1/4 pound	35.00

Item	Milk White
Cake plate, 10-1/2" d	65.00
Cake plate, 11" d, ftd, skirt	70.00
Candelabra, three-lite	500.00
Candleholder, 4", octagonal	18.00
Candleholder, 5" h, handle	40.00
Candleholder, 9" h, two-lite	30.00
Candy jar, cov, 6-1/4"	35.00
Canister, cov, 7" h	175.00
Canister, cov, 9-1/2" h	185.00
Canister, cov, 11" h	195.00
Celery vase, 6-1/2" h	50.00
Champagne	35.00
Cheese, cov, 7" d	60.00
Chocolate box, cov, 6-1/2" l	55.00
Chop plate, 14" d	125.00
Cigarette lighter, goblet or toothpick shape	25.00
Cologne, gold trim	60.00
Compote, cov, 7" d, ftd	45.00
Compote, cov, 9" d, ftd, crimped	48.00
Compote, open, 4-1/2" d, crimped	30.00
Condiment set, five pcs	130.00

Paneled Grape, white milk dinner plate, **$65**.

Item	Milk White
Cordial, 2 oz.	20.00
Creamer, individual	12.00
Creamer, table	22.50
Creamer, tall	30.00
Cruet, stopper	40.00
Cup, flared	20.00
Decanter	165.00
Dresser set, four pcs	215.00
Egg plate, 10" d, center handle	75.00
Egg plate, 12" d	70.00
Epergne, 8-1/2" h	60.00
Epergne, 9" d bowl, two pcs	185.00
Flower pot	45.00
Fruit cocktail, 3-1/2" or 4-1/2"	12.00
Goblet, 8 oz	18.00
Iced tea tumbler, 12 oz	25.00
Ivy ball	65.00

Item	Milk White
Jardinière, 5", cupped or straight, ftd	25.00
Jardinière, 6-1/2" h, cupped or straight, ftd	35.00
Jelly, cov, 4-1/2" d	25.00
Juice tumbler, 5 oz	24.00
Ladle	10.00
Marmalade	55.00
Mayonnaise, 4" d, ftd	40.00
Napkin ring	12.00
Nappy, 4-1/2" d	20.00
Nappy, 5" d, bell shape	22.00
Nappy, 5" d, round, handle	30.00
Nappy, 7" d	26.00
Nappy, 8-1/2" d	28.00
Nappy, 9" d	30.00
Nappy, 10" d	35.00
Oil or vinegar bottle, stopper	40.00
Old fashioned tumbler, 6 oz	28.00

Item	Milk White
Parfait, 6" h	25.00
Pickle dish, oval	20.00
Pitcher, 16 oz	50.00
Pitcher, 32 oz	48.00
Planter, 3" x 8-1/2"	30.00
Planter, 4-1/2" x 4-1/2"	45.00
Planter, 5" x 9"	45.00
Plate, 6" d, bread and butter	8.00
Plate, 7" d, salad	25.00
Plate, 8-1/2" d, luncheon	25.00
Plate, 10-1/2" d, dinner	65.00
Puff box, cov	35.00
Punch bowl, 13" d, bell or flared	300.00
Punch cup	15.00
Punch ladle	65.00
Relish, three parts, 9" l	45.00
Rose bowl, 4" d	20.00
Rose bowl, 4-1/2" d, cupped, ftd	35.00
Salt and pepper shakers, pr, ftd, three sizes	45.00
Sauce boat	45.00
Sauce boat underplate	20.00
Saucer	9.50
Serving plate, 18" d	165.00
Sherbet, 3-3/4" h	15.00
Sherbet, 4-3/4" h	17.50
Soap dish	100.00
Spooner, 6" h	40.00
Sugar, cov, individual	10.00
Sugar, cov, large	35.00
Sugar, cov, table	20.00
Sugar, open, 4-1/4"	10.00
Tidbit tray, metal handle, 8-1/2" d	30.00
Tidbit tray, metal handle, 10-1/2" d	50.00
Toothpick holder	25.00
Tray, 9" l, oval	55.00
Tray, 13-1/2" l, oval	90.00
Tumbler, 8 oz	20.00
Vase, 6" h, bell shape	20.00
Vase, 8-1/2" h or 9" h, bell shape	35.00

Item	Milk White
Vase, 8-1/2" h or 9" h, bell shape	35.00
Vase, 9-1/2" h, straight sides	30.00
Vase, 11-1/2" h, bell or straight sides	35.00
Vase, 14" h, 16" h, 18" h, swung	65.00
Wall pocket, 6"	85.00
Wall pocket, 8"	95.00
Wine, 3 oz	24.00

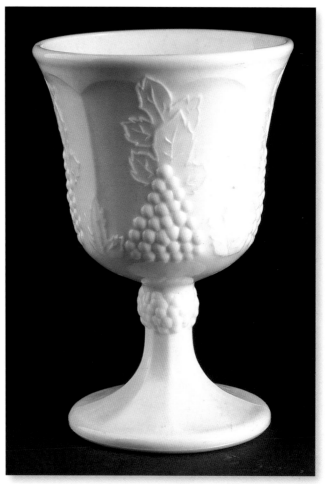

Paneled Grape, white milk goblet, $18.

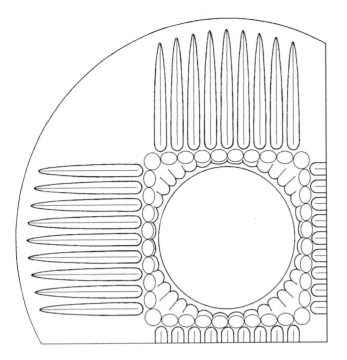

PARK AVENUE

Manufactured by Federal Glass Company, Columbus, Ohio, 1941 to the early 1970s.

Pieces are made in amber, crystal, and crystal with gold trim. Values for crystal and crystal with gold trim are the same.

Park Avenue, crystal juice tumbler with gold band, $5.

Item	Amber	Crystal
Ashtray, 3-1/2" sq	—	5.00
Ashtray, 4-1/2" sq	—	6.50
Candleholder, pr, 5" d	—	10.00
Dessert bowl, 5" d	8.50	5.00
Iced tea tumbler, 12 oz	12.00	6.50
Juice tumbler, 4-1/2 oz	5.00	5.00
Tumbler, 9 oz	7.50	5.50
Tumbler, 10 oz	9.00	6.00
Vegetable bowl, 8-1/2" d	18.00	10.00
Whiskey tumbler, 1-1/4 oz	—	4.50

PARROT

Sylvan

Manufactured by Federal Glass Company, Columbus, Ohio, from 1931 to 1932.

Pieces are made in amber and green, with limited production in blue and crystal.

Item	Amber	Green
Berry bowl, 5" d	22.50	30.00
Berry bowl, 8" d	75.00	80.00
Butter dish, cov	1,250.00	475.00
Creamer, ftd	65.00	55.00
Cup	35.00	40.00
Fruit bowl	—	40.00
Hot plate, 5" d, pointed	875.00	900.00
Hot plate, round	—	950.00
Jam dish, 7" d	35.00	—
Pitcher, 80 oz, 8-1/2" h	—	2,500.00
Plate, 5-3/4" d, sherbet	45.00	35.00
Plate, 7-1/2" d, salad	—	60.00
Plate, 9" d, dinner	50.00	95.00
Plate, 10-1/2" d, grill, round	35.00	—
Plate, 10-1/2" d, grill, square	—	60.00
Platter, 11-1/4" l, oblong	65.00	70.00

Item	Amber	Green
Salt and pepper shakers, pr	—	270.00
Saucer	18.00	18.00
Sherbet, ftd, cone	22.50	27.50
Soup bowl, 7" d	35.00	60.00
Sugar, cov	450.00	320.00
Tumbler, 10 oz, 4-1/4" h	100.00	130.00
Tumbler, 10 oz, 5-1/2" h, ftd, Madrid mold	145.00	—
Tumbler, 12 oz, 5-1/2" h	115.00	160.00
Tumbler, 5-3/4" h, ftd, heavy	100.00	120.00
Vegetable bowl, 10" l, oval	75.00	65.00

Parrot, amber jam dish, $35; green sherbet plate, $35.

PATRICIAN

Spoke

Manufactured by Federal Glass Company, Columbus, Ohio, from 1933 to 1937.

Pieces are made in amber (also called Golden Glo), crystal, green, and pink.

*Patrician, amber cream soup bowl, **$20**; sherbet, **$14**; and cup, **$14**.*

Item	Amber	Crystal	Green	Pink
Berry bowl, 5" d	12.50	10.00	12.50	18.50
Berry bowl, 8-1/2" d	35.00	15.00	37.50	35.00
Butter dish, cov	100.00	100.00	215.00	225.00
Cereal bowl, 6" d	30.00	27.50	27.50	25.00
Cookie jar, cov	75.00	80.00	500.00	—
Cream soup, 4-3/4" d	20.00	25.00	24.50	22.00
Creamer, ftd	12.50	9.50	12.50	12.50
Cup	10.00	12.00	15.00	18.50
Iced tea tumbler, 14 oz, 5-1/2" h	45.00	40.00	42.00	45.00
Jam dish	30.00	25.00	35.00	30.00
Mayonnaise, three toes	—	—	—	165.00
Pitcher, 75 oz, 8" h, molded handle	120.00	125.00	125.00	115.00
Pitcher, 75 oz, 8-1/4" h, applied handle	150.00	140.00	150.00	145.00
Plate, 6" d, sherbet	10.00	8.50	10.00	10.00
Plate, 7-1/2" d, salad	18.00	15.00	20.00	15.00
Plate, 9" d, luncheon	15.00	12.50	12.00	22.50
Plate, 10-1/2" d, grill	15.00	13.50	20.00	20.00
Plate, 10-1/2 d, dinner	12.50	12.75	32.00	36.00
Platter, 11-1/2" l, oval	35.00	30.00	30.00	28.00
Salt and pepper shakers, pr	65.00	65.00	65.00	85.00
Saucer	10.00	9.25	9.50	12.50
Sherbet	14.00	12.00	14.00	16.00
Sugar	12.50	9.00	18.50	12.50
Sugar lid	55.00	50.00	75.00	60.00
Tumbler, 5 oz, 4" h	40.00	28.50	30.00	32.00
Tumbler, 8 oz, 5-1/4" h, ftd	50.00	42.00	50.00	—
Tumbler, 9 oz, 4-1/4" h	32.00	28.50	25.00	28.00
Tumbler, 12 oz	45.00	—	—	—
Vegetable bowl, 10" l, oval	35.00	30.00	38.50	30.00

Patrician, amber pitcher, molded handle, 8" h, 75 oz, **$120***.*
Photos on this page are courtesy of James Hintz.

Patrician, amber salt and pepper shakers, **$65***.*

*Patrician,
amber sherbet,* **$15***;
cream soup,* **$28***.*

Patrician, back, from left: amber tumbler, 9 oz, 4-1/4" h, **$32***; cup,* **$12.50***, and saucer,* **$10***. Front, from left: amber luncheon plate, 9" d,* **$14***; dinner plate, 10-1/2" d,* **$10***; and salad plate, 7-1/2" d,* **$17.50***.*

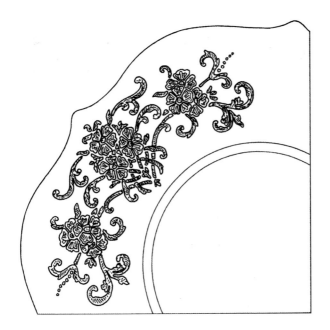

PATRICK

Manufactured by Lancaster Glass Company, Lancaster, Ohio, early 1930s.

Pieces are made in pink and yellow.

Item	Pink	Yellow
Candlesticks, pr	200.00	160.00
Candy dish, three ftd	175.00	175.00
Cheese and cracker set	150.00	130.00
Cocktail, 4" h	85.00	85.00
Console bowl, 11" d	150.00	150.00
Creamer	90.00	40.00
Cup	85.00	40.00
Fruit bowl, 9" d, handle	175.00	130.00
Goblet, 10 oz, 6" h	85.00	75.00
Juice goblet, 6 oz, 4-3/4" h	85.00	75.00

Item	Pink	Yellow
Mayonnaise, three pieces	200.00	140.00
Plate, 7" d, sherbet	20.00	15.00
Plate, 7-1/2" d, salad	25.00	20.00
Plate, 8" d, luncheon	45.00	30.00
Plate, 9" d	60.00	—
Saucer	20.00	12.00
Sherbet, 4-3/4" d	72.00	60.00
Sugar	90.00	40.00
Tray, 11" d, center handle	165.00	120.00
Tray, 11" d, two handles	80.00	65.00

Patrick, yellow luncheon plate, $30.

Patrick, yellow tray with caned center and two handles, $65.

PEACOCK & WILD ROSE

Line #1300

Manufactured by Paden City Glass Company, Paden City, W.V., 1930s.

Pieces are made in amber, black, cobalt blue, crystal, green, light blue, pink and red. A black 6-1/4-inch vase is valued at $100; a black 10-inch vase is valued at $165.

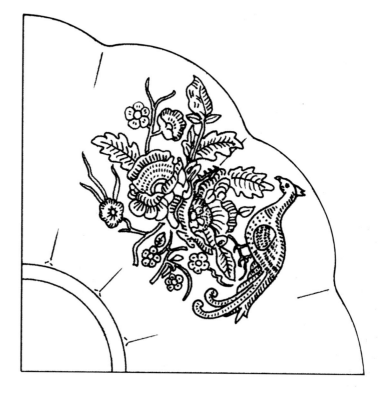

Item	Amber, Cobalt Blue, Crystal Light Blue, Red	Green	Pink
Bowl, 8-1/2" d, flat	110.00	175.00	185.00
Bowl, 8-3/4" d, ftd	115.00	125.00	135.00
Bowl, 9-1/2" d, center handle	175.00	185.00	195.00
Bowl, 9-1/2" d, ftd	85.00	95.00	95.00
Bowl, 10-1/2" d, center handle	85.00	115.00	195.00
Bowl, 10-1/2" d, ftd	95.00	165.00	195.00
Cake plate, low foot	195.00	195.00	150.00
Candlesticks, pr, 5" h	145.00	165.00	165.00
Candy dish, cov, 7"	250.00	250.00	250.00
Cheese and cracker set	195.00	225.00	225.00
Comport, 3-1/4" h, 6-1/4" w	75.00	165.00	115.00
Console bowl, 11" d	165.00	175.00	175.00
Console bowl, 14" d	80.00	120.00	120.00
Fruit bowl, 8-1/2" l, oval, ftd	165.00	175.00	185.00
Fruit bowl, 10-1/2" d	175.00	185.00	185.00
Ice bucket	175.00	175.00	200.00
Ice tub, 4-3/4"	185.00	195.00	195.00
Mayonnaise	115.00	120.00	125.00
Pitcher, 5" h	250.00	250.00	265.00

Item	Amber, Cobalt Blue, Crystal Light Blue, Red	Green	Pink
Relish, three parts	75.00	90.00	90.00
Sandwich tray, 10"	125.00	125.00	150.00
Tumbler, 3" h	55.00	60.00	65.00
Tumbler, 4" h	65.00	70.00	75.00
Tumbler 5-1/4" h	75.00	75.00	75.00
Vase, 8-1/4" h, elliptical	200.00	350.00	425.00
Vase, 10" h	250.00	145.00	225.00
Vase, 12" h	250.00	200.00	200.00

*Peacock & Wild Rose, pink bowl with center handle, **$195**.*

PEANUT BUTTER

Unknown maker, 1950s.

Pieces are made in crystal and milk glass. Some pieces were originally filled with Big Top Peanut Butter.

Peanut Butter, crystal tumbler, **$8**.

Item	Crystal	Milk Glass
Cup	6.50	—
Juice tumbler, 5-1/4" h	10.00	12.00
Plate, 8" d	7.50	—
Saucer	3.50	—
Sherbet, ftd	4.00	5.00
Tumbler, 5-3/4" h	8.00	7.50

PETALWARE

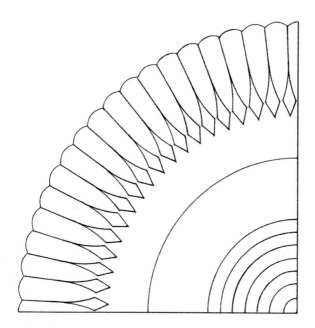

Manufactured by Macbeth-Evans Glass Company, Charleroi, Pa., from 1930 to 1940.

Made in cobalt blue, Cremax, crystal, fired-on red, blue, green and yellow, Monax and pink. Florette is the name given to a floral decorated with a pointed petal. There are other patterns, such as red flowers with a red rim, fruit and other floral patterns.

Crystal values are approximately 50 percent less than those listed for Cremax. Cobalt blue production was limited and the mustard is currently valued at $15 when complete with its metal lid. Monax Regency is priced the same as Monax Florette.

Item	Cremax	Cremax, Gold Trim	Fired-On Colors	Monax, Florette	Monax, Plain	Pink
Berry bowl, 9" d	30.00	32.00	—	35.50	18.00	25.00
Cereal bowl, 5-1/4" d	15.00	17.50	8.50	15.50	9.00	15.00
Cream soup liner	—	—	—	—	18.75	—
Cream soup, 4-1/2" d	12.50	12.00	12.00	15.00	10.00	19.00
Creamer, ftd	12.50	15.00	8.50	15.00	12.00	15.00
Cup	8.00	10.00	9.50	12.00	6.50	6.00
Lamp shade, 9" d	16.50	—	—	14.00	18.00	—
Plate, 6" d, sherbet	4.50	50.00	6.00	6.00	2.50	4.50
Plate, 8" d, salad	12.00	8.00	7.50	15.00	4.50	10.00
Plate, 9" d, dinner	25.00	14.00	8.50	16.50	9.00	20.00
Platter, 13" l, oval	25.00	20.00	20.00	25.00	20.00	17.50
Salver, 11" d	15.00	17.00	14.00	25.00	15.00	17.50
Salver, 12" d	—	—	—	—	24.00	22.50
Saucer	3.50	3.00	4.00	5.00	3.50	5.00
Sherbet, 4" h, low ftd	—	—	—	—	32.00	—
Sherbet, 4-1/2" h, low ftd	15.00	12.00	8.00	12.00	10.00	8.50
Soup bowl, 7" d	65.00	60.00	70.00	65.00	60.00	—
Sugar, ftd	7.50	11.00	12.00	15.00	10.00	9.00
Tumbler, 12 oz, 4-5/8" h	—	—	—	—	—	25.00

Petalware, Monax dinner plate, **$9**.

Petalware, pink sugar, **$9**, and creamer, **$15**; two dinner plates, **$20** each.

Petalware, cremax cream, **$12.50**; cremax sugar with gold rim, **$11**. Photo courtesy of Tina Trautman.

Petalware, monax lampshade with flower decoration, **$18**. Photo courtesy of Tina Trautman.

PINEAPPLE & FLORAL

No. 618

Manufactured by Indiana Glass Company, Dunkirk, Ind., from 1932 to 1937.

Pieces are made in amber, avocado (late 1960s), cobalt blue (1980s), crystal, fired-on green, fired-on red, and pink (1980s).

Reproductions: † A salad bowl and diamond-shaped comport have been reproduced in several different colors, including crystal, pink, and avocado green.

Item	Amber	Crystal	Red
Ashtray, 4-1/2" d	20.00	16.50	20.00
Berry bowl, 4-3/4" d	24.00	20.00	22.00
Cereal bowl, 6" d	24.00	30.00	22.00
Comport, diamond-shape	10.00	3.50	10.00
Creamer, diamond-shape	10.00	9.50	10.00
Cream soup	16.50	18.00	16.50
Cup	10.00	12.00	10.00
Plate, 6" d, sherbet	8.00	7.50	8.00
Plate, 8-3/8" d, salad	12.00	8.00	12.00
Plate, 9-3/8" d, dinner	17.50	18.00	17.50
Plate, 9-3/4" d, indentation	—	25.00	—
Plate, 11" d, closed handles	24.00	20.00	24.00
Plate, 11-1/2" d, indentation	—	25.00	—
Platter, 11" l, closed handles	20.00	8.00	20.00
Relish, 11-1/2" d, divided	28.00	20.00	28.00
Salad bowl, 7" d †	10.00	5.00	10.00
Sandwich plate, 11-1/2" d	24.00	20.00	24.00
Saucer	4.50	5.00	7.50
Sherbet, ftd	28.00	24.00	28.00
Sugar, diamond-shape	10.00	9.50	10.00
Tumbler, 8 oz, 4-1/4" h	40.00	40.00	40.00
Tumbler, 12 oz, 5" h	48.00	46.50	48.00
Vase, cone shape	45.00	42.50	45.00
Vegetable bowl, 10" l, oval	32.00	30.00	32.00

Pineapple & Floral, crystal sugar, **$9.50**; *creamer,* **$9.50**.

*Pineapple & Floral, crystal
footed sherbet,* **$24**.

*Pineapple & Floral,
amber cream soup
bowl,* **$16.50**.

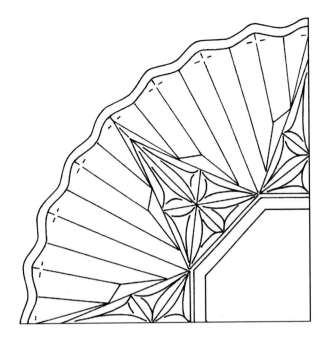

PIONEER

Manufactured by Federal Glass Co., Columbus, Ohio, starting in the 1940s.

Pieces were originally made in pink; crystal was added later. The crystal 11-inch fluted bowl and a 12-inch dinner plate were made until 1973.

Item	Crystal	Pink	Item	Crystal	Pink
Bowl, 7" d, low, fruits center	8.00	10.00	Nappy, 5-3/8" d, fruits center	8.00	10.00
Bowl, 7-3/4" d, ruffled, fruits center	10.00	12.00	Nappy, 5-3/8" d, plain center	6.00	8.00
Bowl, 10-1/2" d, fruits center	12.00	14.00	Plate, 8" d, luncheon, fruits center	6.00	8.00
Bowl, 10-1/2" d, plain center	10.00	12.00	Plate, 8" d, luncheon, plain center	6.00	8.00
Bowl, 11" d, ruffled, fruits center	15.00	18.00	Plate, 12" d, fruits center	10.00	12.00
Bowl, 11" d, ruffled, plain center	12.00	15.00	Plate, 12" d, plain center	10.00	12.00

*Pioneer, pink luncheon plate, fruit center, **$8**.*

PRETZEL

No. 622

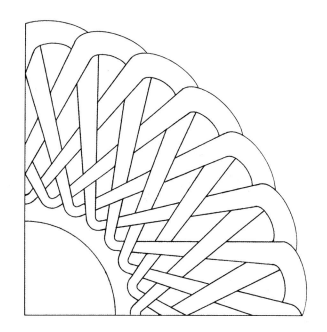

Manufactured by Indiana Glass Company, Dunkirk, Ind., from late 1930s to 1960s.

Pieces are made in avocado, crystal, and teal. Some crystal pieces have a fruit decoration. A teal cup and saucer is valued at $135. There have also been recent amber, blue, and opaque white issues.

Item	Crystal, Plain	Crystal, Fruits
Berry bowl, 9-3/8" d	18.00	—
Bowl, 8" d	7.00	—
Celery tray, 10-1/4" l	5.50	—
Creamer	10.00	—
Cup	6.50	—
Fruit cup, 4-1/2" d	7.50	—
Iced tea tumbler, 12 oz, 5-1/2" h	90.00	—
Juice tumbler	35.00	—
Olive, 7" l, leaf-shape	7.00	—
Pickle, 8-1/2" d, two handles	6.00	—
Pitcher, 39 oz	250.00	—
Plate, 6" d	3.50	5.00
Plate, 6" d, tab handle	7.00	—
Plate, 7" sq, wings	9.00	—
Plate, 7-1/4" w, sq, indent	8.00	—
Plate, 7-1/4" w, sq, indent, three parts	12.00	—
Plate, 8-3/8" d, salad	8.50	4.00
Plate, 9-3/8" d, dinner	10.00	20.00
Plate, 10" d, dinner	12.00	15.00
Relish, 7", three parts	10.00	—
Sandwich plate, 11-1/2" d	12.50	12.00
Saucer	2.00	4.00
Soup bowl, 7-1/2" d	10.00	10.00
Sugar	8.00	—
Tumbler, 5 oz, 3-1/2" h	50.00	—
Tumbler, 9 oz, 4-1/2" h	70.00	—

Pretzel, crystal sugar, *$8*; creamer, *$10*.

Pretzel, milk white celery tray, *$5*.

PRIMO

Paneled Aster

Manufactured by U.S. Glass Company, Pittsburgh, Pa., early 1930s.

Pieces are made in green and yellow.

Item	Green	Yellow	Item	Green	Yellow
Bowl, 4-1/2" d	20.00	25.00	Plate, 7-1/2" d	10.25	12.00
Bowl, 7-3/4" d	38.00	40.00	Plate, 10" d, dinner	27.50	30.00
Cake plate, 10" d, three ftd	40.00	45.00	Plate, 10" d, grill	18.00	22.50
Coaster/ashtray	8.75	8.75	Saucer	3.25	5.00
Creamer	12.00	15.00	Sherbet	14.25	14.50
Cup	14.50	15.00	Sugar	12.00	12.00
Hostess tray, 5-3/4" d, handles	42.00	45.00	Tumbler, 9 oz, 5-3/4" h, ftd	25.00	30.00

Primo, yellow cup, **$15**.

PRINCESS

Manufactured by Hocking Glass Company, Lancaster, Ohio, from 1931 to 1935.

Pieces are made in apricot yellow, blue, green, pink, and topaz yellow.

Reproductions: † The candy dish and salt and pepper shakers have been reproduced in blue, green and pink.

Item	Apricot Yellow	Blue	Green	Pink	Topaz Yellow
Ashtray, 4-1/2" d	110.00	—	72.00	90.00	110.00
Berry bowl, 4-1/2" d	55.00	—	40.00	30.00	55.00
Butter dish, cov	700.00	—	115.00	120.00	700.00
Cake plate, 10" d, ftd	—	—	40.00	100.00	—
Candy dish, cov †	—	—	75.00	95.00	—
Cereal bowl, 5" d	—	—	50.00	45.00	—
Coaster	100.00	—	85.00	65.00	100.00
Cookie jar, cov	—	875.00	85.00	75.00	—
Creamer, oval	25.00	—	15.00	17.50	22.50
Cup	10.00	120.00	15.00	17.50	15.00
Hat-shaped bowl, 9-1/2" d	125.00	—	80.00	50.00	125.00
Iced tea tumbler, 13 oz, 5-1/2" h	45.00	—	125.00	115.00	30.00
Juice tumbler, 5 oz, 3" h	28.00	—	25.00	28.00	30.00
Pitcher, 24 oz, 7-3/8" h, ftd	—	—	550.00	475.00	—
Pitcher, 37 oz, 6" h	775.00	—	60.00	75.00	775.00
Pitcher, 60 oz, 8" h	95.00	—	65.00	80.00	95.00
Plate, 5-1/2" d, sherbet	4.75	65.00	15.00	12.00	4.75
Plate, 8" d, salad	15.00	—	20.00	15.00	20.00
Plate, 9-1/2" d, dinner	25.00	—	30.00	35.00	30.00
Plate, 9-1/2" d, grill	10.00	175.00	20.00	15.00	10.00
Plate, 10-1/2" d, grill, closed handles	10.00	—	15.00	15.00	10.00
Platter, 12" l, closed handles	60.00	—	25.00	25.00	60.00
Relish, 7-1/2" l, divided, four parts	100.00	—	35.00	30.00	100.00
Relish, 7-1/2" l, plain	225.00	—	195.00	195.00	225.00
Salad bowl, 9" d, octagonal	125.00	—	55.00	40.00	125.00
Salt and pepper shakers, pr, 4-1/2" h †	75.00	—	60.00	65.00	85.00
Sandwich plate, 10-1/4" d, two closed handles	175.00	—	30.00	35.00	175.00
Saucer, 6" sq	2.75	65.00	14.50	10.00	3.75
Sherbet, ftd	40.00	—	25.00	25.00	40.00
Spice shakers, pr, 5-1/2" h	—	—	20.00	—	—
Sugar, cov	30.00	—	35.00	65.00	30.00

Item	Apricot Yellow	Blue	Green	Pink	Topaz Yellow
Tumbler, 9 oz, 4" h	25.00	—	28.00	25.00	25.00
Tumbler, 9 oz, 4-3/4" h, sq, ftd	—	—	65.00	25.00	—
Tumbler, 10 oz, 5-1/4" h, ftd	18.00	—	35.00	35.00	30.00
Tumbler, 12-1/2 oz, 6-1/2" h, ftd	25.00	—	180.00	95.00	25.00
Vase, 8" h	—	—	65.00	75.00	—
Vegetable bowl, 10" l, oval	60.00	—	50.00	50.00	65.00

Princess, green cookie jar, $85.

Princess, green salad bowl, octagonal, $55.

PYRAMID

No. 610

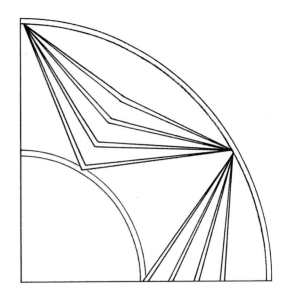

Manufactured by Indiana Glass Company, Dunkirk, Ind., from 926 to 1932.

Made in crystal, green, pink, white, and yellow. Later production in 1974 to 1975 by Tiara produced black and blue pieces. Production limited in blue and white. Prices for black not firmly established in secondary market at this time.

Item	Black	Crystal	Green	Pink	Yellow
Berry bowl, 4-3/4" d	15.00	20.00	35.00	35.00	65.00
Berry bowl, 8-1/2" d	40.00	30.00	65.00	55.00	75.00
Bowl, 9-1/2" l, oval	—	50.00	45.00	40.00	65.00
Creamer	50.00	20.00	35.00	35.00	40.00
Ice tub	—	95.00	145.00	155.00	225.00
Pickle dish, 9-1/2" l, 5-3/4" w	—	30.00	35.00	35.00	65.00
Pitcher	—	395.00	265.00	400.00	550.00
Relish, four parts, handles	27.50	25.00	65.00	60.00	70.00
Sugar	50.00	20.00	35.00	35.00	40.00
Tray for creamer and sugar	85.00	25.00	30.00	30.00	35.00
Tumbler, 8 oz, ftd	—	55.00	50.00	55.00	75.00
Tumbler, 11 oz, ftd	35.00	70.00	75.00	50.00	95.00

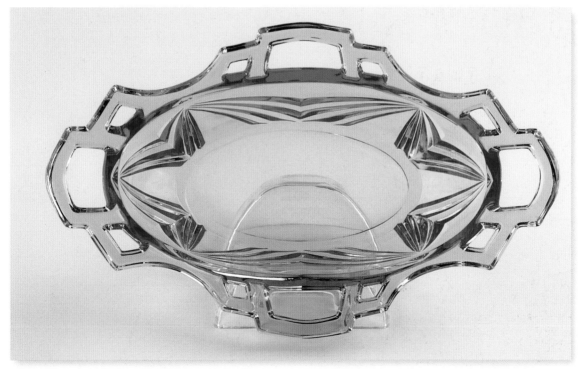

Pyramid, green pickle dish, **$35**.

QUEEN MARY

Prismatic Line, Vertical Ribbed

Manufactured by Hocking Glass Company, Lancaster, Ohio, from 1936 to 1948.

Pieces are made in crystal, pink, and royal ruby.

Item	Crystal	Pink	Royal Ruby
Ashtray, 2" x 3-3/4" l, oval	5.00	5.50	5.00
Ashtray, 3-1/2" d, round	4.00	—	—
Berry bowl, 4-1/2" d	3.00	8.00	—
Berry bowl, 5" d	5.00	15.00	—
Berry bowl, 8-3/4" d	10.00	17.50	—
Bowl, 4" d, one handle	4.00	7.50	—
Bowl, 5-1/2" d, two handles	8.00	15.00	—
Bowl, 7" d	7.50	35.00	—
Bowl, 7-1/2" d, rimmed	—	40.00	—
Butter dish, cov	42.00	125.00	—
Candlesticks, pr, two lite, 4-1/2" h	30.00	—	70.00
Candy dish, cov	70.00	42.00	—
Celery tray, 5" x 10"	10.00	24.00	—
Cereal bowl, 6" d	8.00	30.00	—
Cigarette jar, 2" x 3" oval	6.50	7.50	—
Coaster, 3-1/2" d	4.00	5.00	—
Coaster/ashtray, 4-1/4" sq	4.00	6.00	—
Comport, 5-3/4"	9.00	14.00	—
Creamer, ftd	8.00	40.00	—
Creamer, oval	8.00	12.00	—
Cup, large	6.00	9.50	—
Cup, small	8.00	12.00	—
Custard cup	—	22.00	—
Juice tumbler, 5 oz, 3-1/2" h	9.50	18.00	—
Pickle dish, 5" x 10"	10.00	24.00	—
Plate, 6" d, sherbet	4.00	10.00	—
Plate, 6-1/2" d, bread and butter	6.00	—	—
Plate, 8-1/4" d, salad	6.00	—	—
Plate, 9-1/2" d, dinner	35.00	65.00	—
Preserve, cov	30.00	125.00	—
Relish, clover-shape	15.00	17.50	—
Relish, 12" d, three parts	10.00	15.00	—
Relish, 14" d, four parts	15.00	17.50	—

Item	Crystal	Pink	Royal Ruby
Salt and pepper shakers, pr	30.00	—	—
Sandwich plate, 12" d	20.00	17.50	—
Saucer	2.00	5.00	—
Serving tray, 14" d	15.00	9.00	—
Sherbet, ftd	6.00	15.00	—
Sugar, ftd	—	40.00	—
Sugar, oval	8.00	24.00	—
Tumbler, 9 oz, 4" h	6.00	17.50	—
Tumbler, 10 oz, 5" h, ftd	35.00	70.00	—

*Queen Mary, crystal bowl, 7" d, **$7.50**; candlesticks, pair, **$30**.*

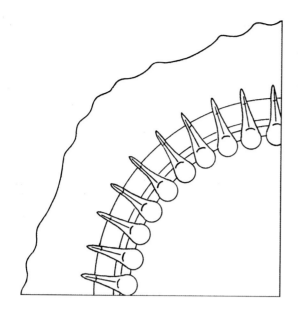

RADIANCE

Manufactured by New Martinsville Glass Company, New Martinsville, W.V., from 1936 to 1939.

Pieces are made in amber, cobalt blue, crystal, emerald green, ice blue, pink, and red. Some pieces are found with an etched design, which adds slightly to the value.

Item	Amber	Cobalt Blue	Crystal	Emerald Green	Ice Blue	Pink	Red
Bonbon, 6" d	16.00	—	8.00	—	32.00	—	32.00
Bonbon, 6" d, cov	48.00	—	24.00	—	95.00	—	95.00
Bonbon, 6" d, ftd	18.00	—	9.00	—	35.00	—	35.00
Bowl, 6" d, ruffled	—	—	—	—	35.00	—	—
Bowl, 6-1/2" d, ftd, metal holder	—	—	—	—	—	—	32.00
Bowl, 10" d, crimped	28.00	—	14.00	—	48.00	—	48.00
Bowl, 10" d, flared	22.00	—	11.00	—	48.00	—	48.00
Bowl, 12" d, crimped	30.00	—	15.00	—	50.00	—	50.00
Bowl, 12" d, flared	28.00	—	14.00	—	50.00	—	50.00
Butter dish, cov	210.00	—	120.00	—	460.00	—	460.00
Butter dish, chrome lid	40.00	—	50.00	—	—	—	—
Cake salver	—	—	—	—	175.00	—	175.00
Candlesticks, pr, two lite	75.00	—	37.50	—	120.00	—	120.00
Candlesticks, pr, 6" h, ruffled	85.00	—	40.00	—	175.00	—	175.00
Candlesticks, pr, 8" h	60.00	—	30.00	—	110.00	—	110.00
Candy dish, cov, three parts	—	125.00	—	—	125.00	—	125.00
Celery tray, 10" l	18.00	—	9.00	—	32.00	—	32.00
Cheese and cracker set, 11" d plate	45.00	—	20.00	—	195.00	—	65.00
Comport, 5" h	18.00	—	9.00	—	30.00	—	30.00
Comport, 6" h	24.00	—	12.00	—	35.00	—	35.00
Condiment set, four pcs, tray	160.00	—	85.00	—	295.00	—	295.00
Cordial, 1 oz	30.00	55.00	15.00	—	45.00	—	45.00
Creamer	15.00	25.00	20.00	—	35.00	32.00	30.00
Cruet, individual	40.00	—	20.00	—	26.00	—	27.50
Cup, ftd	15.00	18.00	8.00	—	18.00	20.00	20.00
Decanter, stopper, handle	90.00	195.00	45.00	—	225.00	—	225.00
Lamp, 12" h	60.00	—	30.00	—	115.00	—	115.00
Mayonnaise, three-pc set	37.50	—	19.00	—	85.00	—	85.00
Nut bowl, 5" d, two handles	12.00	—	6.50	—	20.00	—	24.00
Pickle, 7" d	16.00	—	8.00	—	25.00	—	27.50
Pitcher, 64 oz	185.00	350.00	95.00	—	375.00	—	375.00
Pitcher, silver overlay	—	—	—	—	—	—	125.00
Plate, 8" d, luncheon	10.00	—	5.00	—	12.00	—	25.00
Punch bowl, 9" d	110.00	—	65.00	135.00	185.00	—	185.00
Punch bowl liner, 14" d	48.00	—	24.00	35.00	85.00	—	85.00
Punch cup	8.00	—	5.00	—	20.00	—	15.00

Item	Amber	Cobalt Blue	Crystal	Emerald Green	Ice Blue	Pink	Red
Punch ladle	100.00	—	45.00	—	120.00	—	120.00
Relish, 7" d, two parts	18.00	—	9.00	—	32.00	—	32.00
Relish, 8" d, three parts	28.00	—	15.00	—	35.00	—	35.00
Salt and pepper shakers, pr	50.00	—	25.00	—	90.00	95.00	95.00
Saucer	6.00	7.50	3.50	—	7.50	8.00	8.00
Sugar	16.00	—	20.00	—	30.00	32.00	30.00
Tray, oval	25.00	—	15.00	—	32.00	32.00	32.00
Tumbler, 9" oz	22.50	35.00	12.00	—	30.00	—	35.00
Vase, 10" h, crimped	48.00	75.00	24.00	—	60.00	—	70.00
Vase, 10" h, flared	48.00	75.00	24.00	—	60.00	—	70.00
Vase, 12" h, crimped	60.00	50.00	30.00	—	55.00	—	85.00
Vase, 12" h, flared	70.00	—	50.00	—	175.00	—	175.00

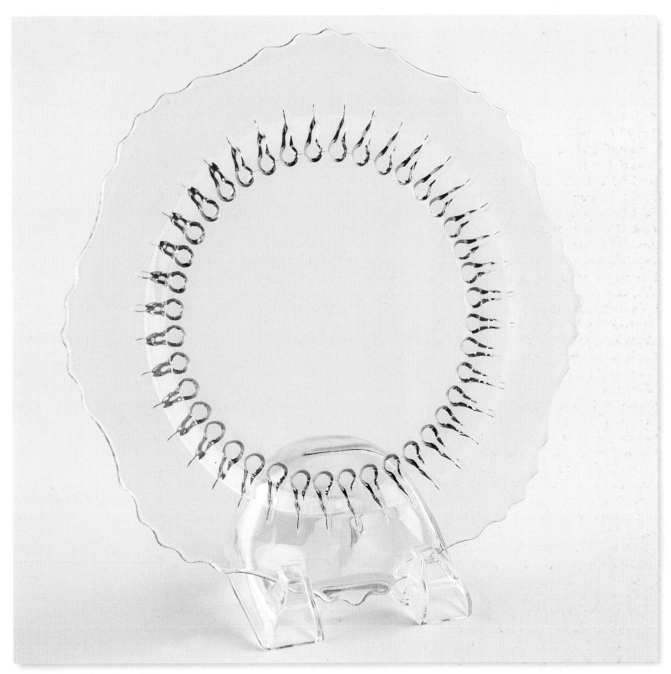

Radiance, ice blue plate, $12.

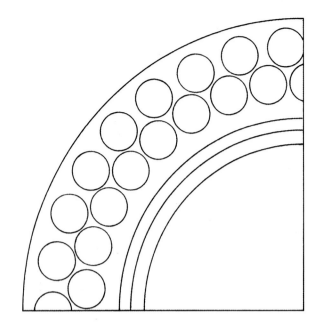

RAINDROPS

Optic Design

Manufactured by Federal Glass Company, Columbus, Ohio, from 1929 to 1933.

Pieces are made in crystal and green.

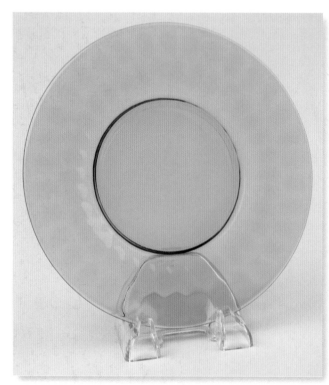

Raindrops, green luncheon plate, $7.50.

Item	Crystal	Green
Berry bowl, 7-1/2" d	30.00	45.00
Cereal bowl, 6" d	10.00	15.00
Creamer	8.00	10.00
Cup	8.50	8.50
Fruit bowl, 4-1/2" d	5.00	12.00
Plate, 6" d, sherbet	1.50	3.00
Plate, 8" d, luncheon	4.00	7.50
Salt and pepper shakers, pr	200.00	350.00
Saucer	3.00	4.50
Sherbet	4.50	7.50
Sugar, cov	7.50	15.00
Tumbler, 2 oz, 2-1/8" h	4.00	7.00
Tumbler, 4 oz, 3" h	4.00	7.00
Tumbler, 5 oz, 3-7/8" h	5.50	9.50
Tumbler, 9-1/2 oz, 4-1/8" h	6.00	12.00
Tumblers, 10 oz, 5" h	6.00	12.00
Tumblers, 14 oz, 5-3/8" h	7.50	15.00
Whiskey, 1 oz, 1-7/8" h	7.50	10.00

RIBBON

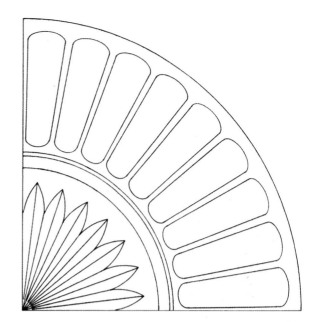

Manufactured by Hazel Atlas Glass Company, Clarksburg, W.V., and Zanesville, Ohio, early 1930s.

Pieces are made in black, crystal, green, and pink. Production in pink was limited to salt and pepper shakers, valued at $40.

Item	Black	Crystal	Green
Berry bowl, 4" d	—	20.00	22.00
Berry bowl, 8" d	—	27.50	45.00
Bowl, 9" d, wide bands	—	—	35.00
Candy dish, cov	45.00	35.00	45.00
Cereal bowl, 5" d	—	20.00	25.00
Creamer, ftd	—	10.00	18.00
Cup	—	4.50	6.50
Plate, 6-1/4" d, sherbet	—	3.50	4.50
Plate, 8" d, luncheon	15.00	7.00	10.00
Salt and pepper shakers, pr	45.00	36.00	32.00
Saucer	—	2.00	3.50
Sherbet	—	6.00	8.00
Sugar, ftd	—	12.00	18.50
Tumbler, 10 oz, 6" h	—	28.00	30.00

Ribbon, green cup, $6.50; creamer, $18.

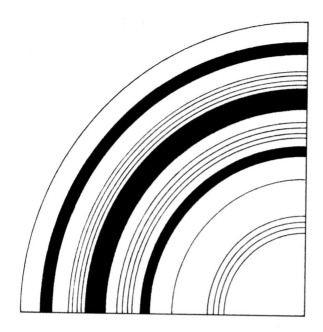

RING
Banded Rings

Manufactured by Hocking Glass Company, Lancaster, Ohio, from 1927 to 1933.

Pieces are made in crystal, crystal with rings of black, blue, pink, red, orange, silver and yellow; and green, Mayfair blue, pink and red. Prices for decorated pieces are quite similar to each other.

Item	Crystal	Decorated	Green
Berry bowl, 5" d	4.00	9.00	6.00
Berry bowl, 8" d	7.50	16.00	16.00
Bowl, 5-1/4" d, divided	12.50	—	—
Butter tub	24.00	25.00	20.00
Cereal bowl	—	5.00	8.00
Cocktail shaker	20.00	30.00	27.50
Cocktail, 3-1/2 oz, 3-3/4" h	12.00	18.00	18.00
Creamer, ftd	5.00	10.00	10.00
Cup	5.00	6.00	5.00
Decanter, stopper	30.00	35.00	32.00
Goblet, 9 oz, 7-1/4" h	7.00	15.00	14.00
Ice bucket	24.00	33.00	30.00
Ice tub	24.00	25.00	20.00
Iced tea tumbler, 6-1/2" h	10.00	15.00	15.00
Juice tumbler, 3-1/2" h, ftd	6.50	10.00	15.00
Old fashioned tumbler, 8 oz, 4" h	15.00	17.50	17.50
Pitcher, 60 oz, 8" h	15.00	25.00	25.00
Pitcher, 80 oz, 8-1/2" h	20.00	35.00	36.00
Plate, 6-1/2" d, off-center ring	5.50	6.50	8.00
Plate, 6-1/4" d, sherbet	3.25	6.50	4.00
Plate, 8" d, luncheon	3.00	6.00	9.00
Salt and pepper shakers, pr, 3" h	20.00	40.00	42.00
Sandwich plate, 11-3/4" d	9.50	15.00	15.00
Sandwich server, center handle	15.00	27.50	27.50
Saucer	1.50	4.00	2.50
Sherbet, 4-3/4" h	6.50	10.00	12.00
Sherbet, flat, 6-1/2" d underplate	12.00	18.00	21.00
Soup bowl, 7" d	10.00	9.00	8.00
Sugar, ftd	5.00	10.00	3.00
Tumbler, 4 oz, 3" h	4.00	6.50	6.00
Tumbler, 5-1/2" h, ftd	6.00	10.00	10.00
Tumbler, 5 oz, 3-1/2" h	5.00	6.50	12.00
Tumbler, 9 oz, 4-1/4" h	4.50	18.00	9.00

Item	Crystal	Decorated	Green
Tumbler, 10 oz, 4-3/4" h	8.50	—	9.00
Tumbler, 12 oz, 5-1/8" h, ftd	10.00	12.00	20.00
Vase, 8" h	20.00	35.00	37.50
Whiskey, 1-1/2 oz, 2" h	8.50	10.00	12.00
Wine, 3-1/2 oz, 4-1/2" h	17.50	20.00	24.00

*Ring, green ice tub, **$20**.*

*Ring, crystal sandwich server with center handle, **$15**.*

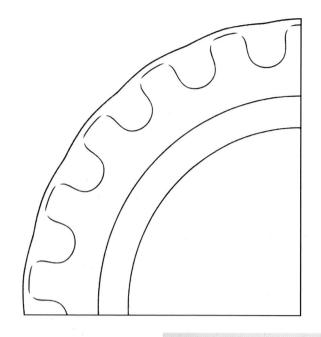

RIPPLE

Crinoline, Petticoat, Pie Crust, Lasagna, No. 6091, No. 6040

Manufactured by Hazel Atlas Glass Company, Clarksburg, W.V., in the early 1950s.

Pieces are made in Platonite white, Jewel Turquoise (white with turquoise trim), and Princess Pink (white with pink trim).

Ripple, Jewel Turquoise luncheon plate, $10.

Item	Jewel Turquoise	Platonite White	Princess Pink
Berry bowl, 5" d	12.00	12.00	7.00
Cereal bowl, 5-5/8" d	9.00	8.50	8.50
Creamer	7.50	7.50	7.50
Cup	4.50	4.50	4.50
Juice tumbler, 5 oz	7.50	7.50	7.50
Plate, 6-7/8" d, salad	5.00	5.00	5.00
Plate, 8-7/8" d, luncheon	10.00	6.00	7.00
Sandwich plate, 10-1/2" d	18.00	18.00	18.00
Saucer, 5-3/8" d	2.00	1.00	1.00
Sugar	7.50	7.50	7.50
Tidbit, three tiers	35.00	35.00	35.00
Tumbler, 6" h, 16 oz	12.00	12.00	12.00
Tumbler, 6-3/4" h, 20 oz	15.00	15.00	15.00

ROCK CRYSTAL

Early American Rock Crystal

Manufactured by McKee Glass Company, Pittsburgh, Pa., in the 1920s and colors in 1930s.

Made in amber, amberina red, amethyst, aquamarine, blue frosted, cobalt blue, crystal, crystal with goofus decoration, crystal with gold decoration, dark red, four shades of green, milk glass, pink and frosted pink, red, red slag, Vaseline, and yellow.

Item	Crystal	Colors	Red
Banana split dish	75.00	—	—
Bonbon, 7-1/2" d, scalloped edge	22.00	35.00	55.00
Bowl, 4" d, scalloped edge	15.00	24.00	35.00
Bowl, 4-1/2" d, scalloped edge	16.00	24.00	35.00
Bowl, 5" d, plain edge	20.00	26.00	45.00
Bowl, 5" d, scalloped edge	20.00	26.00	45.00
Bowl, 8-1/2" d, center handle	—	—	150.00
Bowl, 12-1/2" d, pedestal	80.00	125.00	300.00
Butter dish, cov	345.00	—	—
Cake stand, 11" d, 2-3/4" h, ftd	40.00	55.00	135.00
Candelabra, pr, two-lite	45.00	110.00	250.00
Candelabra, pr, three-lite	70.00	135.00	350.00
Candlesticks, pr, 5-1/2" h, low	45.00	70.00	175.00
Candlesticks, pr, 8" h	95.00	70.00	400.00
Candy dish, cov, ftd, 9-1/2" d	55.00	95.00	225.00
Candy dish, cov, round	50.00	75.00	175.00
Celery tray, 12" l, oblong	30.00	40.00	85.00
Center bowl, 12-1/2" d, ftd	80.00	135.00	310.00
Champagne, 6 oz, ftd	16.50	25.00	35.00
Claret, 3 oz	—	65.00	—
Cocktail, 3-1/2 oz, ftd	17.50	24.00	45.00
Comport, 7" d	35.00	60.00	90.00
Cordial, 1 oz, ftd	25.00	45.00	65.00
Creamer, 9 oz, ftd	20.00	35.00	75.00
Creamer, flat, scalloped edge	40.00	—	—
Cruet, stopper, 6 oz,	95.00	—	—
Cup, 7 oz	20.00	25.00	70.00
Deviled egg plate	50.00	—	—
Eggcup, 3-1/2 oz, ftd	15.00	20.00	65.00
Finger bowl, 5" d bowl, 7" d plate, piecrust edge	35.00	48.00	70.00
Goblet, 8 oz, ftd	20.00	30.00	65.00
Goblet, 8 oz, 7-1/2" h, low, ftd	22.50	30.00	65.00
Ice dish	35.00	—	—

Item	Crystal	Colors	Red
Iced tea goblet, 11 oz	25.00	35.00	72.50
Jelly, 5" d, ftd, scalloped edge	18.00	30.00	50.00
Juice tumbler, 5 oz	24.00	30.00	50.00
Lamp, electric	225.00	375.00	650.00
Old fashioned tumbler, 5 oz	20.00	30.00	60.00
Parfait, 3-1/2 oz, low, ftd	27.50	40.00	75.00
Pickle, 7" l	37.50	40.00	65.00
Pitcher, covered, 9" h	175.00	350.00	675.00
Pitcher, half gallon, 7-1/2" h	130.00	165.00	—
Pitcher, quart, scalloped edge	150.00	220.00	—
Pitcher, tankard	190.00	650.00	900.00
Plate, 6" d, bread and butter, scalloped edge	6.50	9.50	20.00
Plate, 7-1/2" d, piecrust edge	8.00	12.00	22.00
Plate, 7-1/2" d, scalloped edge	8.00	12.00	22.00
Plate, 8-1/2" d, piecrust edge	9.00	12.00	30.00
Plate, 8-1/2" d, scalloped edge	9.00	12.00	30.00
Plate, 9" d, scalloped edge	18.50	24.00	55.00
Plate, 10-1/2" d, center design, scalloped edge	47.50	75.00	175.00
Plate, 10-1/2" d, scalloped edge	27.50	35.00	65.00
Plate, 11-1/2" d, scalloped edge	20.00	30.00	60.00
Punch bowl and stand, 14"	555.00	—	—
Relish, 11-1/2" d, two parts	35.00	50.00	75.00
Relish, 12-1/2" d, five parts	0.00	—	—
Relish, 14" d, six parts	45.00	65.00	—
Roll tray, 13" d	35.00	60.00	125.00
Salad bowl, 7" d, scalloped edge	25.00	40.00	65.00
Salad bowl, 8" d, scalloped edge	32.00	42.00	67.50
Salad bowl, 9" d, scalloped edge	35.00	50.00	85.00
Salad bowl, 10-1/2" d, scalloped edge	25.00	50.00	90.00
Salt and pepper shakers, pr	80.00	135.00	—
Salt dip	35.00	—	—
Sandwich server, center handle	32.00	40.00	175.00
Saucer	5.00	6.50	20.00
Sherbet, 3-1/2 oz, ftd	15.00	20.00	25.00
Spoon tray, 7" l	20.00	40.00	65.00
Spooner	42.00	—	—
Sugar, cov	50.00	65.00	155.00
Sugar, 10 oz, open	18.00	20.00	45.00
Sundae, 6 oz, low, ftd	12.00	15.00	35.00
Syrup, lid	165.00	—	—
Tray, 5-3/8" x 7-3/8", 7/8" h	70.00	—	—
Tumbler, 9 oz, concave	15.00	26.00	30.00
Tumbler, 9 oz, straight	15.00	26.00	30.00
Tumbler, 12 oz, concave	35.00	40.00	70.00
Tumbler, 12 oz, straight	35.00	40.00	70.00
Vase, 11" h, ftd	75.00	95.00	170.00
Vase, cornucopia	70.00	95.00	—
Whiskey, 2-1/2 oz	25.00	35.00	65.00
Wine, 2 oz	22.50	30.00	50.00
Wine, 3 oz	22.50	30.00	55.00

Rock Crystal, amber plate, 8-1/2" d, **$12**.

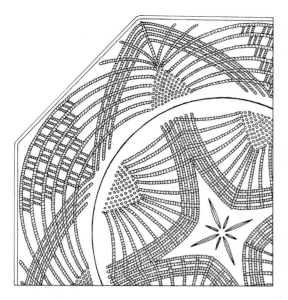

ROMANESQUE

Manufactured by L.E. Smith Glass Company, Mt. Pleasant, Pa., in the early 1930s.

Pieces are made in amber, black, crystal, green, and yellow.

Romanesque, yellow octagonal plate, 8" d, $10.

Item	Amber	Black	Crystal	Green	Yellow
Bowl, 10" d, ftd	75.00	95.00	70.00	75.00	75.00
Bowl, 10-1/2" d	42.00	55.00	40.00	42.00	42.00
Cake plate	40.00	45.00	35.00	40.00	40.00
Candlesticks, pr	27.50	35.00	25.00	27.50	27.50
Plate, 5-1/2", octagonal	6.50	10.00	6.00	6.50	6.50
Plate, 7", octagonal	8.50	14.00	8.50	8.50	8.50
Plate, 8", octagonal	10.00	18.00	9.00	10.00	10.00
Plate, 8" d, round	9.00	15.00	8.00	9.00	9.00
Plate, 10", octagonal	20.00	27.50	18.00	20.00	20.00
Sherbet, plain	8.50	14.00	7.50	8.50	8.50
Sherbet, scalloped	10.00	18.00	9.00	10.00	10.00
Snack Tray	15.00	20.00	14.00	15.00	15.00
Vase, 7-1/2" h, fan	50.00	60.00	45.00	50.00	50.00

ROSE CAMEO

Manufactured by Belmont Tumbler Company, Bellaire, Ohio, in 1931.

Pieces are made in green.

Rose Cameo, green tumbler, $25.

Item	Green
Berry bowl, 4-1/2" d	15.00
Cereal bowl, 5" d	27.50
Bowl, 6" d, straight sides	30.00
Plate, 7" d, salad	16.00
Sherbet	15.00
Tumbler, 5" h, ftd	25.00
Tumbler, 5" h, ftd, sterling silver trim	30.00

ROSEMARY

Dutch Rose

Manufactured by Federal Glass Company, Columbus, Ohio, from 1935 to 1937.

Pieces are made in amber, green, and pink.

Item	Amber	Green	Pink
Berry bowl, 5" d	7.00	17.50	17.50
Cereal bowl, 6" d	30.00	32.00	35.00
Cream soup, 5" d	20.00	25.00	30.00
Creamer, ftd	15.00	16.00	20.00
Cup	7.50	12.50	15.00
Plate, 6-3/4" d, salad	6.25	12.00	12.50
Plate, 9-1/2" d, dinner	10.00	15.00	30.00
Plate, 9-1/2" d, grill	12.00	15.00	22.00
Platter, 12" l, oval	18.00	24.00	35.00
Saucer	4.50	8.50	9.50
Sugar, ftd	15.00	16.00	20.00
Tumbler, 9 oz, 4-1/4" h	35.00	38.00	50.00
Vegetable bowl, 10" l, oval	17.50	40.00	45.00

*Rosemary, amber vegetable bowl, **$17.50**; berry bowl, **$7**.*

*Rosemary, green platter, **$24**.*

ROULETTE

Many Windows

Manufactured by Hocking Glass Company, Lancaster, Ohio, from 1935 to 1939.

Made in crystal, green, and pink.

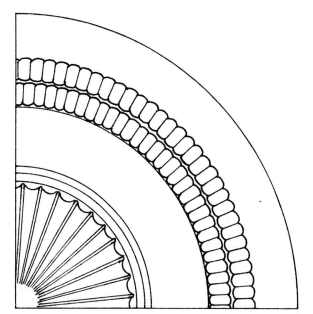

Item	Crystal	Green	Pink
Cup	35.00	8.50	8.50
Fruit bowl, 9" d	12.00	25.00	25.00
Iced tea tumbler, 12 oz, 5-1/8" h	24.00	40.00	35.00
Juice tumbler, 5 oz, 3-1/4" h	10.00	60.00	24.00
Old fashioned tumbler, 7-1/2 oz, 3-1/4" h	24.00	40.00	40.00
Pitcher, 65 oz, 8" h	30.00	35.00	45.00
Plate, 6" d, sherbet	3.50	4.50	5.00
Plate, 8-1/2" d, luncheon	7.00	8.00	6.00
Sandwich Plate, 12" d	15.00	18.50	20.00
Saucer	2.50	4.50	3.00
Sherbet	8.00	6.75	12.00
Tumbler, 9 oz, 4-1/8" h	15.00	20.00	30.00
Tumbler, 10 oz, 5-1/2" h, ftd	18.00	30.00	35.00
Whiskey, 1-1/2 oz, 2-1/2" h	10.00	18.00	17.50

*Roulette, green plate, **$8**; sherbet, **$6.75**.*

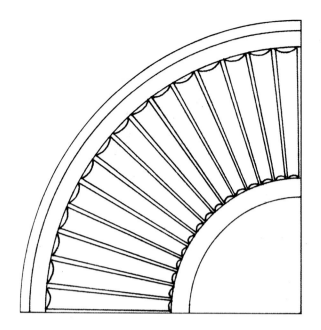

ROUND ROBIN

Unknown maker, early 1930s.

Pieces are made in crystal, iridescent, and green. Crystal, produced as the base for iridescent pieces, is found occasionally.

Item	Iridescent	Green
Berry bowl, 4" d	12.00	10.00
Creamer, ftd	7.50	12.00
Cup	7.50	6.00
Domino tray	—	120.00
Plate, 6" d, sherbet	4.00	6.00

Item	Iridescent	Green
Plate, 8" d, luncheon	9.00	12.00
Sandwich plate, 12" d	15.00	17.50
Saucer	2.50	2.00
Sherbet	8.50	10.00
Sugar	7.50	12.00

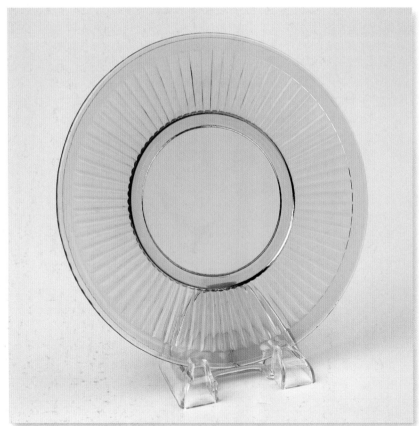

Round Robin, green luncheon plate, $8.

ROXANA

Manufactured by Hazel Atlas Glass Company, Clarksburg, W.V., and Zanesville, Ohio, in 1932.

Pieces are made in crystal, golden topaz, and white. Production in white was limited to a 4-1/2-inch bowl, valued at $15.

Item	Crystal	Gold Topaz
Berry bowl, 5" d	8.50	15.00
Bowl, 4-1/2" x 2-3/8"	8.00	15.00
Cereal bowl, 6" d	9.00	20.00
Plate, 5-1/2" d	5.00	12.00
Plate, 6" d, sherbet	5.00	10.00
Sherbet, ftd	8.00	12.00
Tumbler, 9 oz, 4-1/4" h	12.00	25.00

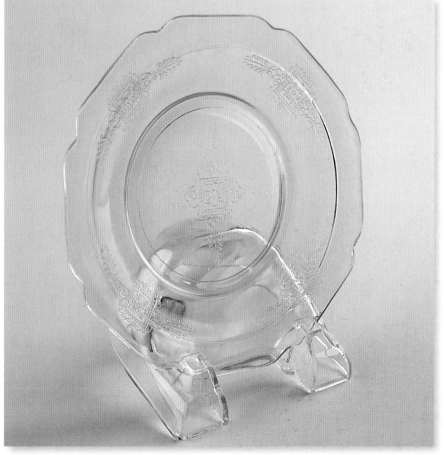

Roxana, gold topaz plate, **$12**.

ROYAL LACE

Manufactured by Hazel Atlas Glass Company, Clarksburg, W.V., and Zanesville, Ohio, from 1934 to 1941.

Pieces are made in cobalt (Ritz) blue, crystal, green, pink, and some amethyst.

Reproductions: † Reproductions include a 5-ounce, 3-1/2-inch high tumbler, found in a darker cobalt blue. A cookie jar has also been reproduced in cobalt blue.

Item	Cobalt Blue	Crystal	Green	Pink
Berry bowl, 5" d	50.00	18.00	65.00	90.00
Berry bowl, 10" d	90.00	20.00	35.00	60.00
Bowl, 10" d, three legs, rolled edge	650.00	225.00	125.00	200.00
Bowl, 10" d, three legs, ruffled edge	750.00	95.00	125.00	165.00
Bowl, 10" d, three legs, straight edge	—	24.00	75.00	65.00
Butter dish, cov	865.00	90.00	275.00	200.00
Candlesticks, pr, rolled edge	—	45.00	85.00	280.00
Candlesticks, pr, ruffled edge	—	28.00	70.00	60.00
Candlesticks, pr, straight edge	—	35.00	75.00	55.00
Cookie jar, cov †	400.00	30.00	75.00	100.00
Cream soup, 4-3/4" d	50.00	18.00	35.00	30.00
Creamer, ftd	65.00	15.00	25.00	20.00
Cup and saucer	60.00	16.00	35.00	32.00
Nut bowl	1,500.00	275.00	425.00	425.00
Pitcher, 48 oz, straight sides	225.00	45.00	110.00	85.00
Pitcher, 64 oz, 8" h	295.00	45.00	120.00	125.00
Pitcher, 68 oz, 8" h, ice lip	320.00	60.00	—	115.00
Pitcher, 86 oz, 8" h	—	60.00	135.00	135.00
Pitcher, 96 oz, 9-1/2" h, ice lip	495.00	115.00	160.00	155.00
Plate, 6" d, sherbet	20.00	8.50	15.00	18.00
Plate, 8-1/2" d, luncheon	60.00	12.00	18.00	24.00
Plate, 9-7/8" d, dinner	55.00	25.00	45.00	40.00
Plate, 9-7/8" d, grill	40.00	20.00	25.00	22.50
Platter, 13" l, oval	60.00	30.00	45.00	48.00
Salt and pepper shakers, pr	395.00	65.00	130.00	85.00
Sherbet, ftd	50.00	18.00	60.00	35.00
Sherbet, metal holder	45.00	18.00	—	—
Sugar, cov	275.00	90.00	40.00	50.00
Sugar, open	—	15.00	25.00	20.00
Toddy or cider set	295.00	—	—	—
Tumbler, 5 oz, 3-1/2" h †	65.00	15.00	60.00	35.00
Tumbler, 9 oz, 4-1/8" h †	60.00	18.00	35.00	30.00
Tumbler, 10 oz, 4-7/8" h	245.00	25.00	60.00	60.00
Tumbler, 12 oz, 5-3/8" h	165.00	25.00	50.00	55.00
Vegetable bowl, 11" l, oval	60.00	25.00	35.00	95.00

*Royal Lace, crystal dinner plate, **$25***.

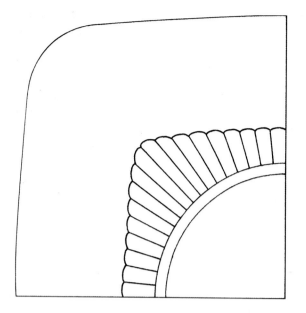

ROYAL RUBY

Manufactured by Anchor Hocking Glass Corporation, Lancaster, Pa., from 1938 to 1967. Pieces are made only in Royal Ruby.

Item	Royal Ruby
Apothecary jar, 8-1/2" h	22.00
Ashtray, 3-1/2", sq	10.00
Ashtray, 4" d, round	10.00
Ashtray, 4-1/4", sq	10.00
Ashtray, 4-1/2", leaf	5.00
Ashtray, 5-7/8", sq	7.50
Ashtray, 7-3/4"	32.00
Beer bottle, 7 oz	42.50
Beer bottle, 12 oz	32.00
Beer bottle, 16 oz	35.00
Beer bottle, 32 oz	40.00
Berry bowl, 4-1/2" d, round	12.00
Berry bowl, 4-5/8" d, small, square	9.50
Berry bowl, 8-1/2" d, round	25.00
Bonbon, 6-1/2" d	20.00
Bowl, 7-3/8" w, sq	18.50
Bowl, 8-1/4" d, round	25.00
Bowl, 11" d, Rachael	50.00
Bowl, 12" l, oval, Rachael	70.00
Cereal bowl, 5-1/4" d	12.00
Cigarette box, card holder, 6-1/8" x 4"	90.00
Cocktail, 3-1/2 oz, Boopie	8.50
Cocktail, 3-1/2 oz, tumbler	10.00
Cordial, ftd	15.00
Creamer, flat	8.00
Creamer, ftd	10.00
Cup, round	12.00
Cup, square	7.50
Dessert bowl, 4-3/4" w, sq	12.00
Fruit bowl, 4-1/4" d	10.00
Goblet, 9 oz	9.00
Goblet, 9-1/2 oz	14.00
Goblet, ball stem	15.00
Ice bucket	55.00
Iced tea goblet, 14 oz, Boopie	20.00
Iced tea tumbler, 13 oz, 6" h, ftd	14.00

Item	Royal Ruby
Ivy ball, 4" h, Wilson	10.00
Juice tumbler, 4 oz	7.00
Juice tumbler, 5-1/2 oz	10.00
Juice tumbler, 5 oz, flat or ftd	8.00
Juice pitcher, tilt, ball	40.00
Lamp	35.00
Marmalade, ruby top, crystal base	22.00
Pitcher, 3 qt, tilted	45.00
Pitcher, 3 qt, upright	38.00
Pitcher, 42 oz, tilted	35.00
Pitcher, 42 oz, upright	40.00
Pitcher, 86 oz, 8-1/2"	35.00
Plate, 6-1/4" d, sherbet	6.50
Plate, 7" d, salad	5.50
Plate, 7-3/4" w, sq, salad	12.50
Plate, 8-3/8" w, sq, luncheon	12.00
Plate, 9-1/8" d, dinner	17.50
Plate, 13-3/4" d	35.00
Popcorn bowl, 5-1/4" d	12.50
Popcorn bowl, 10" d, deep	40.00
Puff box, ruby top, crystal base, orig label	28.00
Punch bowl and Stand	75.00
Punch set, 14 pieces	95.00
Punch cup	3.00
Relish, 3-3/4" x 8-3/4", tab handle	16.00
Roly poly tumbler	6.00
Salad bowl, 8-1/2" d	19.00
Salad bowl, 11-1/2" d	48.00
Saucer, 5-3/8" w, sq	4.00
Saucer, round	4.00
Set, 50 pcs, orig labels, orig box	350.00
Sherbet, Baltic, low collar	8.00
Sherbet, 6-1/2 oz, stemmed	9.50
Sherbet, 6 oz, Boopie	9.00
Shot glass	4.50
Soup bowl, 7-1/2" d	13.00
Sugar, flat	8.00
Sugar, footed	8.00
Sugar lid, notched	11.00
Tray, center handle, ruffled	16.50
Tumbler, 5 oz, 3-1/2" h	15.00
Tumbler, 9 oz, Windsor	8.00

Item	Royal Ruby	Item	Royal Ruby
Tumbler, 10 oz, 4-1/2" h, Baltic	10.00	Vase, 6-3/8" h, Harding	9.00
Tumbler, 10 oz, 5" h, ftd	15.00	Vase, 6-5/8" h, Coolidge	20.00
Tumbler, 12 oz, 4-7/8" h, ftd	16.00	Vase, 9" h, Hoover, plain	20.00
Tumbler, 14 oz, 5" h	9.00	Vase, 9" h, Hoover, white birds on branch dec	25.00
Tumbler, 15 oz, long boy	15.00	Vase, 10" h, fluted, star base	35.00
Tumbler, 16 oz, coupe	12.00	Vase, 10" h, ftd, Rachael	50.00
Vase, 3-3/4" h, Roosevelt	7.50	Vegetable bowl, 8" l, oval	30.00
Vase, 4" h, Wilson, fancy edge	8.00	Wine, 2-1/2 oz, ftd	12.50

Royal Ruby, punch set, includes 14 pieces, punch bowl and six cups are shown, value for the entire set is $95.

Royal Ruby, footed sugar, $8; footed creamer (on pedestal), $10; square cup, $7.50; square saucer, $4.

Royal Ruby, vase with original foil label, $20.

S-PATTERN

Stippled Rose Band

Manufactured by Macbeth-Evans Glass Company, Charleroi, Pa., from 1930 to 1933.

Pieces are made in amber, crystal, crystal with amber, blue, green, pink or silver trims, fired-on red, green, light yellow and Monax.

Item	Amber	Crystal	Crystal with Trims	Fired-On Colors	Yellow
Berry bowl, 8-1/2" d	8.50	12.00	—	—	8.50
Cake plate, 11-3/4" d	50.00	48.00	55.00	—	50.00
Cake plate, 13" d	80.00	65.00	75.00	—	75.00
Cereal bowl, 5-1/2" d	9.50	4.50	6.50	12.00	6.50
Creamer, thick	7.50	6.50	6.00	15.00	7.50
Creamer, thin	7.50	6.50	6.00	15.00	7.50
Cup, thick	5.00	4.00	5.50	10.00	5.00
Cup, thin	5.00	4.00	5.50	10.00	5.00
Pitcher, 80 oz	—	75.00	—	—	—
Plate, 6" d, sherbet	3.50	3.00	4.00	—	3.50
Plate, 8-1/4" d, luncheon	7.00	6.50	8.50	—	5.00
Plate, 9-1/4" d, dinner	9.50	—	12.50	—	9.50
Plate, grill	8.50	6.50	9.00	—	8.50
Saucer	4.00	3.00	4.00	—	4.00
Sherbet, low, ftd	8.00	5.50	8.50	—	8.00
Sugar, thick	7.50	6.50	6.00	15.00	7.50
Sugar, thin	7.50	6.50	6.00	15.00	7.50
Tumbler, 5 oz, 3-1/2" h	6.50	5.00	6.50	—	6.50
Tumbler, 10 oz, 4-3/4" h	8.50	9.00	7.50	—	8.50
Tumbler, 12 oz, 5" h	15.00	10.00	17.50	—	15.00

S-Pattern, crystal luncheon plate with yellow trim,
$8.50

SANDWICH

Line #41

Manufactured by Duncan & Miller Glass Company, Washington, Pa., from 1924 to 1955.

Pieces are made in crystal with limited production in amber, cobalt blue, green, pink, and red. The molds were sold to Lancaster Colony, which continues to produce some glass in this pattern, but in newer brighter colors, such as amberina, blue, and green.

Item	Crystal
Almond bowl, 2-1/2" d	12.00
Ashtray, 2-1/2" x 3-3/4"	10.00
Ashtray, 2-3/4" sq	8.50
Basket, 6-1/2", loop handle	135.00
Basket 10", loop handle, crimped	185.00
Basket, 10", loop handle, oval	185.00
Basket, 11-1/2", loop handle	225.00
Bonbon, 5" w, heart shape	15.00
Bonbon, 6" w, heart shape, ring handle	20.00
Bonbon, cov, 7-1/2" d, ftd,	45.00
Bowl, 5-1/2" d, handle	15.00
Butter, cov, quarter pound	40.00
Cake stand, 11-1/2" d, ftd	95.00
Cake stand, 12" d, ftd	115.00
Cake stand, 13" d, ftd	125.00
Candelabra, with bobeche and prisms, 10" h, one-lite	95.00
Candelabra, with bobeche and prisms, 10" h, three-lite	200.00
Candelabra, with bobeche and prisms, 16" h, three-lite	225.00
Candlesticks, pr, 4" h	30.00
Candlesticks, pr, 5" h, three-lite	90.00
Candy box, cov, 5" d, flat	42.00
Candy comport, 3-1/4" d, low, ftd or flared	25.00
Candy dish, 6" sq	375.00
Candy jar, cov, 8-1/2" d, flat	60.00
Celery tray, 10" l, oval	30.00
Champagne, 5 oz	25.00
Cheese comport, 13" d underplate	60.00
Cheese dish, cov	125.00
Cigarette box, cov, 3-1/2"	24.00
Cigarette holder, 3" d, ftd	30.00
Coaster, 5" d	12.00
Cocktail, 3 oz	15.00
Comport, 2-1/4"	17.50
Comport, 4-1/4" d, ftd	22.00
Comport, 5" d, low, ftd	22.00

Item	Crystal
Comport, 5-1/2" d, ftd, low, crimped	25.00
Comport, 6" d, low, flared	25.00
Condiment set, pr cruets, pr salt and pepper shakers, tray	100.00
Console bowl, 12" d	45.00
Cracker plate, 13" d	32.00
Creamer	10.00
Cup	10.00
Deviled egg plate, 12" d	65.00
Epergne, 9" h	125.00
Epergne, 12" h, three parts	200.00
Finger bowl, 4" h	12.00
Finger bowl underplate, 6-1/2" d	8.00
Flower bowl, 11-1/2" d, crimped	60.00
Fruit bowl, 5" d	10.00
Fruit bowl, 10" d	65.00
Fruit bowl, 11-1/2" d, crimped, ftd	65.00
Fruit bowl, 12", flared	50.00
Fruit cup, 6 oz	12.00
Fruit salad bowl, 6" d	12.00
Gardenia bowl, 11-1/2" d	48.00
Goblet, 9 oz, 6" h	18.00
Grapefruit bowl, 5-1/2" d or 6" d	17.50
Hostess plate, 16" d	100.00
Ice cream dish 5 oz	12.00

Item	Crystal	Item	Crystal
Ice cream plate, rolled edge, 12" d	60.00	Relish, 7" d, two parts, oval	20.00
Ice cream tray, rolled edge, 12" d	45.00	Relish, 10" d, three parts, rect	27.50
Iced tea tumbler, 12 or 13 oz, ftd	20.00	Relish, 10" d, four parts	25.00
Ivy bowl, ftd, crimped	35.00	Relish, 10-1/2" l, three parts, rect	27.50
Jelly, 3" d	8.00	Relish, 12" l, three parts	25.00
Juice tumbler, 5 oz	12.00	Salad bowl, 10" d, deep	75.00
Lazy Susan, 16" d	115.00	Salad bowl, 12" d, shallow	42.00
Lily bowl, 10" d	55.00	Salt and pepper shakers, pr, 2-1/2" h, glass tops	20.00
Mayonnaise set, three pcs	35.00	Salt and pepper shakers, pr, 2-1/2" h, metal tops	20.00
Mint tray, 6" l or 7" l, rolled edge, ring handle	18.00	Salts and pepper shakers, set, pr 3-3/4" h, metal tops, 6" tray	35.00
Nappy, 5" d, two parts	15.00	Service plate, 11-1/2" d, handle	50.00
Nappy, 5" d, ring handle	12.00	Service plate, 13" d	55.00
Nappy, 6" d, ring handle	15.00	Sugar shaker	72.00
Nut bowl, 3-1/2" d	10.00	Sugar bowl, 5 oz	10.00
Nut bowl, 11" d, cupped	55.00	Sugar bowl, 9 oz, 3-1/4" h, ftd	12.00
Oil bottle, orig stopper	35.00	Sundae, 5 oz	15.00
Oil and vinegar tray, 8" l	20.00	Torte plate, 12" d	48.00
Oyster cocktail, 5 oz	18.00	Tray, 8" l	20.00
Parfait, 4 oz, ftd	30.00	Urn, cov, 12" h, ftd	150.00
Pickle tray, 7" l, oval	15.00	Tumbler, 9 oz, 4-3/4", ftd	15.00
Pitcher, 13 oz, metal lip	75.00	Vase, 3" h, crimped	18.00
Pitcher, 64 oz, ice lip	125.00	Vase, 3" h, flared rim	18.00
Plate, 3" d, jelly	5.00	Vase, 4" h, hat shape	20.00
Plate, 6" d, bread and butter	6.00	Vase, 4-1/2" h, crimped	25.00
Plate, 7" d, dessert	7.50	Vase, 5" h, fan	40.00
Plate, 8" d, salad	10.00	Vase, 5" h, flared or crimped	25.00
Plate, 9-1/2" d, dinner	35.00	Vase, 10" h, ftd	70.00
Relish, 5-1/2" d, two parts, ring handle	15.00	Wine, 3 oz	24.00
Relish, 6" d, two parts, ring handle	18.00		

*Sandwich, crystal salad plate, **$10**.*

SANDWICH

Hocking

Manufactured by Hocking Glass Company, and later Anchor Hocking Corporation, from 1939 to 1964.

Pieces are made in crystal, Desert Gold, 1961-64; Forest Green, 1956-1960s; pink, 1939-1940; Royal Ruby, 1938-1939; and white/ivory (opaque), 1957-1960s.

Reproductions: † The cookie jar has been reproduced in crystal.

Item	Crystal	Desert Gold	Forest Green	Pink	Royal Ruby	White
Bowl, 4-5/16" d, smooth	5.00	—	4.00	—	—	—
Bowl, 4-7/8" d, smooth	5.00	6.00	—	7.00	17.50	—
Bowl, 4-7/8" d, crimped	20.00	—	—	—	—	—
Bowl, 5-1/4" d, scalloped	8.00	6.00	—	—	32.00	—
Bowl, 5-1/4" d, smooth	—	—	—	7.00	35.00	—
Bowl, 6-1/2" d, scalloped	7.50	9.00	60.00	—	35.00	—
Bowl, 6-1/2" d, smooth	7.50	6.00	—	—	—	—
Bowl, 7-1/4" d, scalloped	14.00	—	—	—	—	—
Bowl, 8-1/4" d, oval	6.00	—	—	—	—	—
Bowl, 8-1/4" d, scalloped	18.00	—	80.00	20.00	35.00	—
Butter dish, cov	45.00	—	—	—	—	—
Cereal bowl, 6-3/4" d	32.00	12.00	—	—	—	—
Cookie jar, cov † *	40.00	45.00	20.00	—	—	—
Creamer	7.50	—	30.00	—	—	—
Cup, coffee	3.50	12.00	24.00	—	—	—
Cup, tea	3.50	14.00	24.00	—	—	—
Custard cup	7.00	—	4.00	—	—	—
Custard cup liner	5.50	—	1.50	—	—	—
Custard cup, crimped	15.00	—	—	—	—	—
Dessert bowl, 5" d, crimped	18.50	—	—	—	—	—
Juice pitcher, 6" h	115.00	—	145.00	—	—	—
Juice tumbler, 3 oz, 3-3/8" h	12.00	—	6.00	—	—	—
Juice tumbler, 5 oz, 3-9/16" h	6.50	—	4.50	—	—	—
Pitcher, half gallon, ice lip	85.00	—	550.00	—	—	—
Plate, 6" d	5.00	—	—	—	—	—
Plate, 7" d, dessert	20.00	—	—	—	—	—
Plate, 8" d, luncheon	18.00	—	—	—	—	—
Plate, 9" d, dinner	24.00	9.00	125.00	10.00	—	—
Plate, 9" d, indent for punch cup	12.00	—	—	—	—	—
Punch bowl, 9-3/4" d	18.00	—	—	—	—	15.00
Punch bowl and stand	30.00	—	—	—	—	30.00
Punch bowl set, bowl, base, 12 cups	80.00	—	—	—	—	—
Punch cup	4.00	—	—	—	—	2.00
Salad bowl, 7" d	8.00	25.00	—	—	—	—
Salad bowl, 7-5/8" d	—	—	60.00	—	—	—

Item	Crystal	Desert Gold	Forest Green	Pink	Royal Ruby	White
Salad bowl, 9" d	24.00	20.00	—	—	—	—
Sandwich plate, 12" d	14.00	17.50	—	—	—	—
Saucer	3.75	5.00	15.00	—	—	—
Sherbet, ftd	9.00	8.00	—	—	—	—
Snack set, plate and cup	12.50	—	—	—	—	—
Sugar, cov	30.00	—	—	—	—	—
Sugar, no cover	6.00	—	30.00	—	—	—
Tumbler, 9 oz, ftd	32.50	125.00	—	—	—	—
Tumbler, 9 oz, water	8.00	—	7.00	—	—	—
Vase	—	—	27.50	—	—	—
Vegetable, 8-1/2" l, oval	10.00	—	—	—	—	—

*No cover is known for the cookie jar in Forest Green.

*Sandwich, Hocking, crystal oval bowl, **$6**.*

*Sandwich, Hocking, smooth desert gold bowl, 6-1/2" d, **$6**.*

*Sandwich, Hocking, crystal saucer, **$3.75**.*
Photo courtesy of Tina Trautman.

*Sandwich, Hocking, forest green cookie jar, no lid, **$10**.*
Photo courtesy of Tina Trautman.

SANDWICH

Manufactured by Indiana Glass Company, Dunkirk, Ind., 1920s to 1980s.

Pieces are made in crystal, late 1920s to 1990s; amber, late 1920s to 1980s; milk white, mid-1950s; teal blue, 1950s to 1960s; red, 1933 and early 1970s; smoky blue, 1976 to 1977; and green in the late 1960s and 1970s by Taira.

Reproductions: † Reproductions include a butter dish, decanter, and wine. Reproductions are found in dark amber, crystal, green, and pink.

Item	Amber	Crystal	Teal Blue	Red
Ashtray, club	3.25	3.00	—	—
Ashtray, diamond	3.25	3.00	—	—
Ashtray, heart	3.25	3.00	2.00	—
Ashtray, spade	3.00	3.00	—	—
Basket, 10" h	35.00	35.00	—	—
Berry bowl, 4-1/4" d	4.00	4.00	—	—
Bowl, 6" w, hexagonal	6.00	6.00	15.00	—
Bowl, 8-1/2" d	10.00	11.00	—	—
Butter dish, cov †	25.00	25.00	150.00	—
Candlesticks, pr, 3-1/2" h	18.00	20.00	—	—
Candlesticks, pr, 7" h	25.00	25.00	—	—
Celery tray, 10-1/2" l	16.00	14.00	—	—
Cereal bowl, 6" d	12.00	6.50	—	—
Cocktail, 3 oz, ftd	7.50	7.50	—	—
Comport, low, ruffled	15.00	—	—	—
Console bowl, 9" d	17.50	17.50	—	—
Console bowl, 11-1/2" d	20.00	20.00	—	—
Creamer	6.00	6.00	—	48.00
Creamer and sugar, tray	18.00	18.00	35.00	—
Cruet, 6-1/2 oz, stopper	—	—	145.00	—
Cup	4.00	4.00	8.50	30.00
Decanter, stopper †	25.00	25.00	—	90.00
Fairy lamp	15.00	—	—	—
Goblet, 9 oz	12.00	12.50	—	45.00
Iced tea tumbler, 12 oz, ftd	10.00	10.00	—	—
Mayonnaise, ftd	14.00	14.00	—	—
Pitcher, 68 oz	24.00	24.00	—	175.00
Plate, 6" d, sherbet	3.50	3.50	7.50	—
Plate, 7" d, bread and butter	4.00	4.00	—	—
Plate, 8" d, oval, indent	5.00	4.00	6.50	15.00
Plate, 8-3/8" d, luncheon	7.50	8.00	—	20.00
Plate, 10-1/2" d, dinner	9.00	8.50	20.00	—
Puff box	18.00	18.00	—	—
Salt and pepper shakers, pr	18.00	18.00	—	—
Sandwich plate, 13" d	14.50	14.50	25.00	35.00

Item	Amber	Crystal	Teal Blue	Red
Sandwich server, center handle	20.00	20.00	—	50.00
Saucer	3.50	2.50	7.00	7.50
Sherbet, 3-1/4" h	6.50	5.00	12.00	—
Sugar, cov, large	20.00	15.00	—	48.00
Tumbler, 8 oz, ftd, water	10.00	10.00	—	—
Wine, 3" h, 4 oz †	10.00	12.00	—	15.00

Sandwich, Indiana, crystal creamer and sugar with matching tray, $18.

SEVILLE

Manufactured by Fostoria Glass Company, Moundsville, Va., from 1926 to 1931.

Pieces are made in amber and green.

Item	Amber	Green
After dinner cup and saucer	32.00	40.00
Ashtray, 4" d	20.00	24.00
Baker, 9" l, oval	27.50	32.00
Baker, 10-1/2" l, oval	37.50	40.00
Bouillon, flat or ftd	15.00	17.50
Bowl, 7" d, low foot	15.50	17.50
Bowl, 10" d, ftd	35.00	40.00
Bowl, 10-1/2" d, flared, ftd	30.00	32.00
Bowl, 12" d, deep, flared	32.00	35.00
Butter dish, cov, round	195.00	250.00
Canapé plate, 8-3/4" d	37.50	42.00
Candlesticks, pr, 2" h	15.00	20.00
Candlesticks, pr, 4" h	15.00	22.00
Candlesticks, pr, 9" h	32.00	35.00
Candy jar, cov, flat	70.00	85.00
Candy jar, cov, ftd	90.00	125.00
Celery, 11"	17.50	20.00
Cereal bowl, 6-1/2" d	17.50	20.00
Cheese and cracker	42.00	48.00
Chop plate, 12-3/4" d	32.00	35.00
Cocktail	17.50	20.00
Comport, 7-1/2" d	22.00	30.00
Comport, 8"	30.00	37.50
Console bowl, 11" d, rolled edge	30.00	35.00
Console bowl, 13" d, rolled edge	35.00	40.00
Console bowl, 13" l, oval	40.00	45.00
Cordial	70.00	72.00
Cream soup, ftd	15.00	17.50
Creamer, flat or ftd	15.00	20.00
Cup, flat or ftd	12.00	15.00

Item	Amber	Green
Eggcup	30.00	35.00
Finger bowl	10.00	12.50
Fruit bowl, 5-1/2" d	10.00	12.50
Goblet	22.00	25.00
Grapefruit, blown	42.00	48.00
Grapefruit, molded	27.50	35.00
Ice bucket	60.00	65.00
Nappy, 9" d	30.00	35.00
Oyster cocktail	17.50	20.00
Parfait	35.00	37.50
Pickle	15.00	17.50
Pitcher, ftd	250.00	275.00
Plate, 6" d, bread and butter	4.00	6.00
Plate, 7-1/2" d, salad	6.00	7.50
Plate, 8-1/2" d, luncheon	7.50	12.50
Plate, 9-1/2" d, dinner	12.50	17.50
Plate, 10-1/2" d, dinner	30.00	35.00
Platter, 10-1/2" l	24.00	27.50
Platter, 12" l	35.00	40.00
Platter, 15" l	65.00	70.00
Salad bowl, 10" d	35.00	40.00
Salt and pepper shakers, pr	65.00	70.00
Sauce boat and underplate	75.00	95.00
Saucer	3.50	4.00
Serving plate, 15" d	37.50	42.00
Sherbet, high	15.00	17.50
Sherbet, low	12.00	15.00
Soup bowl, 7-3/4" d	24.00	30.00
Sugar bowl lid	75.00	100.00
Sugar bowl, ftd	15.00	15.00

Item	Amber	Green	Item	Amber	Green
Tray, 11" d, center handle	30.00	32.00	Urn	72.00	95.00
Tumbler, 2 oz, ftd	37.50	42.00	Vase, 8" h	50.00	60.00
Tumbler, 5 oz, ftd	15.00	17.50	Vegetable bowl	24.00	30.00
Tumbler, 9 oz, ftd	17.50	20.00	Wine	24.00	27.50
Tumbler, 12 oz, ftd	20.00	24.00			

*Seville, amber dinner plate, 9-1/2" d, **$12**.*

SHARON

Cabbage Rose

Manufactured by Federal Glass Company, Columbus, Ohio, from 1935 to 1939.

Pieces are made in amber, crystal, green, and pink.

Reproductions: † Reproductions include the butter dish, covered candy dish, creamer, covered sugar, and salt and pepper shakers. Reproduction colors include dark amber, blue, green, and pink.

Item	Amber	Crystal	Green	Pink
Berry bowl, 5" d	8.50	5.00	18.50	16.50
Berry bowl, 8-1/2" d	7.50	12.00	40.00	35.00
Butter dish, cov †	50.00	20.00	85.00	65.00
Cake plate, 11-1/2" d, ftd	30.00	10.00	65.00	45.00
Candy dish, cov †	45.00	15.00	100.00	65.00
Cereal bowl, 6" d	24.00	12.00	32.00	30.00
Champagne, 5" d bowl	—	—	—	12.00
Cheese dish, cov †	225.00	1,500.00	—	950.00
Cream soup, 5" d	28.00	15.00	60.00	52.50
Creamer, ftd †	15.00	14.00	22.00	20.00
Cup	9.00	6.00	18.00	18.00
Fruit bowl, 10-1/2" d	24.00	18.00	40.00	50.00
Iced tea tumbler, ftd	85.00	15.00	—	65.00
Jam dish, 7-1/2" d	45.00	—	48.00	215.00
Pitcher, 80 oz, ice lip	165.00	—	150.00	165.00
Pitcher, 80 oz, without ice lip	140.00	—	150.00	150.00
Plate, 6" d, bread and butter	12.00	5.00	9.00	9.50
Plate, 7-1/2" d, salad	22.50	6.50	8.00	30.00
Plate, 9-1/2" d, dinner	17.00	9.50	27.50	26.50
Platter, 12-1/2" l, oval	24.00	—	35.00	35.00
Salt and pepper shakers, pr †	50.00	—	80.00	65.00
Saucer	6.50	4.00	36.00	12.00
Sherbet, ftd	12.50	8.00	35.00	20.00
Soup, flat, 7-3/4" d, 1 7/8" deep	55.00	—	—	60.00

Item	Amber	Crystal	Green	Pink
Sugar, cov †	35.00	12.00	55.00	60.00
Tumbler, 9 oz, 4-1/8" h, thick....................	30.00	—	65.00	47.50
Tumbler, 9 oz, 4-1/8" h, thin	38.00	—	65.00	50.00
Tumbler, 12 oz, 5-1/4" h, thick	55.00	—	95.00	50.00
Tumbler, 12 oz, 5-1/4" h, thin	55.00	—	95.00	62.00
Tumbler, 15 oz, 6-1/2" h, thick	125.00	18.00	—	65.00
Vegetable bowl, 9-1/2" l, oval....................	22.00	—	45.00	36.00

*Sharon, pink sherbet, **$20**; berry bowl, 8-1/2 d, **$35**; creamer, **$20**; berry bowl, 5 d, **$16.50**.*

REPRODUCTION! Sharon, pink covered candy dish.

SHIPS

Sailboat, Sportsman Series

Manufactured by Hazel Atlas Glass Company, Clarksburg, W.V., and Zanesville, Ohio, late 1930s.

Pieces are made in cobalt blue with white, yellow, and red decoration. Pieces with yellow or red decoration are valued slightly higher than the traditional white decoration.

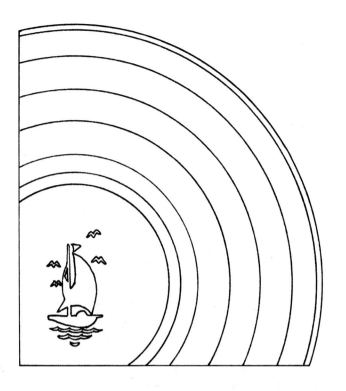

Ships, cobalt blue cocktail shaker, $25.

Item	Cobalt Blue with White Decoration
Ashtray	60.00
Ashtray, metal sailboat	120.00
Box, cov, three parts	250.00
Cocktail mixer, stirrer	45.00
Cocktail shaker	25.00
Cup	15.00
Ice bowl	45.00
Iced tea tumbler, 10-1/2 oz, 4-7/8" h	22.00
Iced tea tumbler, 12 oz	24.00
Juice tumbler, 5 oz, 3-3/4" h	12.50
Old fashioned tumbler, 8 oz, 3-3/8" h	22.00
Pitcher, 82 oz, no ice lip	85.00
Pitcher, 86 oz, ice lip	75.00
Plate, 5-7/8" d, bread and butter	40.00
Plate, 8" d, salad	27.50
Plate, 9" d, dinner	32.00
Roly Poly, 6 oz	10.00
Saucer	18.00
Shot glass, 2 oz, 2-1/4" h	250.00
Tumbler, 4 oz, 3-1/4" h, heavy bottom	27.50
Tumbler, 4 oz, heavy bottom	12.00
Tumbler, 9 oz, 3-3/4" h	18.00
Tumbler, 9 oz, 4-5/8" h	18.00
Whiskey, 3-1/2" h	45.00

*Ships, cobalt blue salad plate, **$27.50***.

*Ships, cobalt blue dinner plate, **$32***.

SIERRA

Pinwheel

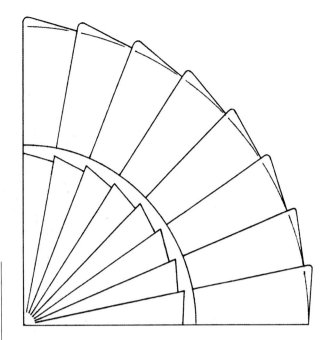

Manufactured by Jeannette Glass Company, Jeannette, Pa., from 1931 to 1933.

Pieces are made in green and pink. A few forms are known in Ultramarine.

Item	Green	Pink
Berry, small	25.00	25.00
Berry bowl, 8-1/2" d	40.00	47.50
Butter dish, cov	80.00	85.00
Cereal bowl, 5-1/2" d	35.00	30.00
Creamer	25.00	25.00
Cup	18.50	15.00
Pitcher, 32 oz, 6-1/2" h	170.00	150.00
Plate, 9" d, dinner	30.00	30.00
Platter, 11" l, oval	70.00	55.00
Salt and pepper shakers, pr	50.00	50.00
Saucer	12.00	8.00
Serving tray, 10-1/4" l, two handles	25.00	28.00
Sugar, cov	48.00	48.00
Tumbler, 9 oz, 4-1/2" h, ftd	90.00	80.00
Vegetable bowl, 9-1/4" l, oval	185.00	95.00

*Sierra, green butter dish, **$80**; and pink cup, **$15**; and saucer, **$8**.*

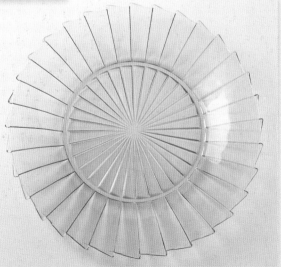

*Sierra, pink dinner plate, **$30**.*

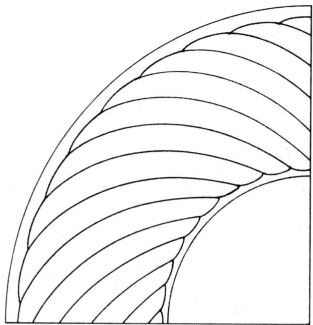

SPIRAL

Manufactured by Hocking Glass Company, Lancaster, Ohio, from 1928 to 1930.

Pieces are made in crystal, green, and pink. Collector interest is strongest in green.

Item	Green
Berry bowl, 4-3/4" d	8.00
Berry bowl, 8" d	16.50
Butter tub	27.50
Candy, cov	35.00
Creamer, flat	8.00
Creamer, footed	8.00
Cup	6.50
Ice tub	25.00

Item	Green
Juice tumbler, 5 oz, 3" h	5.00
Mixing bowl, 7" d	9.00
Pitcher, 58 oz, 7-5/8" h	35.00
Plate, 6" d, sherbet	5.00
Plate, 8" d, luncheon	6.00
Platter, 12" l	32.00
Preserve, cov	50.00
Salt and pepper shakers, pr	37.50
Sandwich server, center handle	30.00
Saucer	5.00
Sherbet	5.00
Sugar, flat	8.00
Sugar, footed	8.00
Tumbler, 5-7/8" h, ftd	24.00
Tumbler, 9 oz, 5" h	12.00

*Spiral, green luncheon plate, **$6**; sherbet, **$5**.*

STAR

Manufactured by Federal Glass Company, Columbus, Ohio, 1950s.

Pieces are made in amber, crystal and crystal with gold trim. Crystal pieces with gold trim are valued the same as plain crystal.

Item	Amber	Crystal
Bowl, 5-5/8" d	—	7.00
Creamer	7.00	9.00
Cup	10.00	10.00
Dessert bowl, 4-5/8" d	4.00	5.00
Iced tea tumbler, 12 oz, 5-1/8" h	8.00	9.00
Juice pitcher, 36 oz, 5-3/4" h	10.00	18.00
Juice tumbler, 4-1/2 oz, 3-3/8" h	4.00	5.00
Pitcher, 60 oz, 7" h	15.00	14.00
Pitcher, 85 oz, 9-1/4" h, ice lip	15.00	15.00
Plate, 6-3/16" d, salad	5.00	6.00
Plate, 9-3/8" d, dinner	12.00	14.00
Saucer	4.00	3.00
Sugar, cov	15.00	15.00
Tumbler, 9 oz, 3-7/8" h, water	15.00	7.50
Vegetable bowl, 8-3/8" d	10.00	15.00
Whiskey, 1-1/2 oz, 2-1/4" h	4.00	5.00

*Star, crystal bowl, **$7**; 85-oz pitcher with ice lip, **$15**; and 60-oz pitcher, **$14**.*

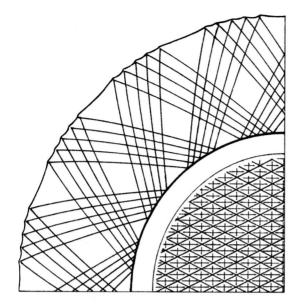

STARLIGHT

Manufactured by Hazel Atlas Glass Company, Clarksburg, W.V., and Zanesville, Ohio, from 1938 to 1940.

Pieces are made in cobalt blue, crystal, pink and white. Production in cobalt blue was limited to a bowl 8-1/2 inches in diameter and valued at $30.

Item	Crystal	Pink	White
Berry bowl, 4" d	9.50	—	—
Bowl, 8-1/2" d, two handles	18.00	20.00	18.00
Bowl, 11-1/2" d, deep	25.00	—	25.00
Bowl, 12" d, 2-3/4" deep	25.00	—	25.00
Cereal bowl, 5-1/2" d, two handles	7.00	12.00	7.00
Creamer, oval	10.00	—	5.00
Cup	7.00	—	4.00
Plate, 6" d, sherbet	4.50	—	4.00
Plate, 7-1/2" d, salad	5.00	—	4.50
Plate, 8-1/2" d, luncheon	5.00	—	5.00
Plate, 9" d, dinner	8.50	—	8.50
Relish dish	15.00	—	15.00
Salad bowl, 11-1/2" d, deep	27.50	—	27.50
Salt and pepper shakers, pr	30.00	—	30.00
Sandwich plate, 13" d	25.00	20.00	—
Saucer	4.00	—	2.50
Sherbet	15.00	—	12.00
Sugar, oval	10.00	—	10.00

Starlight, crystal salt and pepper shakers, ***$30.***

Starlight, crystal dinner plate, 9" d, ***$8.50.***

STRAWBERRY

Manufactured by U.S. Glass Company, Pittsburgh, Pa., in the early 1930s.

Pieces are made in crystal, green, pink, and some iridescent.

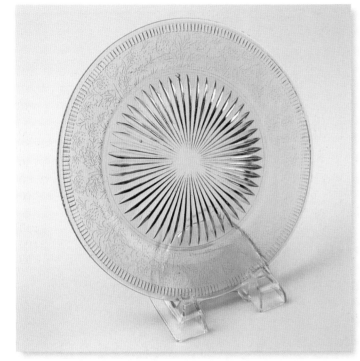

*Strawberry, pink salad plate, **$15**.*

Item	Crystal	Green	Iridescent	Pink
Berry bowl, 4" d	7.50	12.00	7.50	32.50
Berry bowl, 7-1/2" d	20.00	45.00	20.00	24.00
Bowl, 6-1/4" d, 2" deep	40.00	60.00	40.00	60.00
Butter dish, cov	125.00	225.00	135.00	195.00
Comport, 5-3/4" d	55.00	60.00	55.00	60.00
Creamer, large, 4-5/8" h	24.00	35.00	24.00	35.00
Creamer, small	12.00	18.50	12.00	18.50
Olive dish, 5" l, one handle	8.50	14.00	8.50	25.00
Pickle dish, 8-1/4" l, oval	8.00	14.00	8.00	15.00
Pitcher, 7-3/4" h	150.00	275.00	150.00	195.00
Plate, 6" d, sherbet	5.00	13.50	5.00	8.00
Plate, 7-1/2" d, salad	10.00	14.00	10.00	15.00
Salad bowl, 6-1/2" d	15.00	20.00	15.00	20.00
Sherbet	6.00	13.50	6.00	13.50
Sugar, large, cov	60.00	85.00	60.00	85.00
Sugar, small, open	12.00	32.00	12.00	32.00
Tumbler, 8 oz, 3-5/8" h	20.00	32.00	20.00	40.00

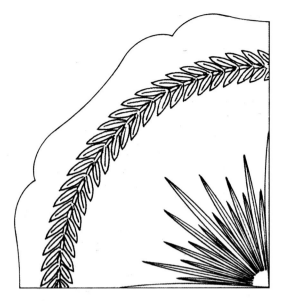

SUNBURST

Herringbone

Manufactured by Jeannette Glass Company, Jeannette, Pa., late 1930s.

Pieces are made in crystal.

Item	Crystal
Berry bowl, 4-3/4" d	9.00
Berry bowl, 8-1/2" d	18.00
Bowl, 10-1/2" d	25.00
Candlesticks, pr, double	35.00
Creamer, ftd	16.00
Cup	7.50
Cup and saucer	10.00
Plate, 5-1/2" d	12.00

Item	Crystal
Plate, 9-1/4" d, dinner	25.00
Relish, two parts	14.50
Salad bowl, 11" d	30.00
Sandwich plate, 11-3/4" d	15.00
Saucer	4.00
Sherbet	12.00
Sugar	16.00
Tumbler, 4" h, 9 oz, flat	18.50

*Sunburst, crystal sandwich plate, **$15**.*

SUNFLOWER

Manufactured by Jeannette Glass Company, Jeannette, Pa., 1930s.

Pieces are made in Delphite, green, pink, and some opaque colors. Look for a creamer in Delphite that is valued at $85.

Sunflower, green cake plate, **$20**.

Item	Delphite	Green	Pink	Opaque
Ashtray, 5" d	—	15.00	15.00	—
Cake plate, 10" d, three legs	—	20.00	30.00	—
Creamer	90.00	20.00	20.00	85.00
Cup	—	15.00	18.00	75.00
Plate, 9" d, dinner	—	27.50	24.00	—
Saucer	—	13.50	12.00	85.00
Sugar	—	25.00	22.00	—
Trivet, 7" d, three legs, turned up edge	—	325.00	315.00	—
Tumbler, 8 oz, 4-3/8" h, ftd	—	35.00	32.00	—

SWIRL

Petal Swirl

Manufactured by Jeannette Glass Company, Jeannette, Pa., from 1937 to 1938.

Pieces are made in amber, Delphite, ice blue, pink and Ultramarine. Production was limited in amber and ice blue.

Item	Delphite	Pink	Ultramarine
Berry bowl	15.00	—	18.50
Bowl, 10" d, ftd, closed handles	—	25.00	35.00
Butter dish, cov	—	220.00	245.00
Candleholders, pr, double branch	—	40.00	60.00
Candleholders, pr, single branch	115.00	—	—
Candy dish, cov	—	235.00	150.00
Candy dish, open, three legs	—	20.00	20.00
Cereal bowl, 5-1/4" d	15.00	15.00	16.00
Coaster, 1" x 3-1/4"	—	18.00	18.00
Console bowl, 10-1/2" d, ftd	—	20.00	35.00
Creamer	12.00	9.50	18.00

*Swirl, Ultramarine sugar, **$18**; creamer, **$18**.*

Item	Delphite	Pink	Ultramarine
Cup and saucer	17.50	16.00	20.00
Plate, 6-1/2" d, sherbet	6.50	8.00	9.00
Plate, 7-1/4" d, luncheon	—	6.50	15.00
Plate, 8" d, salad	9.00	8.50	18.00
Plate, 9-1/4" d, dinner	12.00	17.50	25.00
Plate, 10-1/2" d, dinner	18.00	—	30.00
Platter, 12" l, oval	35.00	—	—
Salad bowl, 9" d	30.00	18.00	32.50
Salad bowl, 9" d, rimmed	—	20.00	30.00
Salt and pepper shakers, pr	—	—	55.00
Sandwich plate, 12-1/2" d	—	20.00	32.50
Sherbet, low, ftd	—	24.00	28.00
Soup, tab handles, lug	—	25.00	52.50
Sugar, ftd	—	12.00	18.00
Tray, 10-1/2" l, two handles	25.00	—	—
Tumbler, 9 oz, 4" h	—	18.00	35.00
Tumbler, 9 oz, 4-5/8" h	—	18.00	—
Tumbler, 13 oz, 5-1/8" h	—	45.00	90.00
Vase, 6-1/2" h, ftd, ruffled	—	22.00	—
Vase, 8-1/2" h, ftd or flat	—	—	30.00

*Swirl, Ultramarine dinner plate, 10-1/2" d, **$30**; bowl with closed handles, **$35**.*

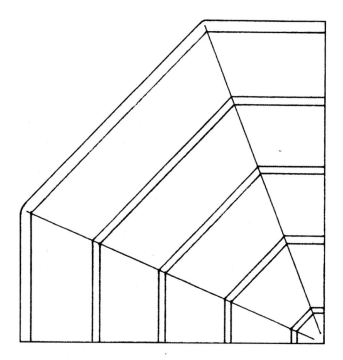

TEA ROOM

Manufactured by Indiana Glass Company, Dunkirk, Ind., from 1926 to 1931.

Pieces are made in amber, crystal, green and pink.

Item	Amber	Crystal	Green	Pink
Banana split bowl, 7-1/2" l	—	95.00	200.00	215.00
Candlesticks, pr, low	—	—	80.00	95.00
Celery bowl, 8-1/2" d	—	15.00	35.00	27.50
Creamer, 3-1/4" h	—	—	30.00	28.00
Creamer, 4-1/2" h, ftd	80.00	—	20.00	25.00
Creamer and sugar on tray	—	—	95.00	85.00
Cup	—	—	65.00	60.00
Finger bowl	—	80.00	50.00	40.00
Goblet, 9 oz	—	—	75.00	65.00
Ice bucket	—	—	85.00	80.00
Lamp, electric	—	140.00	175.00	195.00
Mustard, cov	—	145.00	160.00	140.00
Parfait	—	—	72.00	65.00
Pitcher, 64 oz	425.00	400.00	150.00	200.00
Plate, 6-1/2" d, sherbet	—	—	35.00	32.00
Plate, 8-1/4" d, luncheon	—	—	37.50	35.00
Plate, 10-1/2" d, two handles	—	—	50.00	45.00
Relish, divided	—	—	30.00	25.00
Salad bowl, 8-3/4" d, deep	—	—	150.00	135.00
Salt and pepper shakers, pr, ftd	—	—	60.00	55.00
Saucer	—	—	30.00	25.00
Sherbet	—	22.00	40.00	35.00
Sugar, 3" h, cov	—	—	115.00	100.00
Sugar, 4-1/2" h, ftd	80.00	—	30.00	30.00
Sugar, cov, flat	—	—	200.00	170.00
Sundae, ftd, ruffled	—	—	85.00	70.00

Item	Amber	Crystal	Green	Pink
Tumbler, 6 oz, ftd	—	—	55.00	32.00
Tumbler, 8 oz, 5-1/4" h, ftd	75.00	—	32.00	40.00
Tumbler, 11 oz, ftd	—	—	45.00	45.00
Tumbler, 12 oz, ftd	—	—	60.00	55.00
Vase, 6-1/2" h, ruffled edge	—	—	145.00	90.00
Vase, 9-1/2" h, ruffled	—	45.00	175.00	100.00
Vase, 9-1/2" h, straight	—	130.00	95.00	225.00
Vase, 11" h, ruffled edge	—	—	350.00	395.00
Vase, 11" h, straight	—	—	200.00	395.00
Vegetable bowl, 9-1/2" l, oval	—	—	75.00	65.00

*Tea Room, pink footed sugar, **$30**; footed creamer, **$35**.*

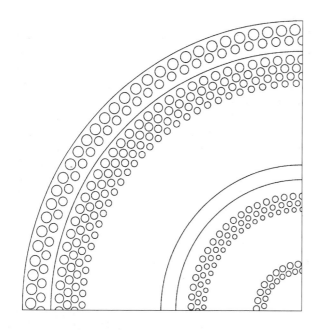

TEARDROP

Line #301

Manufactured by Duncan & Miller Glass Company, Washington, Pa., from 1936 until 1955. Pieces are made only in crystal.

Item	Crystal
Ale, 8 oz	18.50
Ashtray, 3" d	6.50
Ashtray, 5" d	9.00
Bonbon	12.00
Butter dish, cov, two handles	25.00
Cake salver, 13" d, ftd	50.00
Canapé set	30.00
Candlesticks, pr, 4" h	20.00
Candlesticks, pr, 7" h, two lite	40.00
Candlesticks, pr, 7" h, bobeches, prisms	125.00
Candy basket, 5-1/2" x 7-1/2"	80.00
Candy box, cov, 7", two parts	60.00
Candy box, cov, 8" d, three parts	65.00
Candy dish, 7-1/2" w, heart shape	30.00
Celery tray, 11" l, two handles	18.00
Celery tray, 11" l, two handles, two parts	20.00
Celery tray, 12" l, three parts	24.00
Champagne, 5 oz	12.00
Cheese and cracker	48.00
Claret, 4 oz	20.00
Coaster, 3" d	6.50
Cocktail, 3-1/2 oz	17.50
Comport, 4-3/4", ftd	15.00
Comport, 6"	18.00
Condiment set, salt and pepper shakers, two cruets, 9" tray	120.00
Cordial, 1 oz	32.00
Creamer and sugar tray, two handles, 8" or 10"	10.00
Creamer, 3 oz	6.50
Creamer, 5 oz	9.00
Creamer, 8 oz	12.00
Cruets tray	12.50
Cup	8.50

Item	Crystal
Demitasse cup and saucer	12.00
Dessert bowl, 6" d	6.50
Finger bowl, 4-1/4" d	7.50
Flower basket	125.00
Flower bowl, 12" d, ftd	48.00
Flower bowl, 8" x 12"	48.00
Fruit bowl, 6" d	7.00
Gardenia bowl, 13" d	40.00
Goblet, 5-3/4" h	12.00
Goblet, 7"	15.00
Hi-ball, 10 oz	12.00
Ice bucket	70.00
Iced tea tumbler, 12 oz or 14 oz	20.00
Juice tumbler, 3-1/2 oz, flat or footed	7.50
Juice tumbler, 4-1/2 oz, ftd	10.00
Lazy Susan, 18" d	75.00
Lemon plate, 7" d, two handles	15.00
Marmalade, cov	37.50
Mayonnaise, ladle, underplate	35.00
Milk pitcher, 5"	20.00
Mustard jar, cov	30.00
Nappy, 5" d	6.50
Nappy, 7" d	12.00
Nappy, 9", two handles	25.00
Nut dish, 6"	12.00
Oil bottle, 3 oz	22.00
Old fashioned, 7 oz	7.50
Olive dish	15.00
Oyster cocktail, 3-1/2 oz, ftd	9.00
Pickle dish	15.00
Pitcher, 64 oz, ice lip	120.00
Plate, 6" d, bread and butter	6.00
Plate, 7-1/2" d, salad	6.00

Item	Crystal	Item	Crystal
Plate, 8-1/2" d, luncheon	9.00	Sherry, 1-3/4" oz	32.00
Plate, 10-1/2" d, dinner	32.00	Sugar, 3 oz	6.00
Punch bowl, 15-1/2"	115.00	Sugar, 6 oz	7.50
Punch bowl underplate, 18" d, rolled edge	65.00	Sugar, 8 oz	10.00
Relish, 7" l, two parts, two handles	12.50	Sweetmeat, center handle, 6-1/2"	36.00
Relish, 7-1/2" d two parts, heart shape	22.00	Sweetmeat, star shape, two handles, 5-1/2" or 7"	40.00
Relish, 9" l, three parts, three handles	32.00	Torte plate, 13" d, rolled edge	32.00
Relish, 11" l, three parts, two handles	32.00	Torte plate, 14" d, rolled or plain edge	37.50
Relish, 12" d, five parts	30.00	Torte plate, 16" d, rolled edge	40.00
Relish, 12" d, six parts	37.50	Tumbler, 8 oz, ftd	10.00
Relish, 12" l, three parts	35.00	Tumbler, 9 oz, flat or footed	10.00
Salad bowl, 9" d	30.00	Urn, cov, 9" h, ftd	125.00
Salt and pepper shakers, pr	25.00	Vase, 9" h, ftd, fan	32.00
Salt and pepper shakers tray	12.00	Vase, 9" h, ftd, round	40.00
Saucer	6.00	Whiskey, 2 oz, flat or footed	15.00
Sherbet, 5 oz	6.50	Wine, 3 oz	20.00

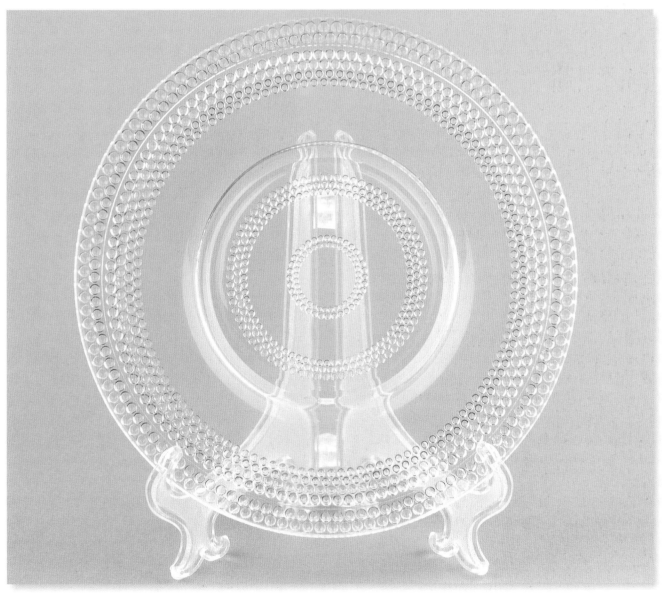

*Teardrop, crystal salad plate, **$6***.

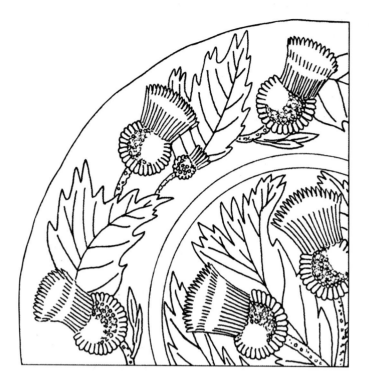

THISTLE

Manufactured by Macbeth-Evans, Charleroi, Pa., about 1929 to 1930.

Pieces are made in crystal, green, pink, and yellow. Production was limited in crystal and yellow pieces.

Reproductions: † Recent reproductions have been found in pink, a darker emerald green, and wisteria. Several of the reproductions have a scalloped edge. Reproductions include the cake plate, fruit bowl, pitcher, salt and pepper shakers, and a small tumbler.

Item	Green	Pink
Cake plate, 13" d, heavy †	195.00	225.00
Cereal bowl, 5-1/2" d	50.00	50.00
Cup, thin	36.50	24.00
Fruit bowl, 10-1/4" d †	295.00	495.00
Plate, 8" d, luncheon	30.00	32.00
Plate, 10-1/4" d, grill	35.00	30.00
Saucer	12.00	12.00

*Thistle, green luncheon plate, **$30**.*

THUMBPRINT

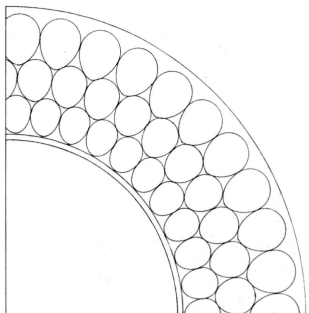

Manufactured by Federal Glass Company, Columbus, Ohio, from 1927 to 1930.

Pieces are made in green.

*Thumbprint, green luncheon plate, **$7**.*

Item	Green
Berry bowl, 4-3/4" d	10.00
Berry bowl, 8" d	25.00
Cereal bowl, 5" d	10.00
Creamer, ftd	12.00
Cup	8.00
Fruit bowl, 5" d	10.00
Juice tumbler, 4" h	6.00
Plate, 6" d, sherbet	4.50
Plate, 8" d, luncheon	7.00
Plate, 9-1/4" d, dinner	24.00
Salt and pepper shakers, pr	65.00
Saucer	4.00
Sherbet	9.00
Sugar, ftd	12.00
Tumbler, 5" h	25.00
Tumbler, 5-1/2" h	10.00
Whiskey, 1-7/8" h	18.00
Whiskey, 2-1/4" h	6.50

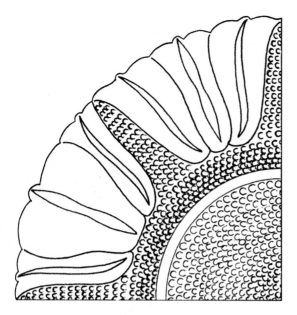

TULIP

Manufactured by Dell Glass Company, Millville, New Jersey, early 1930s.

Pieces are made in amber, amethyst, blue, crystal, and green.

Item	Amber	Amethyst	Blue	Crystal	Green
Bowl, 6" d	20.00	18.00	18.00	20.00	20.00
Bowl, 13-1/4" l, oblong oval	90.00	100.00	110.00	90.00	90.00
Candleholders, pr, 3-3/4" h	24.50	30.00	30.00	24.50	24.50
Candy, cov	175.00	195.00	195.00	150.00	165.00
Creamer	20.00	25.00	30.00	20.00	30.00
Cup	15.00	20.00	24.00	15.00	18.00
Decanter, orig stopper	—	500.00	500.00	—	—
Ice tub, 4-7/8" wide, 3" deep	70.00	95.00	95.00	65.00	90.00
Juice tumbler	15.00	40.00	40.00	15.00	15.00
Plate, 6" d	10.00	12.00	12.00	9.50	10.00
Plate, 7-1/4" d	12.00	20.00	22.00	13.50	24.00
Plate, 10-1/4" d	35.00	40.00	42.50	20.00	40.00
Saucer	10.00	8.50	10.00	5.00	7.50
Sherbet, 3-3/4" h, flat	20.00	24.00	24.00	18.00	20.00
Sugar	20.00	25.00	25.00	20.00	20.00
Whiskey	22.00	35.00	35.00	20.00	25.00

Tulip, green creamer, $30.

TWIGGY

Manufactured by Indiana Glass Company, Dunkirk, Ind., in the 1950s and early 1960s.

Pieces are made in crystal, some green and pink, and rarely in light blue with an opalescent edge. Collector interest is highest in the crystal. A green jelly dish is valued at $18.

Item	Crystal
Jelly, 8" d	12.00
Nappy, 4-1/2" d	5.00
Nappy, 8" d	8.00
Plate, 8" d	10.00
Punch bowl	45.00

Item	Crystal
Punch cup	12.00
Relish, 10" d, divided	15.00
Relish, 8" d	12.00
Snack plate, 10" d	10.00

Twiggy, green nappy, **$18**. *Photo courtesy of Tina Trautman.*

Twiggy, crystal nappy, 8" d, **$8**.

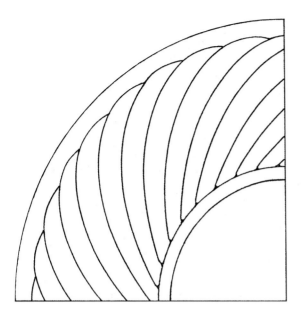

TWISTED OPTIC

Manufactured by Imperial Glass Company, Bellaire, Ohio, from 1927 to 1930.

Pieces are made in amber, blue, canary, green, and pink.

Item	Amber	Blue	Canary	Green	Pink
Basket, 10" h	55.00	95.00	95.00	60.00	60.00
Bowl, 7" d, ruffled	—	—	—	—	18.00
Bowl, 9" d	18.50	28.50	28.50	18.50	18.50
Bowl, 11-1/2" d, 4-1/4" h	24.00	48.00	48.00	24.00	24.00
Candlesticks, pr, 3" h	22.00	40.00	40.00	35.00	22.00
Candlesticks, pr, 8" h	30.00	50.00	50.00	30.00	30.00
Candy jar, cov, flat	25.00	50.00	50.00	25.00	25.00
Candy jar, cov, flat, flange edge	50.00	90.00	90.00	55.00	55.00
Candy jar, cov, ftd, flange edge	50.00	90.00	90.00	55.00	55.00
Candy jar, cov, ftd, short	55.00	100.00	100.00	60.00	60.00
Candy jar, cov, ftd, tall	55.00	100.00	100.00	60.00	60.00
Cereal bowl, 5" d	8.50	15.00	15.00	10.00	10.00
Cologne bottle, stopper	60.00	85.00	85.00	60.00	60.00
Console bowl, 10-1/2" d	25.00	45.00	45.00	25.00	25.00
Cream soup, 4-3/4" d	12.00	25.00	25.00	15.00	15.00
Creamer	8.00	14.00	14.00	8.00	8.00
Cup	7.50	12.50	12.50	5.00	8.00
Mayonnaise	20.00	50.00	50.00	30.00	30.00
Pitcher, 64 oz	45.00	—	—	40.00	45.00
Plate, 6" d, sherbet	3.00	6.50	6.50	3.00	3.00
Plate, 7" d, salad	4.00	8.00	8.00	4.00	4.00
Plate, 7-1/2" x 9" l, oval	6.00	12.00	12.00	6.00	6.00
Plate, 8" d, luncheon	6.00	9.00	10.00	6.00	5.00
Powder jar, cov	38.00	65.00	65.00	38.00	38.00
Preserve jar	30.00	—	—	30.00	30.00
Salad bowl, 7" d	12.00	25.00	25.00	15.00	15.00
Sandwich plate, 10" d	12.00	20.00	20.00	15.00	15.00
Sandwich server, center handle	22.00	35.00	35.00	22.00	22.00
Sandwich server, two-handles, flat	15.00	20.00	20.00	15.00	15.00
Saucer	2.50	4.50	4.50	2.50	5.00
Sherbet	7.50	12.00	12.50	7.00	7.50
Sugar	8.00	14.00	14.00	8.00	10.00
Tumbler, 4-1/2" h, 9 oz	6.50	—	—	6.50	7.00
Tumbler, 5-1/4" h, 12 oz	9.50	—	—	9.50	10.00
Vase, 7-1/4" h, two handles, rolled edge	35.00	65.00	65.00	40.00	40.00
Vase, 8" h, two handles, fan	45.00	95.00	95.00	50.00	50.00
Vase, 8" h, two handles, straight edge	45.00	95.00	95.00	50.00	50.00

U.S. SWIRL

Manufactured by U.S. Glass Company, late 1920s. Pieces are made in crystal, green, iridescent, and pink. Production in crystal and iridescent was limited.

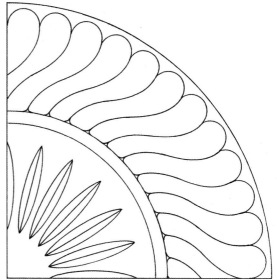

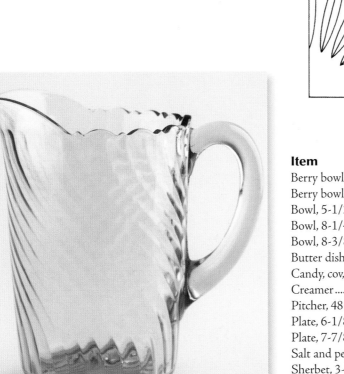

*U.S. Swirl, green pitcher, **$55**.*

Item	Green	Pink
Berry bowl, 4-3/8" d	8.00	10.00
Berry bowl, 7-7/8" d	15.00	17.00
Bowl, 5-1/2" d, handle	10.00	12.00
Bowl, 8-1/4" l, 2 3/4" h, oval	40.00	40.00
Bowl, 8-3/8" l, 1-3/4" h, oval	50.00	50.00
Butter dish, cov	115.00	115.00
Candy, cov, two handles	30.00	32.00
Creamer	15.00	17.50
Pitcher, 48 oz, 8" h	55.00	50.00
Plate, 6-1/8" d, sherbet	3.00	2.50
Plate, 7-7/8" d, salad	6.00	6.50
Salt and pepper shakers, pr	48.00	45.00
Sherbet, 3-1/4" h	5.00	6.00
Sugar, cov	35.00	32.00
Tumbler, 8 oz, 3-5/8" h	12.00	12.00
Tumbler, 12 oz, 4-3/4" h	15.00	17.50
Vase, 6-1/2" h	25.00	25.00

VERNON

No. 616

Manufactured by Indiana Glass Company, Dunkirk, Ind., from 1930 to 1932.

Pieces are made in crystal, green, and yellow.

Item	Crystal	Green	Yellow
Creamer, ftd	12.00	25.00	30.00
Cup	10.00	15.00	18.00
Plate, 8" d, luncheon	7.00	10.00	15.00
Sandwich plate, 11-1/2" d	14.00	25.00	30.00
Saucer	4.00	6.00	6.00
Sugar, ftd	18.00	25.00	30.00
Tumbler, 5" h, ftd	16.00	40.00	45.00

*Vernon, yellow tumbler, **$45**.*

VICTORY

Manufactured by Diamond Glass-Ware Company, Indiana, Pa., from 1929 to 1932.

Pieces are made in amber, black, cobalt blue, green, and pink.

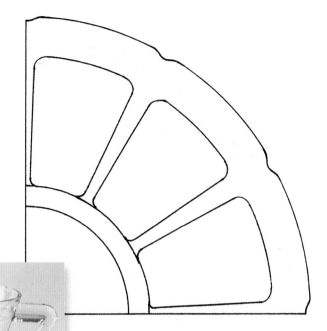

Victory, pink creamer, $15; sugar, $15.

Item	Amber	Black	Cobalt Blue	Green	Pink
Bonbon, 7" d	15.00	20.00	20.00	15.00	15.00
Bowl, 11" d, rolled edge	30.00	50.00	50.00	30.00	30.00
Bowl, 12-1/2" d, flat edge	30.00	60.00	60.00	30.00	30.00
Candlesticks, pr, 3" h	35.00	100.00	100.00	35.00	35.00
Cereal bowl, 6-1/2" d	15.00	30.00	30.00	15.00	15.00
Cheese and cracker set, 12" d indented plate and comport	45.00	—	—	45.00	45.00
Comport, 6" h, 6-1/4" d	18.00	—	—	18.00	18.00
Console bowl, 12" d	35.00	65.00	65.00	35.00	35.00
Creamer	17.50	45.00	45.00	15.00	15.00
Cup	10.00	35.00	40.00	10.00	10.00
Goblet, 7 oz, 5" h	20.00	—	—	20.00	20.00
Gravy boat, underplate	185.00	325.00	325.00	185.00	185.00
Mayonnaise set, 3-1/2" h, 5-1/2" d bowl, 8-1/2" d indented plate, ladle	55.00	100.00	100.00	55.00	55.00
Plate, 6" d, bread and butter	6.50	17.50	17.50	6.50	6.50
Plate, 7" d, salad	7.50	20.00	20.00	8.00	7.00
Plate, 8" d, luncheon	10.00	40.00	30.00	8.00	8.00
Plate, 9" d, dinner	20.00	40.00	40.00	22.00	20.00
Platter, 12" l, oval	30.00	70.00	70.00	32.00	32.00
Sandwich server, center handle	35.00	65.00	65.00	40.00	30.00
Saucer	5.00	12.50	12.50	5.00	6.00
Sherbet, ftd	15.00	27.50	27.50	15.00	15.00
Soup bowl, 8-1/2" d, flat	20.00	45.00	45.00	20.00	20.00
Sugar	15.00	45.00	45.00	15.00	15.00
Vegetable bowl, 9" l, oval	35.00	85.00	85.00	35.00	35.00

VITROCK

Flower Rim

Manufactured by Hocking Glass Company, Lancaster, Ohio, from 1934 to 1937.

Pieces are made in white and white with fired-on colors.

Item	Fired-On Colors	White
Berry bowl, 4" d	9.50	7.50
Cereal bowl, 7-1/2" d	12.00	8.50
Cream soup, 5-1/2" d	16.00	14.00
Creamer, oval	10.00	7.50
Cup	8.50	6.00
Fruit bowl, 6" d	10.00	8.00
Plate, 7-1/4" d, salad	7.50	6.00
Plate, 8-3/4" d, luncheon	12.00	6.50

Item	Fired-On Colors	White
Plate, 10" d, dinner	15.00	12.00
Platter, 11-1/2" l	50.00	35.00
Saucer	7.50	3.50
Soup bowl, flat	48.00	35.00
Sugar	12.00	8.50
Vase, 3-1/4" h, ruffled	—	12.50
Vegetable bowl, 9-1/2" d	24.00	18.00

Vitrock, white salad plate, **$6**; *cereal bowl,* **$8.50**.

WATERFORD

Waffle

Manufactured by Hocking Glass Company, Lancaster, Ohio, from 1938 to 1944.

Pieces are made in crystal, Forest Green (1950s), pink, white, and yellow. Forest Green production was limited; currently an ashtray is valued at $5. Yellow was also limited. Collector interest is low in white.

Item	Crystal	Pink
Ashtray, 4" d	8.00	—
Berry bowl, 4-3/4" d	8.50	18.00
Berry bowl, 8-1/4" d	10.00	36.00
Bonbon, cov	45.00	—
Butter dish, cov	30.00	250.00
Cake plate, 10-1/4" d, handles	15.00	25.00
Cereal bowl, 5-1/2" d	18.50	32.00
Coaster, 4" d	5.50	—
Creamer, Miss America style	35.00	—
Creamer, oval	5.00	15.00
Cup	8.50	18.00
Cup, Miss America style	—	45.00
Goblet, 5-1/4" h	16.00	—
Goblet, 5-1/2" h, Miss America style	35.00	85.00
Goblet, 5-5/8" h	20.00	—
Juice pitcher, 42 oz, tilted	30.00	—
Juice tumbler, 5 oz, 3-1/2" h, Miss America style	—	65.00
Lamp, 4" spherical base	45.00	—
Pitcher, 80 oz, tilted, ice lip	50.00	165.00
Plate, 6" d, sherbet	5.00	9.50
Plate, 7-1/8" d, salad	8.00	18.00
Plate, 9-5/8" d, dinner	12.00	24.00
Platter, 14" l	14.00	—
Relish, 13-3/4" d, five parts	12.00	—
Relish, 14" d, six parts	35.00	—
Salt and pepper shakers, pr	14.50	—
Sandwich plate, 13-3/4" d	15.00	32.00
Saucer	5.00	5.00
Sherbet, ftd	5.00	15.00
Sherbet, ftd, scalloped base	8.00	—
Sugar	6.50	15.00
Sugar, Miss America style	30.00	—
Sugar lid, oval	5.00	25.00
Tray, 10-1/4" l, handles	15.00	—
Tray, 13" d	15.00	45.00
Tumbler, 10 oz, 4-7/8" h, ftd	12.00	30.00

Waterford, crystal dinner plate, $12.

WEXFORD

Manufactured by Anchor Hocking Glass Corp. Pieces are made in crystal.

Item	Crystal
Bowl, 7-3/4" d, ftd	30.00
Bud vase	12.00
Butter dish, cov	30.00
Candlestick	9.00
Candy dish, cov, 7-3/4" d	15.00
Canister, cov, coffee, 5-3/8" h	15.00
Canister, cov, flour, 9-1/4" h	22.00
Canister, cov, sugar, 6-3/8" h	18.00
Centerpiece bowl	18.00
Champagne, 3-5/8" h	8.00
Chip and dip set	20.00
Claret, 5-3/8" h	10.00

Wexford, crystal serving plate, **$20**.

Item	Crystal
Creamer, 4-1/4" h	10.00
Cruet, 7-1/2" h	15.00
Cup, ftd, 3" h	6.00
Decanter, 11-3/4" h	30.00
Decanter, 14-1/2" h	35.00
Dessert bowl, 5-1/2" d	4.00
Fruit bowl, 10" d, ftd	30.00
Goblet, 6-5/8" h	12.00
Iced tea tumbler, 5-1/2" h, 12 oz	12.00
Juice tumbler	9.00
Old fashioned tumbler, 3-3/4" h	9.00
Pitcher, 5-1/4" h, pint	18.00
Pitcher, 9-3/4" h, two quart	35.00
Plate, luncheon	9.00

Item	Crystal
Plate, salad	6.00
Punch bowl	10.00
Punch cup, 3" d	3.00
Relish	20.00
Relish, three parts, 8-5/8" l	18.00
Salad bowl, 9-3/4" d	15.00
Serving plate	20.00
Sherbet, low	6.50
Sugar, cov, 5-1/4" h, ftd	15.00
Toothpick holder	12.00
Torte plate, 14" d	24.00
Tumbler, 5-1/2" h, flat	6.00
Vase, ftd	40.00
Wine, 4-1/2" h	10.00

Wexford, crystal decanter, 11-3/4" h, **$30**.

Wexford, crystal goblet, **$12**.

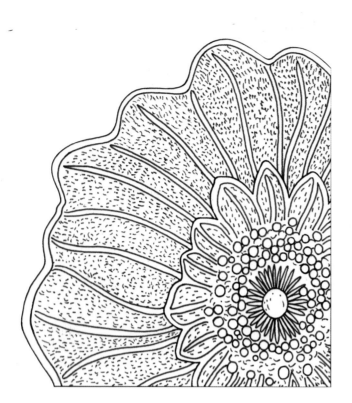

WILD ROSE WITH LEAVES & BERRIES

Manufactured by Indiana Glass Company, Dunkirk, Ind., from the early 1950s to the 1980s.

Pieces are made in crystal, iridescent, milk glass, multicolored blue, green, pink, and yellow, satinized crystal, satinized green, pink, and yellow, sprayed green lavender, and pink.

Item	Crystal, Satinized Crystal	Iridescent, Satinized colors, Sprayed colors	Multicolored
Bowl, large	10.00	15.00	40.00
Candleholder	5.00	8.00	20.00
Relish, handle	6.50	10.00	25.00
Relish, handle, divided	7.50	12.00	25.00
Sauce bowl, handle	4.00	7.00	12.00
Sherbet	5.00	6.50	15.00
Sherbet plate	2.50	3.50	9.00
Tray, two handles	15.00	20.00	35.00

Wildrose with Leaves & Berries, crystal bowl, $10.

WINDSOR

Windsor Diamond

Manufactured by Jeannette Glass Company, Jeannette, Pa., from 1936 to 1946.

Pieces are made in crystal, green, and pink, with limited production in amberina red, Delphite, and ice blue.

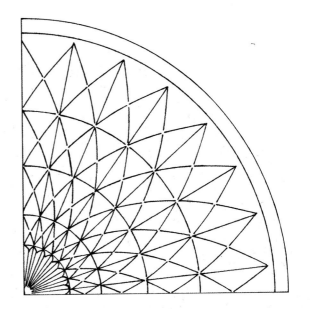

Item	Crystal	Green	Pink
Ashtray, 5-3/4" d	15.00	55.00	45.00
Berry bowl, 4-3/4" d	5.00	5.00	12.00
Berry bowl, 8-1/2" d	7.50	18.50	25.00
Bowl, 5" l, pointed edge	10.00	—	70.00
Bowl, 7" x 11-3/4", boat shape	30.00	40.00	32.00
Bowl, 7-1/2" d, three legs	8.00	—	24.00
Bowl, 8" d, two handles	9.00	24.00	20.00
Bowl, 8" l, pointed edge	10.00	—	48.00
Bowl, 10-1/2" l, pointed edge	25.00	—	32.00
Butter dish, cov	30.00	95.00	60.00
Cake plate, 10-3/4" d, ftd	12.00	22.00	20.00
Candlesticks, pr, 3" h	24.00	—	265.00
Candy jar, cov	18.00		—
Cereal bowl, 5-3/8" d	10.00	32.50	32.00
Chop plate, 13-5/8" d	24.00	55.00	45.00
Coaster, 3-1/4" d	8.50	22.00	25.00
Comport	9.00	—	—
Cream soup, 5" d	6.00	30.00	25.00
Creamer	8.00	15.00	20.00
Creamer, Holiday shape	7.50	—	—
Cup	7.00	18.00	12.00
Fruit console, 12-1/2" d	45.00	—	115.00
Iced tea tumbler, 12 oz, 5" h	—	55.00	—
Pitcher, 16 oz, 4-1/2" h	25.00	—	115.00
Pitcher, 52 oz, 6-3/4" h	20.00	65.00	40.00
Plate, 6" d, sherbet	3.75	8.00	6.00
Plate, 7" d, salad	4.50	30.00	18.00
Plate, 9" d, dinner	10.00	25.00	25.00
Platter, 11-1/2" l, oval	7.00	25.00	30.00
Powder jar	20.00	—	55.00
Relish platter, 11-1/2" l, divided	30.00	—	200.00
Salad bowl, 10-1/2" d	12.00	—	—
Salt and pepper shakers, pr	20.00	55.00	45.00
Sandwich plate, 10" d, closed handles	10.00	—	24.00
Sandwich plate, 10" d, open handles	12.50	18.00	20.00

Item	Crystal	Green	Pink
Saucer	2.50	5.00	4.50
Sherbet, ftd	3.50	18.50	15.00
Sugar, cov	24.00	40.00	42.00
Sugar, cov, Holiday shape	12.00	—	135.00
Tray, 4" sq	5.00	12.00	10.00
Tray, 4" sq, handles	6.00	—	40.00
Tray, 4-1/8" x 9"	5.00	16.00	10.00
Tray, 4-1/8" x 9", handles	9.00	—	50.00
Tray, 8-1/2" x 9-3/4"	7.00	35.00	25.00
Tray, 8-1/2" x 9-3/4", handles	15.00	45.00	85.00
Tumbler, 4" h, ftd	7.00	—	—
Tumbler, 5 oz, 3-1/4" h	9.00	36.50	26.50
Tumbler, 7-1/4" h, ftd	19.00	—	—
Tumbler, 9 oz, 4" h	7.50	36.50	18.00
Tumbler, 10 oz, 5-1/4" h, ftd	12.00	—	—
Tumbler, 11 oz, 4-5/8" h	8.00	—	—
Tumbler, 11 oz, 5" h, ftd	12.00	—	—
Tumbler, 12 oz, 5" h	11.00	55.00	32.50
Vegetable bowl, 9-1/2" l, oval	7.50	32.50	25.00

*Windsor, crystal chop plate, **$24**; pink pitcher, 16 oz, **$115**.*

YORKTOWN

Manufactured by Federal Glass Company, in the mid-1950s.

Pieces are made in crystal, iridescent, smoke, white, and yellow. Values for all the colors are about the same.

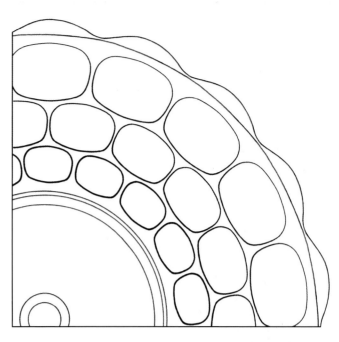

Item	Crystal
Berry bowl, 5-1/2" d	4.50
Berry bowl, 9-1/2" d	10.00
Celery tray, 10" l	10.00
Creamer	5.00

Item	Crystal
Cup	3.50
Fruit bowl, 10" d, ftd	18.00
Iced tea tumbler, 5-1/4" h, 13 oz	7.50
Juice tumbler, 3-7/8" h, 6 oz	4.50

Yorktown, yellow sandwich server with gold metal center handle, ***$4.50***.

Item	Crystal	Item	Crystal
Mug	15.00	Saucer	1.00
Plate, 8-1/4" d	4.50	Sherbet, 7 oz	3.50
Plate, 11-1/2" d	8.50	Snack cup	2.50
Punch bowl set	40.00	Snack plate with indent	3.50
Punch cup	2.50	Sugar	5.00
Relish	3.00	Tumbler, 4-3/4" h, 10 oz	6.00
Sandwich server	4.50	Vase, 8" h	15.00

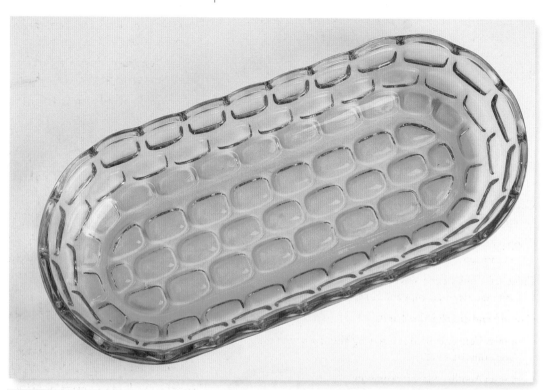

*Yorktown,
yellow relish, $3*.

*Yorktown, crystal
fruit bowl, $18*.

GLOSSARY

AOP: All-over pattern; often found in descriptions to indicate a design that covers the entire piece rather than in just one location.

Berry bowl: Used to describe both individual serving dishes and a master bowl used as a set to serve different kinds of berries. Often accompanied by a creamer or milk pitcher and sugar bowl.

Bouillon: Generally, a cup-shaped bowl for serving broth or clear soups; usually has handles.

Cheese and cracker set: Serving set often consists of a comport to hold cheese and large plate for crackers; forms differ. Sometimes a sherbet is used as a comport.

Cheese dish: Serving dish, often with domed top, to cover a cheese wedge.

Children's wares: Dish and tea sets designed to be used by children for play.

Chop plate: Large round plate used to serve individual portions of meat and fowl.

Cider set: Consists of covered cookie jar (used to hold cider), tray and roly-poly cups and ladle.

Closed handle: Solid glass handle.

Comport: Container used as a serving dish, open with handles, sometimes covered.

Compote: Another name for comport.

Console set: Decorative large bowl with matching candlesticks.

Cream soup: Bowl used to serve cream-type or chilled soups, usually has handles.

Cup and saucer: Used to refer to place-setting cup and saucer; some patterns include larger coffee cup or more diminutive tea cup.

Demitasse cup and saucer: Term used to describe smaller cup and saucer used for after-dinner beverage.

Domino tray: Tray used to hold sugar blocks shaped like dominoes.

Eggcup: Stemware with short stem used to hold an egg, usually used with an underplate.

Goblet: Stemware used to hold water.

Grill plate: Dinner-sized plate with lines that divide plate into compartments.

Ice lip: Small piece of glass inside of top of pitcher to hold ice in the pitcher. May also mean a pinched lip that prevents ice from falling from a pitcher.

Icer: Vessel with compartment to hold crushed ice to keep main vessel cold, i.e., mayonnaise, cream soup, shrimp, etc.

Individual-sized pieces: Smaller sized pieces, often designed for bed tray use. Not to be confused with children's wares.

Liner: Underplate or under bowl used to accompany another piece, i.e., finger bowl or sherbet.

Light (Lite): Branch found on candlestick used to hold additional candles, i.e., two light, three light.

Nappy: Shallow bowl used as serving dish or in a place setting; often has small handle.

Oil/vinegar: Term used to describe a cruet or bottle with a stopper to hold oil and/or vinegar for salads.

Platter: Small, medium or large oval plate used to serve roasts and fowl.

Ring handle: Figural round handle, ring-shaped.

Salver: Large round plate used as serving piece.

Sandwich server: Round plate, often with center handle (made of glass or metal) used to serve tea-type sandwiches.

Sherbet: Part of a place setting used to hold sherbet, often served with matching underplate about the same size as a saucer.

Snack set: Plate or small tray with indent to hold punch or coffee-type cup.

Spooner: Small, often squatty, open vase-type vessel used to hold spoons upright. Typically, part of table set.

Spoon tray: Small bowl-shaped vessel used to hold spoons horizontally, often oval. Often used on buffets, etc., to hold extra place-setting spoons.

Stand: Base or additional piece used to hold punch bowl, etc.

Table set: Name given to set of matching covered butter dish, creamer, covered (or open) sugar and spooner. An extended table service may include syrup, toothpick holder and salt and pepper shakers.

Tab handle: Small solid glass handle useful to grab bowl, etc.

Toddy set: Set consists of covered cookie jar (used to hold toddy), tray and roly-poly cups and ladle.

Tumbler: Any footed or flat vessel used to hold water or other liquids. Specialized tumblers include ginger ale, juice, iced tea, lemonade, old fashioned and whiskey.

Wine: Term used to describe stemware used to hold wine. Depression-era wines have a small capacity, by today's standards.

REFERENCES

General Depression Glass References

Tom and Neila Bredehoft, *Fifty Years of Collectible Glass, 1920-1970*, Antique Trader Books, Volume 1, 1997, Volume 2, 2000.

Monica Lynn Clements and Patricia Rosser Clements, *Cobalt Blue Glass*, Schiffer Publishing, 2001.

—*Green Depression Era Glass*, Schiffer Publishing, 2000.

—*Price Guide to Pink Glass*, Schiffer Publishing, 1999.

Debbie and Randy Coe, *Elegant Glass: Early, Depression & Beyond*, Schiffer, 2004.

Gene Florence, *Collectible Glassware from the 40s, 50s, & 60s, 8th Edition*, Collector Books, 2005.

—*Collector's Encyclopedia of Depression Glass, 17th Edition*, Collector Books, 2005.

—*Elegant Glassware of the Depression Era, 11th Edition*, Collector Books, 2004.

—*Florence's Glassware Pattern Identification Guide*, Collector Books, 2005.

—*Kitchen Glassware of the Depression Era, 6th Edition*, Collector Books, 1995, revised 2005.

—*Pocket Guide to Depression Glass, 14th Edition*, Collector Books, 2004.

—*Stemware Identification*, Collector Books, 1996.

—*Treasures of Very Rare Depression Glass*, Collector Books, 2003.

—*Very Rare Glassware of the Depression Years*, 1st Series (1988, 1990 value update), 2nd Series (1990), 3rd Series (1993, 1995 value update), 4th Series (1995), 5th Series (1996), 6th Series (1999), Collector Books.

Philip Hopper, *Anchor Hocking Catalogs, 1940-Present*, Schiffer Publishing, 2003.

—*Anchor Hocking Decorated Pitchers & Glasses*, Schiffer Publishing, 2001.

—*Forest Green Glass with Price Guide*, Schiffer Publishing, 2000.

—*Royal Ruby*, Schiffer Publishing, 1998.

—*More Royal Ruby*, Schiffer Publishing, 1999.

Ralph and Terry Kovel, *Kovel's Depression Glass & Americana Dinnerware Price List, 6th Edition*, Three Rivers Press, 1998.

Carl F. Luckey and Debbie Coe, *Identification and Value Guide to Depression Era Glassware, 4th Edition*, Krause Publications, 2002.

Barbara and Jim Mauzy, *Mauzy's Comprehensive Handbook of Depression Glass Prices*, Schiffer Publishing, 2002.

—*Mauzy's Depression Glass, A Photographic Reference with Prices*, Schiffer Publishing, 1999.

—*Mauzy's Cake Plates*, Schiffer Publishing, 2004.

Naomi L. Over, *Ruby Glass of the 20th Century*, Antique Publications, 1990, 1993-94 value update.

—*Ruby Glass of the 20th Century, Book 2*, Antique Publications, 1999.

Marlene Toohey, *A Collector's Guide to Black Glass*, Antique Publications, 1988.

—*A Collector's Guide to Black Glass, Book 2*, Antique Publications, 1999.

Kent G. Washburn, *Price Survey, 4th Edition*, published by author, 1994.

Hazel Marie Weatherman, *Colored Glassware of the Depression Era, Book 2*, published by author, 1974, available in reprint.

—*1984 Supplement & Price Trends for Colored Glassware of the Depression Era, Book 1*, published by author, 1984.

Specific Company Reference

Duncan: Gail Krause, *The Encyclopedia of Duncan Glass*, published by author, 1984; *A Pictorial History of Duncan & Miller Glass*, published by author, 1986; *The Years of Duncan*, published by author, 1980; Leslie Piña, *Depression Era Glass By Duncan*, Schiffer Publishing, 1992.

Fenton: Carrie and Gerald Domitz, *Fenton Glass Made for Other Companies, 1907-1980*, Collector Books, 2005; Mark Moran, *Warman's Fenton Glass*, Krause Publications, 2005; Ferill J. Rice (ed.), *Caught in the Butterfly Net*, Fenton Art Glass Collectors of America, The Glass Press, 1995; John Walk, *The Big Book of Fenton Glass, 1940-70*, Schiffer, 2004; Margaret and Kenn Whitmyer, *Fenton Art Glass 1907-1939*, Collector Books, 2002; *Fenton Art Glass, 1939-1980*, Collector Books, 2004; *Fenton Art Glass, Hobnail Pattern*, Collector Books, 2005.

Fire King: Monica Clements and Patricia Rosser Clements, *Unauthorized Guide to Fire King Glassware*, Schiffer Publishing, 2002; Gene Florence, *Anchor Hocking's Fire-King & More*, Collector Books, 2000; Philip A. Hopper, *The Fire-King Years*, Schiffer Publishing, 2003; Joe Keller and David Ross, *Fire-King—An Identification and Price Guide*, Schiffer Publishing, 2002; Garry and Dale Kilgo, Jerry and Gail Wilkins, *Collectors Guide to Anchor Hocking's Fire-King Glassware*, K & W Collectibles Publisher, 1997; *Fire King Glassware, A Collector's Guide to Anchor Hocking, 2nd Edition*, K & W Collectibles Publisher, 1998.

Fostoria: Fostoria Glass Co., *Fine Crystal and Colored Glassware, Cut, Etched, & Plain*, L-W Books, 2000; Ann Kerr, Milbra Long and Emily Seate, *Fostoria Stemware, The Crystal for America Value Guide*, Collector Books, 2003; *Fostoria Tableware, 1924-1943*, Collector Books, 1999; *Fostoria Tableware, 1944-1986*, Collector Books, 1999.

Imperial: Margaret and Douglas Archer, *Imperial Glass*, Collector Books, 1978, 1993 value update; Myrna and Bob Garrison, *Candlewick: Colored and Decorated Lines*, Schiffer Publishing, 2003; *Candlewick: The Crystal Line*, Schiffer Publishing, 2004; *Imperial Cape Cod*, Schiffer Publishing, 2003; *Milk Glass: Imperial Glass Corporation*, Schiffer Publishing, 2000; Laura J. Marsh, *Imperial Glass: Lace Edge Pattern*, Schiffer Publishing, 2004; James Measell, *Imperial Glass Encyclopedia, Volume III, M-Z*, Antique Publications, 1999; National Imperial Glass Collectors Society, *Imperial Glass Encyclopedia, Volume I: A-Cane*, Antique Publications, 1995; —, *Imperial Glass Encyclopedia, Volume II: Cape Cod to L*, Antique Publications, 1998; Mary M. Wetzel-Tomalka, *Candlewick: The Jewel of Imperial*, Book II, published by author, 1995.

Morgantown: Jerry Gallagher, *A Handbook of Old Morgantown Glass, Volume I: A Guide to Identification and Shape*, published by author, 1995; Jeffrey B. Snyder, *Morgantown Glass: Depression through 1960s*, Schiffer Publishing, 1998.

New Martinsville: James Measell, *New Martinsville Glass*, Antique Publications, 1994.

Tiffin: Fred Bickenhauser, *Tiffin Glassmasters, Book I (1979), Book II (1981), Book III (1985)*, Glassmasters Publications; Ed Goshe, Ruth Hemminger and Leslie Piña, *Tiffin Depression-Era Stems and Tablewares*, Schiffer Publishing, 1998; *Tiffin Glass, 1940-80*, Schiffer Books, 2001; Kelly O'Kane, *Tiffin Glassmasters, The Modern Years*, published by author, 1998; Bob Page and Dale Fredericksen, *Tiffin Is Forever*, Page-Fredericksen, 1994; Leslie Piña and Jerry Gallagher, *Tiffin Glass 1914-1940*, Schiffer Publishing, 2000.

Westmoreland: Lorraine Kovar, *Westmoreland Glass, Volumes I and II (1991), Volume III (1998)*, Antique Publications, 1991; *Westmoreland Glass 1950-1984 Volume I Comprehensive Price Guide*, published by author, 1998; *Price Guide to Westmoreland's Paneled Grape Pattern*, published by author, 1997; *Westmoreland Glass, The Popular Years, 1940-85*, Collector Books, 2004.

RESOURCES

Collectors' Clubs

International Associations

Canadian Depression Glass Association
119 Wexford Road
Brampton, Ontario L6Z 2T5 Canada
Web site: http://www.waltztime.com/CDGA

Fenton Art Glass Collectors of America, Inc.
P.O. Box 384
Williamstown, WV 26187

Fire-King Collectors Club
1406 E. 14th St.
Des Moines, IA 50316

Fostoria Glass Collectors, Inc.
P.O. Box 1625
Orange, CA 92856
Web site: http://www.fostoriacollectors.org

Fostoria Glass Society of America, Inc.
P.O. Box 826
Moundsville, WV 26041
Web site: http://fostoriaglass.org

H. C. Fry Glass Society
P.O. Box 41
Beaver, PA 15009
Web site: http://www.thenostalgialeague.com/fryglass/society.htm

Heisey Collectors of America, Inc.
169 N. Church St.
Newark, OH 43055
Web site: http://www.heiseymuseum.org/hca

Indiana Glass Society
P. O. Box 444
Hampstead, MD 21074

National Cambridge Collectors Inc.
P.O. Box 416
Cambridge, OH 43725
Web site: http://www.cambridgeglass.org

National Depression Glass Association
P.O. Box 8264
Wichita, KS 67208-0264
Web site: http://www.ndga.net

National Duncan Glass Society
P.O. Box 965
Washington, PA 15301

National Fenton Glass Society
P.O. Box 4008
Marietta, OH 45750
Web site: http://www.fentonglasssociety.org

National Imperial Glass Collectors Society
P.O. Box 534
Bellaire, OH 43906
Web site: http://www.Imperialglass.org

National Westmoreland Glass
Collectors Club
P.O. Box 372
Westmoreland City, PA 15692

Old Morgantown Glass
Collectors Guild Inc.
P.O. Box 894
Morgantown, WV 26507-0894
Web site: http://www.oldmorgantown.org

Tiffin Glass Collectors' Club
P.O. Box 554
Tiffin, OH 44883
Web site: http://www.tiffinglass.org

Westmoreland Glass Society, Inc.
P. O. Box 2883
Iowa City, IA 52244-2883
Web site: http://www.westmorelandglassclubs.org

20-30-40 Society, Inc.
P. O. Box 856
LaGrange, IL 60525
Web site: http://www.20-30-40society.org

Regional

There are many regional clubs where people gather to discuss Depression-era glassware. Regional clubs may change mailing addresses or meeting locations frequently, so check your favorite Web site for more information. Check with the National Depression Glass Association for a club in your region if none are listed here.

Arizona Depression Glass Club
2242 E. Campbell St.
Phoenix, AZ 85016

Big "D" Pression Glass Club
10 Windling Creek Trail
Garland, TX 75043

Candlewick Collectors Club of Florida
120 Red Sky Court
Lake Mary, FL 32746
Web site: http://www.candlewickfl.com

Central Florida Glassaholics
P. O. Box 2319
Lakeland, FL 33806

Central Jersey Depression Glass Club
181 Riviera Drive
Brick Town, NJ 08723
Web site: www.cjdgclub.homestead.com

Charter Oak Depression Glass Club
P.O. Box 604
Chester, CT 06412

Crescent City Depression Glass Society
1624 Metairie Road
Metairie, LA 70055
Web site: http://www.crescentcityglass.org

Dayton Area Heisey Club
Huber Heights Public Library
6363 Brandt Pike
Huber Heights, OH 45424

Depression Era Glass
Society of Wisconsin
1534 S. Wisconsin Ave.
Racine, WI 53403

Duncan and Miller Glass Club
P. O. Box 965
Washington, PA 15301

Fenton Finders
P. O. Box 384
Williamstown, WV 26187

Fenton Finders of Illiana
Riley Junior High School
15555 Henry Ruff
Livonia, MI 48154

Fire King Collectors Club
1406 E. 14th St.
Des Moines, IA 50316

Gateway Depressioners Glass Club of Greater St. Louis
2040 Flight Drive
Florissant, MO 63031-2216

Greater San Diego
Depression Glass Club
4750 Mission Gorge Place
San Diego, CA 92103-3573

Greater Tulsa Depression Era
Glass Club
Hardesty South Regional Library
6737 N. 85th Ave.
P.O. Box 470763
Tulsa, OK 74147-0763

Hoosier Depression Era Glass Club
Warren Library
21st and Post Road
Indianapolis, IN 46229

Kansas City Depression Glass Club
12950 East 51st Terrace
Independence, MO 64055

Land of Sunshine Depression
Glass Club
589 S Longview Place
P.O. Box 560275
Orlando, FL 32856-0275

Liberty Bell Glass Club
Central Baptist Church
106 W. Lancaster Ave.
Wayne, PA 19087

Lincoln Land Depression Glass Club
1625 Dial Court
Springfield, IL 62704

Long Island Depression Glass Society
P.O. Box 147
West Sayville NY 11796

Miami Valley Cambridge Club
Huber Heights Public Library
6363 Brandt Pike
Huber Heights, OH 45424

Michiana Association of Candlewick Collectors
17370 Battles Road
South Bend, IN 46614
Web site: www.macc-candlewick.org

Michigan Depression Glass Society
Livonia Senior Center
Five Mile and Farmington
Livonia, MI 48154
Web site: http://www.michigandepressionglass.com

North Jersey Dee Geer's
P. O. Box 741
Oradell, NJ 07649

Nutmeg Depression Glass Club
230 Hillside Ave.
Naugatuck, CT 06770

Ohio Candlewickers
613 S. Peterson St.
Gibsonburg, OH 43431

Old Dominion Depression
Glass Club
8415 W. Rugby Road
Manassas, VA 22111

Peach State Depression Glass Club
East Marietta Library
2051 Lower Roswell Rd
Marietta, GA 30068

Permian Basin Depression Glass Club
1412 Alamosa St.
Odessa, TX 79763

Pikes Peak Depression Glass Club
2029 Devon
Colorado Springs, CO 80909

Portland's Rain of Glass, Inc.
P.O. Box 819
Portland, OR 97207-0819

Rocky Mountain Depression Glass Society
790 S. Corona
Denver, CO 80209
Web site: www.rmdgs.org

Sandlapper Depression Glass Club
503 Leyswood Drive
Greenville, SC 29615

South Bay Depression Glass Society
P.O. Box 7400
Torrance, CA 90504-7400

Southern Illinois Diamond H Seekers
1203 N. Yale
O'Fallon, IL 62269

Sparkling Clearwater Depression Glass Club
607 Indiana Ave.
Clearwater, FL 33756
Web site: scdgc.com

Three Rivers Depression Era Glass Society
Donna Hennen
3275 Sylvan Road
Bethel Park, PA 15102
412-835-1903

Texas Regional Imperial Glass Collectors
2613 Hawk Drive
Mesquite, TX 75181
Web site: www.awantiques.com/tricc.htm

Western North Carolina
P.O. Box 116
Mars Hill, NC 28743

Western Reserve Depression Glass Club
5168 Lake Vista Drive
Solon, OH 44139

Internet Sites

The following Internet Web sites offer information about Depression-era glassware in the form of online articles, references, chats, etc. There are hundreds of Web sites to purchase Depression-era glassware as well as numerous e-auctions.

Depression Glass Forum
http://www.glassforum.net

Dictionary of Glass Marks
http://www.heartland-discoveries.com

Facets Antiques & Collectibles Mall
http://www.Facets.net

Fire-King.Net
http://www.fire-king.net
29 Pleasant St.
Bar Harbor, ME 04609-1604

Just Glass
http://www.justglass.com
P.O. Box 20146
Cincinnati, OH 45220

Mega Show
http://www.glassshow.com

Antique & Collector's
Reproduction News
P.O. Box 12130
Des Moines, IA 50312
Web site: www.repronews.com

PATTERNS
BY MANUFACTURER

Anchor Hocking Glass Co.
Early American Prescut, 102
Fire-King, Alice, 109
Fire-King, Charm, 110
Fire-King, Dinnerware, 111
Fire-King, Jane Ray, 112
Fire-King, Laurel Leaf, 113
Fire-King, Philbe, 114
Fire-King, Primrose, 115
Fire-King, Swirl, 116
Fire-King, Turquoise Blue, 117
Forest Green, 127-128
Manhattan, 157-158
Moonstone, 172-173
Oyster & Pearl, 192
Royal Ruby, 234-235
Wexford, 272-273

Belmont Tumbler Co.
Rose Cameo, 227

Dell Glass Co.
Tulip, 264

Diamond Glass-Ware Co.
Victory, 269

Duncan & Miller Glass Co.
Sandwich, 237-238
Teardrop, 260-261

Federal Glass Co.
Colonial Fluted, 74
Columbia, 77
Diana, 96-97
Georgian, 131
Heritage, 135
Madrid, 155-156
Mayfair, 159
Normandie, 182-183
Park Avenue, 196
Parrot, 197
Patrician, 198-199
Pioneer, 208
Raindrops, 218
Rosemary, 228
Sharon, 245-246
Star, 251
Thumbprint, 263
Yorktown, 277-278

Fenton Art Glass
Lincoln Inn, 152-153

Fostoria Glass Co.
American, 30-33
Coin, 69-70
Colony, 75-76
Fairfax, 107-108
Jamestown, 145
Seville, 243-244

Hazel Atlas Glass Co.
Aurora, 40
Cloverleaf, 68
Colonial Block, 73-74
Florentine No. 1, 122
Florentine No. 2, 123-124
Fruits, 130
Moderntone, 166-167
New Century, 178-179
Newport, 180
Ovide, 191
Ribbon, 219
Ripple, 222
Roxana, 231
Royal Lace, 232-233
Ships, 247-248
Starlight, 252

Hazel Ware, Continental Can
Capri, 60
Moroccan Amethyst, 174

Hocking Glass Co.
Block Optic, 45-46
Bubble, 48-49
Cameo, 52-53
Circle, 66-67
Colonial, 71-72
Coronation, 80
Fortune, 129
Hobnail, 137
Lake Como, 149
Mayfair, 160-162
Miss America, 164-165
Old Café, 184-185
Old Colony, 186-187
Princess, 211-212
Queen Mary, 214-215
Ring, 220-221
Roulette, 229
Sandwich, 239-240
Spiral, 250
Vitrock, 270
Waterford, 271

INDEX BY PATTERN